Research Reports ESPRIT

Project 6310 · MMTCA · Volume 1

Edited in cooperation with the European Commission

M. K. Crowe (Ed.)

Cooperative Work with Multimedia

ESPRIT 6310:
MULTIMEDIA
TOOLBOX FOR
COOPERATIVE
APPLICATIONS

Springer-Verlag
Berlin Heidelberg New York
London Paris Tokyo
Hong Kong Barcelona
Budapest

Volume Editor

Malcolm K. Crowe
University of Paisley, Department of Computing
and Information Systems
High Street, Paisley PA1 2BE, UK

ESPRIT Project 6310, MMTCA (Multimedia Toolbox for Cooperative Applications) belongs to the Software and Advanced Information Processing sector of the ESPRIT Programme (European Specific Programme for Research and Development in Information Technologies) supported by the European Commission.

The objective of ESPRIT Project 6310, MMTCA, was to design and build a toolbox for the development of cooperative applications with special attention to the requirements of multimedia applications. The project results are: a client-server system which allows for the execution of cooperative applications; tools to manage such cooperative applications, the existing applications employed, the documents created, etc.; and a set of applications developed by endusers.

MMTCA is targeted on a range of environments of particular economic importance such as: banking, including financial services; public administration sector and large corporations; and health sector, including hospital management.

CR Subject Classification (1991): H.5.3, H.4.3

ISBN 3-540-58315-7 Springer-Verlag Berlin Heidelberg New York
ISBN 0-387-58315-7 Springer-Verlag New York Berlin Heidelberg

Publication No. EUR 15916 EN of the
European Commission,
Dissemination of Scientific and Technical Knowledge Unit,
Directorate-General Information Telecommunications, Information Market and
Exploitation of Research,
Luxembourg.

Typesetting: Camera-ready by the editor
SPIN: 10132176 45/3140-543210 – Printed on acid-free paper

Preface

The purpose of this book is to present a project from the ESPRIT Specific Programme of European Research and Development in Information Technology, project number 6310, known as MMTCA: Multimedia Toolbox for Cooperative Applications. This project ran from 1992 to 1994, and concluded with a product which is probably of great usefulness to all business organisations.

MMTCA enables managers to set up arrangements or to delegate tasks involving cooperation between people in different places using standard Windows software tools for what-you-see-is-what-I-see (WYSIWIS) cooperation. MMTCA is the only product that delivers all of these points.

Several trends in 1994 lead the authors to believe that MMTCA will become more important over the coming months:

- the continuing popularity of personal computers and Microsoft's Windows operating system,
- the growing importance of computer-supported cooperative work, and
- the availability of powerful networks and satellites for wide-area communications.

In MMTCA it is not necessary for the manager to know anything about computer programming, but merely to have a user's working knowledge of the application software (spreadsheets etc.) that is used in his office. The MMTCA approach envisages two stages where MMTCA's facilities are used:

- by the manager: setting up or organising work to be done,
- by the participants: carrying out the resulting tasks.

A workflow control mechanism in addition to relevant tools is built into MMTCA, so that sophisticated *procedures,* which may contain both synchronous and asynchronous *tasks,* can be constructed. Consequently various requirements from different organisations could be satisfied. MMTCA provides end users with a collaborative environment (a toolbox) under which users build their own multimedia applications and perform them collaboratively.

Part 1 of this book examines computer supported cooperative work, and how MMTCA can be useful in typical business situations.

Part 2 presents a user's view of the way MMTCA's tools can be used in practice, including details of demonstrators that were built with the prototype version developed in the project. Since MMTCA is intended for end-users, many standard kinds of computer support for cooperative work can be provided with a minimum of effort.

Finally, in Part 3, some technical details are given that enable advanced use to be made of MMTCA's facilities, such as macros for automating interactions with the MMTCA environment.

The MMTCA project consortium consisted of Intrasoft (Greece), Novosoft (Spain), Robotiker (Spain), and University of Paisley (UK), with associated partners Intracom (Greece), Banco del Comercio (Spain), and Institut für Seeverkehrswirtschaft und Logistik (Germany).

The associated partners were responsible for ensuring that the project addressed real industrial needs and that the resulting concepts were reasonable for the types of users envisaged. As a result, MMTCA has retained a strongly practical emphasis throughout, with types of user cooperation and facilities considered by the users to be the most significant.

The consortium is committed to exploiting the results of the project, and enquiries should be addressed to the Project Manager: Alexis Argyris, Intrasoft SA, 2 Adrianiou Street, Athens, tel +30 1 649 6620, fax +30 1 692 5259, or any member of the consortium.

This book represents the final report of the research and development project. It presents the ideas and software generated in the project, and details of how MMTCA can be used.

It has been based on contributions from many authors:

From Intrasoft SA, Athens: Yiannis Galanos, Alexis Argyris, Platon Velonias, Kostas Tzelepis, Akis Hamamtzoglou.

From Robotiker SA, Zamudio, Spain: Guillermo Gil Aguirrebeitia, Carmen Pastor, Jesus Herrero, Silvia Renteria, Cristina Martinez.

From Novosoft SA, Madrid: Pierre Roucher, Jesus Toral, Carlos Oramas, José Oramas, Alfredo Alonso, Rafael Ruiz.

From University of Paisley, Paisley, UK: Malcolm Crowe, Sandy Kydd, Stuart McColl, Shichen Tian, Paul Oldfield, John Galloway.

From Institut für Seeverkehrswirtschaft und Logistik (ISL), Bremen: Andreas Stern, Lars Riekers, Hubert Hoffmann.

From Banco del Comercio, Madrid: José-Maria Alfonsel, José-Miguel Redondo, Fenando Martinez, Juan-Manuel Menendez.

From Intracom SA, Athens: Nikos Ioannides, Veronika Samara, Theodoros Bozios.

Paisley, June 1994 Malcolm Crowe

Table of Contents

Part 1 Computer Supported Cooperative Work and MMTCA

There is a technical achievement at the heart of the MMTCA project that makes it unique and a "world first". This is to add some software to the PC so that, with no changes to the Windows operating system or the standard multimedia applications running on it, applications can be operated as required in a strict what-you-see-is-what-I-see manner (WYSIWIS, Stefik et al 1987) by exchanging input events. This achievement is startling in itself and contradicts earlier wisdom (e.g. Ellis et al 1991). It is made particularly important by the success of the Windows operating system and the availability of a very large number of applications for it, most of which can be integrated with MMTCA.

It is hard to imagine business organisations without cooperative work: by most definitions (cf Jackson 1992), the concept of *organisation* is based on the notion of people working together for some purpose, and much research has been done on the many approaches to information systems that can serve business organisations (Lyytinen, 1987). With the rise in the power and sophistication of computers and networking technology, it has become natural to look for ways in which technology can provide support to cooperative work. Research in this area (surveyed in Greif 1988, Wilson 1991) has involved expertise from many fields including management science, sociology and psychology in addition to information technology.

The term Computer Supported Cooperative Work (CSCW) was coined by Greif and Cashman for the first workshop of that name in 1986. Many researchers were inspired by the promise of those early days, and a very large number of interesting experiments have been done: but apart from electronic mail, few of these attempts at computer support for cooperative work have become widely accepted. It is arguable, with the hindsight afforded by the results of the MMTCA project, presented here, that a number of key technical ground rules have changed since 1991, making the background analysis for these experiments no longer trustworthy.

The technical success of sharing applications allowed the MMTCA project to examine the most acceptable kinds of WYSIWIS cooperation using such standard applications, and to develop a coherent philosophy for CSCW in which *synchronous* cooperation is used only where a meeting would normally be unavoidable, such as in the concluding stages of negotiations. This contrasts with earlier CSCW approaches where synchronous cooperation was used in tasks such as co-authorship (Stefik et al 1987) that would not normally be attempted in meetings.

The MMTCA project as a whole offers an integrated environment for end-user empowerment, which includes administration, browsing, and procedure design tools enabling true workflow management in addition to supporting cooperative sessions. A videoconference facility is available as an optional extra. MMTCA is an open environment, in which new applications can be integrated as they become popular, and new workflow arrangements added as they are developed by end-users. Equally, MMTCA's cooperative sessions can be included in existing office automation procedures. All of these aspects are presented in later parts of the book.

In Part 1, the nature of cooperative work, the possible kinds of available computer support, and the opportunities afforded by MMTCA are explored from the point of view of the user and the organisation.

Chapter 1 discusses the nature of cooperative work, and considers a number of experiments and projects that have aimed at providing computer support.

In chapter 2, these requirements are analysed critically, bearing in mind recent developments and new perspectives on what kinds of computer support might be desirable. This leads to the MMTCA approach to computer-supported cooperative work, which is outlined in chapter 3.

1. Cooperative Work

Most computing systems now in use aid the work of separate individuals rather than their work in groups, although for a long time computers have supported simple asynchronous group work through shared file systems, explicit file transfer, remote login, and electronic message exchange. The development of powerful low-cost personal computing equipment has offered us the opportunity to use computing and communication technology to support group activity. This has led the needs of business organisations in the area of computer-supported cooperative work to be re-assessed. In this chapter, the discussion begins with the nature of business organisations and the work that needs to be carried out to achieve their business goals.

1.1 Business Organisations and Group Work

Business organisations (Jackson 1992), by their nature, are notional wholes which serve a business purpose, through the cooperation of the people who belong to them. Such cooperation can be considered to be work of the set of people, and group work in this sense, but the business purpose of the organisation is also achieved through the success of a number of business processes which serve the larger purpose of the organisation. These business processes are extremely varied in nature, ranging from routine operations such as taking on new staff, or effecting a sale or a purchase, to non-routine operations such as responding to major events or carrying out strategic reorganisation.

Such business activities are very often entrusted to a more or less cohesive and identifiable group of people (including clients and other outsiders where appropriate). The term *group work* is used to refer to such a set of people working together on a common project.

Group work is therefore important to most organisations because their success depends on staff co-ordinating their efforts to reach common goals. Routine operations will usually involve following standard (implicit) procedures, while non-routine operations will be set up on an ad hoc basis, though probably with

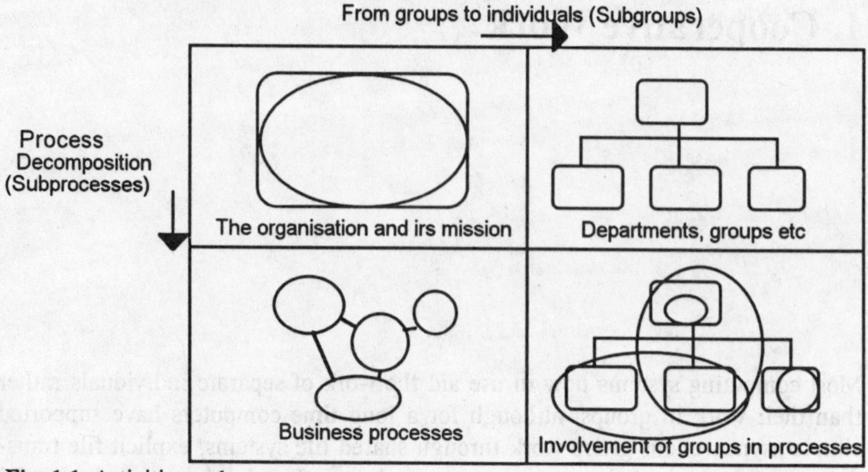

Fig. 1.1. Activities and groups

regard to some recognised responsibilities and management groupings, and "good practice".

Even where routine procedures are being followed, it is often the case that the people involved do not form a cohesive group. In the case of sales, for example, the client is not a part of the sales team but is obviously an important player in agreeing the terms; or in recruitment, different departments of the organisation need to work with the personnel department, providing interviewers, etc.

Table 1.1. Group Cohesion and Business Processes

	Low Group Cohesion	High Group Cohesion
Ad hoc arrangement	Relocation Innovation	Strategic Planning Development Project
Routine procedure	Sales Recruitment Training	Accounts Manufacture

It is obvious that the availability of computer technology to support group activities will vary greatly from one business organisation to another. For example, an army unit might be expected to have good support for relocating its operations; the stock exchange has good computerised support for share trading; some manufacturers have CIM systems, an airline may have computer support for training, and so on. It is worth examining this range of business activities to appreciate the potential of CSCW and the ambition of the MMTCA project.

1.2 Group Processes

From the previous section it can be seen that group processes are at the heart of the operation of all business organisations. Groups set up to solve a particular business problem may collaborate over a problem for months, or even years, during which time participants will undoubtedly operate both independently (asynchronous cooperation) and collectively (synchronous cooperation). Also, within the lifetime of the problem, members of the group may leave – perhaps to begin a new job – but their role in the group can usually be adopted by a newcomer.

In 1984, Grief and Cashman introduced the term “computer supported cooperative work” (CSCW) as a way of describing how computing technology can help people to work together in groups, and since then, CSCW has been increasing its profile dramatically. Paradoxically though, attempts at the provision of computer support for group activities have resulted in a realisation that no clear understanding exists of how people work together. Malone and Crowston (1990) suggested that although common sense might do, sound theories on how groups work would lead to the design of more useful cooperative tools. Indeed, Grudin (1991) cites research into individual and group behaviour in the workplace as being a fundamental element of CSCW.

Wilson (1991) observes that five aspects need to be addressed in understanding and supporting group processes. First, groups consist of individuals, and thus it is necessary to understand and support the individual. Secondly, individuals and groups work within organisation contexts, which place demands and constraints on what they do, so that the organisational context in which the work is done should be considered. Thirdly, discussions between the individuals who are involved in the same process of group work are common, so it is important to investigate how the process of designing group work can be supported. Fourthly, the principles of group dynamics (how people work together) must be taken into account if appropriate tools are to be developed.

When groups meet, its members cooperate interactively. Synchronous CSCW systems support this form of collaboration. When a group object (document, memo, code fragment, etc.) is passed between members, the group is cooperating without the active participation of all members. Asynchronous CSCW systems support this form of collaboration. Actual observation of group activity reveals the need for a CSCW system incorporating elements to support both synchronous and asynchronous cooperation. Mixed systems such as this require a coherent conceptual construct of the group's activities, together with a set of consistent goals or target products (Jeffay et al 1992).

Process models (Christie 1993) can be built for several reasons:

- in order to understand the nature of how one does business. This can help with communication, training, and process improvement with the implied aim of increasing product quality.

- as a basis for automating the process. This type of activity is much more ambitious, in that such models have to be rigorously specified, designed and programmed. Even if such an endeavour is technically successful, it may yet fail by not considering the adoption and user issues critical to its success.
- as part of a process reuse library. Such models may either be descriptive or enactable. Automation and reuse have yet to make significant inroads into commercial software development organisations.

Thus (Ould, 1992), it is proper to start by asking "what sort of things happen in real-world processes?", i.e. "what sorts of things do we want to be able to model?" There are five key aspects to consider:

1. What the organisation is trying to achieve with the process: the business *goals*.

For instance, the goals of an organisation might be to deliver computer systems, to maintain positive cash flow, or manage a research budget. It should be possible to see from process models how a process is achieving the objectives or goals set for it, and ideally to be able to identify the point(s) in the process where those goals can be said to have been achieved or maintained.

2. What constraints the organisation puts on what people can do and how they should operate: the business *rules*.

An organisation might have a policy of buying in the management of its computer facilities, or strict procedures for reporting, or standard for the use of particular tools or forms, and above all, an organisation prescribes responsibility levels and means for authorisation and delegation that prescribe who can do what and how they are empowered.

All these are rules about "how things get done around here", and from the perspective of the group that is carrying out the process, it could be useful to be able to capture them in process models.

3. What individuals do to achieve the goals.

Individuals do more than just produce or make things (such as preparing a design, or preparing an invoice). They may wait, collect, check, organise, monitor, chase, interact, distribute, identify, re-organise, report, plan, create routines and so on: a multiplicity of "non-productive" activities which, however, add value to the process they are part of. Management activity is particularly composed of such non-productive activities which are supposed to organise the process.

We want to be able to model both productive and managerial activity.

4. How processes are divided over "roles".

A role is a set of activities that are generally carried out by an individual or group within the organisation.

An important role is that of *project managing*. This role would be *acted* by one person at a time, and within the role there are many activities that that person would undertake: planning, reporting, monitoring, managing staff, liaising with suppliers, working with the client, and so on. The role of project managing project X could be acted by one person today, and by another person tomorrow. The role is separate from the people who act it.

A role could be carried out by a group. The work of a whole Division of a typical company may be about the process of *doing projects*. A model of how this company worked in a broad brush way might identify the Division and the activities in it as one role, even though a whole group of people were involved in acting the role and, indeed, that group changes in time as people arrive and leave.

5. How individuals within groups *interact* to work collaboratively in order to get the job done.

People do not only operate as individuals. Processes almost invariably involve the collaboration of a group of individuals, and that collaboration takes place through many sorts of interaction, such as:

- I pass you some information
- I delegate a task to you
- I give you authority to do something
- We agree on an action
- We approve something, such as a plan
- You report your status to me
- You pass me the results of your work
- I wait for you to do something
- I chase the progress of something

To model a process comprehensively it is therefore useful to be able to model goals, rules, activities, roles and interactions.

A model of a process can provide a vehicle for carrying out a number of analyses. Typical of the sorts of *qualitative* analysis that become possible are:

- checking that commitments made are kept and reported back: does the Board ever get to hear the results of the budget pruning exercise it requests?
- checking that the information flow is sound: does the Supervisor have the facts necessary from Sales at the right moment?
- checking that all activities and interactions add value: what does it add if the Line Manager is involved in that decision?
- understanding the effect of mapping activity onto roles in a different way: could responsibility for deciding credit worthiness be moved down the organisation?

Similarly, a process model can provide the information to carry out *quantitative* analysis. By assigning durations to activities and interactions, and delays or frequencies to external events, once can examine critical paths, case transit times and other properties of a process.

1.3 Availability of Technology

Computing systems have improved greatly compared with those of a decade ago. Terminals have been replaced with desktop computers, and often these computers are connected by networks. Sophisticated software tools with 'wimp' (window, icon, menu and pointer) user interfaces are common. These changes to computing systems are recognised as a trend towards networks and organisational computing, and the evidence for this trend is overwhelming (Pinella 1990). Consequently, higher quality documents can be produced and propagated in less time, and office work has been improved. However, when considering to what extent today's computing systems can support people in carrying out collaborative activities, the situation is not encouraging. Most computing systems in use aid the work of separate individuals rather than their work in groups, although computers have allowed simple asynchronous group work through shared file systems, explicit file transfer, remote login, and electronic message exchange.

Wilson (1991) notes that the fundamental requirement for supporting group work is two-way communication. Once this is in place, it can be used in two complementary ways: to share information, for example via a multi-user database, and to share a virtual work space for example using remote screens. Fourthly, special applications can support ideas generation, priority setting, and procedure processing.

According to Wilson (1991), the Greif and Cashman conference in 1986 (Greif 1988) also made something else clear: CSCW tools will only work if they reflect and augment the way people actually talk, work and live together. This is more than just making the tools easy to use – their functionality must be derived from an accurate understanding of human traits, practices, communication and motivation.

Two main characteristics are used to describe CSCW enabling technology (Ellis, 1991): the style of interaction and the geographical location of the participants. The former includes synchronous (same time) cooperation such as brainstorming, and asynchronous (different time) cooperation such as tasks being carried out without the presence of other group members.

Potential applications for CSCW are very wide in scope. For example (Wilson, 1991):

Table 1.2. Styles of interaction and distance

	Same Time	Different Time
Same Place	Face-to-face interaction	Asynchronous interaction
Different Places	Synchronous distributed interaction	Asynchronous distributed interaction

- *collaboration tools* can help working groups agree what has to be done, allocate tasks and roles, and undertake specific group activities.
- *meeting room systems* can support face-to-face meeting activities such as the presentation and manipulation of information, decision making, minute taking and action review
- *desktop video conferencing* enables two or more geographically separated people to interwork using a common screen display, video images of the other people in separate windows on the screen, and an integrated voice connection.
- *procedure processing* or *workflow* technology can automate paper-based forms handling and, at the same time, provide full summary information about status, whereabouts, and over-runs.

The communication technology can this be used in three complementary ways, which are examined in the next three sections:

- to help with coordination of activity by keeping participants advised of what awaits their attention, so that they can schedule their work;
- to help to reduce the need for meetings or equivalently to provide facilities additional to the telephone; and
- to provide a shared information space.

Among existing systems, four kinds of enabling technologies can be classified (Rodden, 1991): message systems, computer conferencing, meeting rooms, and co-authoring and argumentation systems.

Message systems: These evolved from the early electronic mail facility which just supported message transfer between a user using a central machine and others on the same machine. Message systems are now very mature, with international standards such as the ITU-TSS X.400 recommendations. Different control models can be classified for structured message systems: formal, semiformal, and informal. The formal control model has the highest degree of task-prescriptivity: this approach was adopted by the Cosmos project (Bowers and Churcher, 1988), which developed a configurable message system to support structured group working; while the project Information Lens (Malone and Lai, 1988) adopted the informal control approach.

Table 1.3 shows a range of research projects using message-based techniques and the form of control they use.

Conferencing Systems: The first computer conferencing system, EMISARI, was developed in the USA in the early 1970's (Hiltz and Turoff, 1978). It worked as an electronic network linking remote regional offices to eliminate the constraints of time and geographic location. There were two parts in EMISARI: Party-Line, point-to-point communication between two users, and Discussion, on-line file

Table 1.3. Message systems (from Rodden 1991)

Coordinator (Winograd, 1987)	Formal Speech-Act	Network
Information Lens (Malone and Lai, 1987)	Informal	Production Rules
Chaos (de Cindio et al, 1986)	Formal Speech-Act	Network
Domino (Kreifelts and Woetzel, 1986)	Formal Procedure System	Script Based
Cosmos (Wilbur and Young, 1988)	Formal Augmented Systems	Script Based
Amigo (Danielson et al, 1986)	Formal Augmented System	Script Based
Strudel (Shepherd et al, 1990)	Semi-formal	Production Rules

storage of topic-specific messages for all users to access. These two elements are building blocks for traditional computer conferencing systems.

The progress of high bandwidth local area networks resulted in the development of real-time conferencing systems, which support real-time cooperation and concurrent access to the shared information space. Multimedia desktop conferencing systems are the latest development in this area and the result of the integration of different media within workstations.

Traditional conferencing systems: In a typical computer conferencing system, there are several conferences, each of which has some members and a sequence of messages. Conferences are arranged to address different topics; and users join conferences which are of interest to them. Traditional computer conferencing systems are built upon the bulletin board concept, which developed from early electronic mail systems. Compared with bulletin board systems which offer a fixed set of topics, conferencing systems have more flexibility in organising new conferences and comments within a conference. Users of a conference can interact with others who have common interests and access information about changes to the conferees. Users also can access conference comments according to criteria such as date, author and keyword. There are many conferencing systems each of which has different properties and peculiarities (Rodden, 1991); several problems associated with supporting groups using computer conferencing systems have been identified from on-field observations: activity level of a conference's leader, appropriateness of discussion topics and overload and pruning. These three factors influence a conference's success or failure.

Real-time conferencing systems: While traditional computer conferencing systems addressing asynchronous group activity, real-time conferencing systems cater for synchronous group activity such as crisis management. RTCAL (in Greif, 1988) is such a system which highlights the principles of real-time conferencing. It supports meeting scheduling among a group of users by providing a shared workspace of information from participants' on-line calendars. There are a number of features which are common to most real-time conferencing systems

- shared and private views which display information for the whole user community or a single user,
- the alignment of related information between the shared and private views to be displayed appropriately,
- an on-line voting mechanism allowing users to express opinions on several proposals,
- user autonomy addressing a user's ability to act independently of the user community,
- different priority allowing a chairperson to control a conference,
- presentation of status information such as topics, participants, chairpersons, floor-holders, etc. and
- user commands which contain those relating to conference control (e.g. requesting the floor) and those concerned with applications (e.g. editing information).

Studying these features is important when CSCW support systems are developed using the real-time computer conferencing technology.

Desktop conferencing systems are considered further in the next chapter.

Meeting Room Systems: These are a recent and distinct research development in cooperative working. A meeting room system often consists of a screen projector and some networked workstations or terminals, and can be used to conduct decision conferences that focus on improving decision-making by groups rather than individuals. Four software elements have been identified in (Kraemer and Kling, 1988) for the construction of decision conferences: decision analysis software, modelling software, voting tally and display software. CoLab (Stefik et al, 1987) developed at Xerox Parc USA is one well-known example of meeting room systems. It does not adopt formal decision models and quantitative techniques, but supports writing and argumentation using verbal models and qualitative technique through the manipulation of text and graphical images. CoLab consists of a number of workstations connected through an Ethernet and a shared electronic chalkboard. Text and images can easily be manipulated (e.g. moved, erased, stored, etc.) on the chalkboard. Providing a co-ordinated interface for participants has been identified as a fundamental requirement for meeting tools and such an interface based on the WYSIWIS abstraction has been implemented by the developers of CoLab. Strict WYSIWIS has several problems (Stefik and Bobrow, 1987), and CoLab used a relaxed version of the abstraction. It is considered to be useful to design two kinds of windows: public interactive windows accessible to the entire group and private windows with limited access. TEAMWORKER (PC Plus, 1993) is one of the latest commercial products supporting face-to-face meeting. It augments communications and aids decision-making in meetings. TEAMWORKER is based on hand-held keypads, enabling each participant to send message by radio to a PC. Messages are displayed on a large electronic board. It can help users to run better meetings by saving time, ensuring full participation, and increasing commitment.

Co-authoring and Argumentation Systems: By their nature these are multi-user hypertext systems (Rodden, 1991). where the hypertext document (or network) is created by several users adding nodes to the text, graphics, and other media. Hypertext documents consist of nodes with each link between nodes representing an association between the information held in the nodes. Hypertext systems can enhance user's ability to process information (Marchionini and Schneiderman, 1988). In some hypertext systems where changes made in a shared storage space, conflicts may occur if several users attempt to collaborate on the production of a document. Four deficiencies with those systems have been identified (Delise and Schwartz, 1986).

- *Limited organisation*: a means of organising related sets of hypertext nodes and links should be provided, therefore a set may contain all the nodes and links that comprise a specific document.
- *Lack of partitioning*: a mechanism allowing teams of authors to work together in independent hypertext partitions without interfering each other and then allowing thosc independent partitions to be joined at carefully controlled intervals.
- *Little version and configuration control*: the ability of building version trees and provision of configuration management support should be provided.
- *Lack of distribution*: the hypertext database should be distributed to support large teams collaborating on a common project.

A system called Contexts has been developed by the authors of (Delise and Schwartz, 1986) in an effort to resolve these deficiencies. In Contexts, two views are used: a private view (context) allowing users to make modifications in it and a shared master view allowing users to merge the private view. Other systems similar to Contexts include Intermedia (Garret et al, 1986), Xanadu (Nelson, 1980) and Notecards (Trigg et al, 1986).

1.4 Coordination and Group Process

Malone and Crowston (1990) note that coordination is about the interdependency of the work being done by members of the group. Coordination is attributed to a situation by observers: the actors involved in a situation may or may not all agree on the identification of all of its components. One very important case of this occurs when the actors have *conflicting goals*. One strange effect of providing computer support for coordination of group activity (not examined by Malone and

Table 1.4. Interdependence of group tasks (from Malone and Crowston 1990)

Kinds of interdependence	Common object	Example of interdependence in manufacturing	Examples of coordination processes for managing interdependence
Generic:			
Prerequisite	Output of one activity which is required by the next activity	Parts must be delivered in time to be used	Ordering activities, moving information from one activity to the next
Shared resource	Resource required by multiple activities	Two parts installed with a common tool	Allocating resources
Simultaneity	Time at which more than one activity must occur	Installing two matched parts at the same time	Synchronising activities
Domain-specific:			
Manufacturability	Part	Part designed by engineering must be made by manufacturing	Decision-making (e.g. negotiation, appeal to authority)
Customer relations	Customer	Both field service and sales personnel deal with same customer	Information sharing (e.g. sharing problem reports)

Crowston) is that one view of the interdependency of the activities becomes privileged by being represented in the form of computer data.

Another approach to processing modelling is provided by ProNet (Christie, 1993). Representationally, a ProNet model has similarities to an entity-relationship model in that it defines entities that are connected by relationships. However, the entities all belong to a small set of predefined classes. For example, a central concept in the language is the class *activity*. The notion of control and hence behavioural modelling) can also be embedded in the diagram through the *condition* class. There is also a small set of predefined relationships which link the entities. Because of the central importance of activities in the language, ProNet diagrams also have some of the characteristics similar to Petri nets in that ProNet's notion of activities corresponds in some ways to the Petri net notion of transitions while the other entities in ProNet correspond to the Petri net notion of places.

It is noteworthy that the formal model of the process provides three benefits. First, it graphically defines roles, activities, products, etc., and their relationships and dependencies. It also defines communication links in the process and under what conditions activities can occur. Such a formal model provides a level of precision and rigour for defining the process that is difficult to attain through

Table 1.5. Process levels (from Malone and Crowston 1990)

Process Level	Components	Examples of Generic Processes
Coordination	goals, activities, actors, resources, interdependencies	identifying goals, ordering activities, assigning activities to actors, allocating resources, synchronising activities
Group decision-making	goals, actors, alternatives, evaluations, choices	proposing alternatives, evaluating alternatives, making choices (e.g. by authority, consensus, or voting)
Communication	senders, receivers, messages, languages	establishing common languages, selecting receiver (routing), transporting message (delivering)
Perception of common objects	actors, objects	seeing same physical objects, accessing shared databases

textual description. Second, such a model is useful as a basis to start process improvement. Often what is ineffective in a process is clear, but having an agreed-upon definition of the process provides a means for communication about change. Finally, defining a formal model of the process provides a vehicle for training new members and providing a corporate memory in 'how things are done'. It provides a means for new project members rapidly to understand and visualise the environment in which they will be working; and it establishes continuity of process when experienced members leave the project.

1.5 Workflow

Among the various methods for analysing group processes in the literature, an interesting approach is offered by the STRIM approach (Ould, 1992). The STRIM analyst gathers facts about an existing group process by interviewing those who carry out the process, ideally as a group. The aim of the questioning is to flush out the roles, activities, entities, and role interactions that form the organisation's process. At each stage, the business rules and goals that govern the process are also recorded. A series of questions can be asked under a number of general headings:

- What are the overall structures and their business goals? This elicits the overall command structure of the major functions in terms of the relevant business rules: objectives, targets, goals, plans, etc.

- What are the roles and what are their business goals? This starts the process of eliciting the roles that are present in the organisation.
- How do the roles interact? This explores the interactions between roles and the organisational motivation for those interactions.
- How does a role work? This looks at the activities of a role that are "private" to that role.
- What entities are essential to the process? Data that records state is not important for this modelling. For instance, a written instruction by a customer to open an account is essential data: it causes further activities (i.e. it changes the process state rather than recording it), and it plays an essential part in a transaction between two roles. On the other hand, the account record is not essential data: it simply records the state of the customer-bank part of the process, in particular the history of previous interactions.

It is often useful to get the group of people who actually carry out the process to do the modelling, with the assistance of a process analyst. The notation is intuitively simple and it is found that people readily model in it, provided that the analyst does the drafting for them on a white-board. The notation is sufficiently transparent for people to work on the *process* during a modelling session, rather than working on (struggling with) the notation. There appears to be little or no need for the analyst to translate the actors' words into a model or to interpret the model for the actors.

From a consideration of roles and activities the next step is to decompose the activity into tasks. In many cases it is obvious that several tasks (refinement of a document, creation of dependent documents) need to occur in sequence.

At some points in the process, what happens next might depend on some condition or state. In this case, one can think of a token passing down the leg of the case refinement that corresponds to the predicate that is true; the role goes in different directions depending on the state of things. Case refinement is a kind of *case* statement in a programming language or as a decision box in a conventional flowchart. However, unlike a decision box, there is no activity going on "in" the symbol for case refinement – no person or machine is doing anything to make the decision: the process is simply going in different directions depending on the state it is in. So, the value of a *Design OK?* predicate will be determined as a result of some prior activity in the process, such as the quality control activity in this case; the case refinement does not itself "contain" any activity to make the check.

A role can also split into a number of separate threads of activity that can be carried out concurrently. The state of the role is being refined (divided) into a number of separate parts. (To follow a Petri Net analogy, think of the single token that enters the part refinement becoming a number of tokens, each of which passes down one leg of the part refinement; the role "divides" in different directions.) It often happens that all the concurrent threads should be complete before the role proceeds to further activity. In some cases however, a process does not operate this way: a project manager's activity might be considered as two quite separate "sub-roles": keeping staff occupied with work and liaising with the client. These might be the two legs of an early part refinement of the role, which need not recombine. Similar reasoning applies to case refinement, where we do not require all the alternative threads to come back to the same point in the process.

Organisational activity often ambles around from role to role, dividing and recombining, ducking and weaving, jumping off at tangents, sometimes coming back. A useful notation must model the untidiness of the real world.

Each task involves processing some documents.

An *interaction* between roles is shown in Ould's (1992) diagrams as a white box in one role connected by a horizontal line to a white box in another role. An interaction can involve any number of roles performing coincident actions. An interaction signifies that the roles involved must pass through it together - they synchronise.

An interaction often involves the transfer of some entity, *a gram*, from the sphere of concern of one role to that of the other. For example the *Managing a Division* role will interact with the *Project Managing* role so that the Divisional Manager can pass the Project Manager some terms of reference for the project they are to manage. However, it should be remembered that an interaction need not involve the transfer of a gram: for instance, you and I might interact simply to agree on something – "nothing changes hands".

The synchronisation aspect in the rendezvous or join operation is important: if I reach my side and you are not ready, I must wait until you are; as soon as we both are ready the interaction can take place.

An interaction can be very simple (e.g. "I give you same terms of reference"), or very complex (e.g. "the three parties meet to negotiate and agree the price of a piece of work, drawing up the agreement as legal document and obtaining financial securities from a bank").

An interaction that is shown as a single line on a workflow diagram might, if "opened up", show the involvement of other roles not mentioned otherwise, new interactions between them and other roles, and all the richness of organisational behaviour. Specific techniques for handling these aspects are needed in workflow systems.

1.6 Desktop Conferencing Systems

Group activity normally involves meetings. As Stefik et al (1987) observed, many managers consider that little benefit is to be gained from personal computers in the workplace unless they help replace or reduce the number of meetings:

Table 1.6. Flow and Tasks

1.	Simple Flow 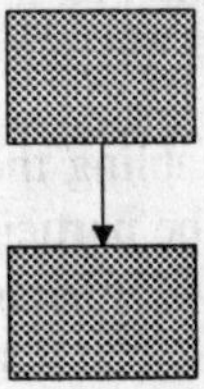		This is the simplest case. The tasks are executed sequentially. The first task must end before the following one begins.
2.	Fork 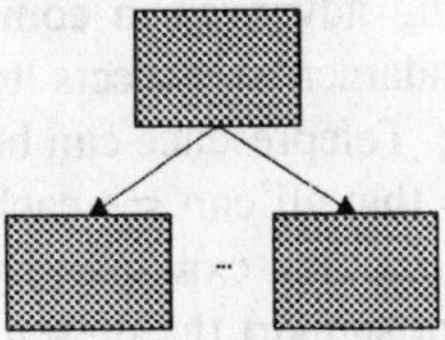		When the first task is finished two (or more) flows are initiated in parallel. These flows may in turn include other parallel flows, etc.
3.	Rendezvous 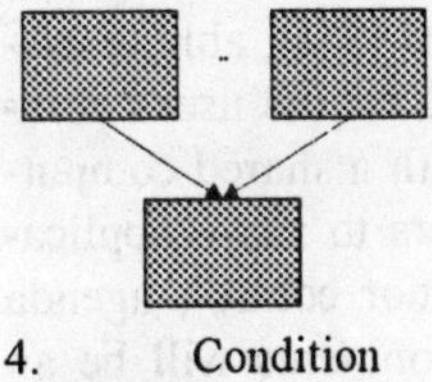		A Parallel flow may end in a rendezvous (or join) task. This task may start only after two (or more) tasks which belong to different flows have ended.
4.	Condition 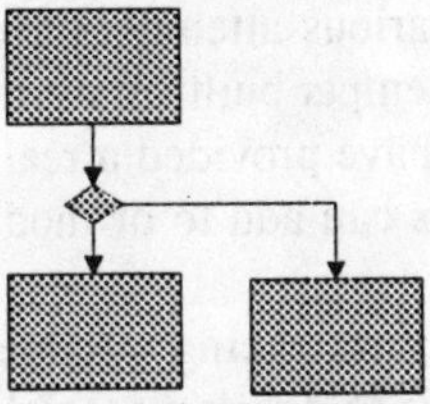		This is the simplest condition. According to the value of a variable either the left or the right flow will be followed at run-time. Note that the alternatives are not executed in parallel.
5.	Alternate 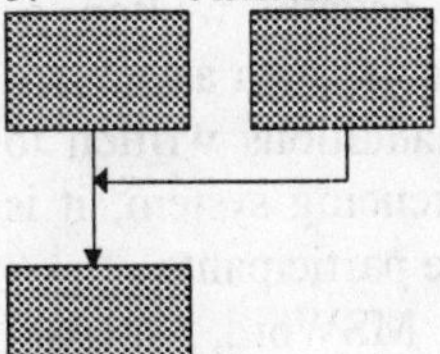		Where alternative paths have been followed because of a condition, it often happens that a task can be the successor of a number of alternatives. It will start when any one of its predecessor tasks terminates.
6.	Loop 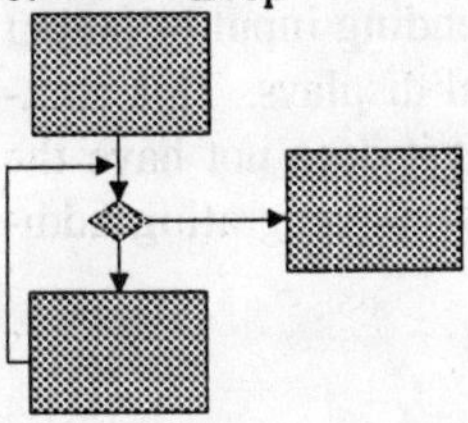		By combining the last two constructs the user may build a loop, as shown in this diagram. Similarly, the user may build more sophisticated constructs (e.g. repeat...until, while...wend, etc)

> One day, in a burst of frank evaluation, one of his charges told him that .. he did not expect [the computer] to save him more than 30 minutes a day... The reason was that this individual was not in his office for more than 30 minutes: he spent almost all his time in meetings! ... Meetings are important. They are at the core of the way most organisations do business.

Desktop conferencing systems aim to provide desktop equipment enabling the activities normally associated with meetings to be carried out without the participants physically meeting. The telephone already very successfully provides some functionality in this direction, and can be coupled with fax so that people can discuss and agree changes to draft documents.

To enhance and extend these successful approaches using advances in computer and communication technology, there are two fundamental aspects to desktop conferencing systems: telepresence and teleworking. Telepresence can be enhanced by adding video images of the people involved so that all can see each other as they confer. This is sometimes considered essential (for example, by banks in dealing with customers), but, on its own, it does not support the presentation of text or diagrams.

Gale (1993) notes that video conferencing is more than just being able to display the video on the computer screen and mount the camera on the user's computer – it is the integration of this conferencing capability with a shared computing environment. This environment will not only allow users to share applications, but could also augment the interaction process via floor control, agenda management, etc. He considers that shared computer environments will be an essential part of any desktop video conferencing system. Various attempts have been made to provide such a shared environment. Early attempts built on asynchronous electronic messaging (or "bulletin boards"). Some have provided a real-time electronic version of the chalkboard, that multiple users can add to or modify; and others have seen this as a co-authoring tool.

Basically, there are two strategies for building desktop conferencing systems (Crowley et al 1990, Lauwers et al 1990). The first strategy is to develop specialised *collaboration-aware* tools. Most of these tools are usually written as (multimedia) editors (Ahuja et al 1990); extensions to these tools, such as spreadsheet commands, must be built as specialised, distributed additions written to accommodate multiple users. In this kind of desktop conferencing system, it is the specialised tools that maintain a consistent state for all the participants.

The second strategy is to use *existing single-user* tools (e.g. MSWord, Notepad, etc.). These single-user tools produce data for user collaboration, while the systems are responsible for maintaining a consistent state by sending input or output commands to each conferee's computer to produce identical displays. This strategy generally produces more traffic (Ahuja et al 1990), but it does not have the same need for extension, since new capabilities are gained by integrating additional single-user tools into conferencing systems.

1.7 Information Sharing in Cooperative Work

Sharing information among a group of users amounts to creating a conceptual *shared workspace*. The form that this workspace takes, and its representation to the user, depends on the individual system. The underlying structure of the information is also important, especially since designing computer-mediated work processes might involve the automation of existing manual procedures. However, it should be noted that by attempting to support existing manual procedures with computer technology, those procedures themselves may evolve due to the new features that CSCW systems provide (Bannon and Schmidt 1991). Information shared in cooperative applications will always have some overhead in terms of the information needed to organise a number of individuals into a workgroup with shared goals. A CSCW system needs to cater for these overheads, and provide some facilities in which the information and work can be structured to help users to work together.

Many organisations (and CSCW system designers) do not have a clear idea of how people work together, and what kind of information they need to share. Categorising the information, and finding out which parts are most important to share among users is a major task. Once the shared information has been identified, a model needs to be developed, so that the information can be structured in a suitable way for incorporation into a shared workspace. Once the model of the shared workspace information is complete, tools need to be designed so that users of the system can access and manipulate the information.

Over the last decade the advent of inexpensive personal computers and the explosion in the ability to network them have resulted in a large number of users who regularly use computers in their daily work to access information in a distributed environment. Until recently, there has been little support for users wishing to work together in such an environment. This is a main focus of Computer Supported Cooperative Work (CSCW) research - providing support for computer-mediated workgroups (Ellis et al. 1991).

Creating a workgroup in a distributed computing environment who have access to the same store of information involves a shared workspace. The information in the workspace has to be structured if it is going to be useful, and there are bound to be some main categories into which the shared information can fall. Users should be able to work on different types of tasks – these will either be tasks that they complete on their own using shared information or as part of a shared objective (*asynchronous tasks*), or those which need the simultaneous participation of a number of users at once (*synchronous tasks*). A system intending to provide a comprehensive package to allow information sharing should consider supporting both cases.

The information which workgroup users are going to share needs a structure. Users will be working towards some shared goals in a particular work process. If there are pre-ordained goals, there will be a plan of how they should be achieved.

On the way to these goals, users will perform tasks, sometimes individually, sometimes in groups. Information will be created along the way, in the form of a history of their actions, and documents (parts of the end target) they have produced. Therefore the CSCW system needs to be able to store the plan and historical records of its use, as will as any documents that are created and used whenever the plan is carried out. In practical terms this means providing a database and a document store.

In the resulting shared workspace, five categories of information that users need to share can be identified:

- *System Definitions* – the system information, including the users, user groups and node machines used in the system,
- *Procedure Definitions* – the work process models for the procedures used in the system,
- *Procedure Instances* – the actual instances of the work processes in the system,
- *Shared Awareness* – transient information on the current activities of users, and
- *Dynamic Control* – transient information used to control the execution of procedures, and the coordination of current workgroup activities.

The information in the first two categories is used by the system as a template for activities within the shared workspace: this is the base information. The last three categories carry out the actual process of work - the procedure instances carrying out and recording information for an occurrence of a work process, while the shared awareness and dynamic control are transient information that gives users feedback on the activities of others, and provide control for them to collaborate successfully.

1.8 Use of Existing Applications and Distributing Documents

It has been observed by other writers on CSCW (e.g. Bullen and Bennett 1990) that users report most benefit from tools paralleling non-electronic activities. It seems also to be the case that cooperative applications are most readily accepted if they provide, as far as possible, they same user interface as the standard single-user tools that are used by the intended beneficiaries of the CSCW system.

Users simply do not want to throw away their existing single-user applications. Even if they did, it would be expensive in development time to replicate the required functionality for a shared environment. The obvious answer is to try to integrate the existing single-user applications into the CSCW system. This does not pose too much of a technical problem for asynchronous tasks, only for synchronous tasks, where the shared environment needs to ensure that all participants in a task see the same representation of a shared application, i.e. *What You See Is What I See* (WYSIWIS).

However, the screen operation is not the whole of the story, since in most environments, each workstation has its local disk storage, and not all documents will be in shared file systems. A number of categories of documents can be considered. Documents can have various roles in a task: they may be downloaded from a standard original or saved previous version, created, read-accessed, updated, published, archived, or deleted in the task. Numerous combinations of these cases are possible, though some are not useful together.

1.9 Groupware Systems

A very large number of groupware products are now available, making a complete listing unpractical (Malm, 1994). Some of the most interesting groupware systems are profiled here. Some are available commercially, while others are experimental systems under exploration in various high-technology research laboratories.

1.9.1 BBN/Slate

BBN/Slate is a powerful groupware product for Sun, Digital, and IBM RISC workstations. BBN/Slate offers support for multilingual word processing, spreadsheets, graphics, bitmapped and colour raster images, voice, and audio, all built around TCP/IP compatible networks.

Documents can be edited by a group of users, with BBN/Slate providing collaboration for both local and remote sites. BBN/Slate allows users to create live links with other data files, so when changes are made to the data, they are reflected in the compound document.

At the Rensselaer Polytechnic Institute (RPI) in Troy, New York, BBN/Slate provides 500 instructional assistants scattered across the campus, in classrooms, faculty offices, the library, and student dormitories. Although this is not really a groupwork application, it nonetheless sets an exciting precedent.

Spreadsheets, graphics, screen shots, colour plots, text, and even symbolic algebra equations can be put into BBN/Slate documents. (BBN/Slate also supports sound and video, but the RPI stations are not equipped to use them.)

Students can embed programs in a BBN/Slate document that are launched when clicked. They use BBN/Slate's e-mail component to mail their work off to the professors and human teaching assistants, who correct and change the documents and e-mail them back to the students.

BBN/Slate is available from BBN Software Products of Cambridge, Massachusetts.

1.9.2 Xerox Analyst

Analyst is presented as an "integrated hypermedia system". It mixes a wide range of object-oriented applications, including word processing, desktop publishing, spreadsheets, forms, graphics, images, databases, and maps, with rule-based organisation tools and an expert system shell. Analyst runs on Macintosh and DOS machines, and on Sun, Apollo, 11P, Tektronix, and Xerox workstations. Analyst is available from Xerox Special Information Systems of Pasadena, California.

1.9.3 Lotus Notes

Lotus Notes provides a shared multimedia-database system where workgroups can build applications like customer tracking, status reporting, project management, and information distribution. Lotus Notes also supports video, images, voice, and even "phonemail" via VoxLink's add-ons. The various media modes that Lotus Notes supports are very important, since users demand this power and flexibility.

These larger systems include NewWave Office from Hewlett Packard, OfficeVision from IBM, NCR Corporation from NCR Corporation, Alis from Applix Inc., AT&T Rhapsody from AT&T Computer Systems, and Cliq from Quadratron Systems Inc.

Action Workflow, available from Action Technologies Inc, Alameda, CA, uses Lotus Notes. It provides rapid application development for integrating business processes. The system includes workflow software, business process re-engineering analysis tools and educational courses on process analysis.

1.9.4 MARS (Multi-User Archival and Retrieval System)

MARS is an image management system that stores scanned paper documents and full-color photographs, digital sound and video.

MARS runs on a network of Macintoshes, with a dedicated directory server for maintaining document descriptions, a dedicated optical server for reading images from and writing them to WORM (write-once-read-many-times) optical devices, and Mac workstations for archiving and retrieving documents.

MARS is available from Micro Dynamics of Silver Springs, Maryland.

1.9.5 The Coordinator

This groupware product shows the significance of hierarchy within cooperation systems.

Winograd and Flores (1986) examines this software program in the context of artificial intelligence theory-building, specifically in the area of speech act theory.

> There are a surprisingly few basic conversational building-blocks (like request/promise, offer/acceptance, and report/acknowledgement) that frequently recur in conversations for action. The development of a conversation requires selection among a certain finite set of possibilities that is defined by the opening directive and the subsequent responses. It is like a dance, giving some initiative to each partner in a specific sequence. (p. 159)

Based on the principles of speech act theory, The Coordinator transposes conversational routines to a networked format, in which groupwork team members "declare" their agreements and commitments. The computer then holds them accountable for the commitments in a public record.

The software structures two conversations: "Conversations for Possibilities" and "Conversations for Action." Its formulas ask participants to "declare," to "promise", and "commit", and to articulate the "conditions of satisfaction" of a "request".

Perin (1991) says The Coordinator has been criticised for forcing clarity and commitment from participants, for assigning authority to the software system, and for promoting a top-down approach, which indeed is contrary to the nature of collaboration.

1.9.6 The Virtual Meeting

This is a Macintosh software package for desktop videoconferencing. The Virtual Meeting uses networks mostly to control the screens of widely separated participants.

With this system, companies can run meetings that include QuickTime movies or other video, audio, and high-quality graphics without incurring the costs of real-time videoconferencing. This material must be distributed before the meeting and physically available at all sites taking part.

Control information, which can cause the same video or graphics to appear on all screens simultaneously, is distributed in real time, using ordinary analogue telephone lines. The Virtual Meeting includes an electronic whiteboard feature that lets users real time. The participants' images appear on screen. They can "raise their hands" electronically if they wish to take an active role.

The package can launch ordinary Mac applications and display participant's documents on all screens with System 7. The Virtual Meeting costs $3,600 for a ten-user system. It includes broadcast server software.

The Virtual Meeting is available from RTZ Software of Cupertino, California.

1.9.7 Bell Labs' Rapport System

This is an experimental groupware system that allows co-workers to jointly edit computer files while discussing them. Participants may communicate through voice and data only, or add full-motion video.

This system presents a uniform interface for e-mail, voice, video, and computer communications. It allows favourite word processor, CAD system, or financial planning program to be used on almost any project.

Researchers at AT&T Bell Laboratories in Holmdel, New Jersey, are pursuing an egalitarian approach to multimedia communications, using the metaphor of a "virtual meeting room".

Participants see video images of each other in separate windows on a Sun workstation. The documents they discuss are seen in another window. Although only one person at a time can control the software, everyone can see the results.

To "raise a hand" or point to various sections of a document, users control a mouse that controls an arrow with their name on it.

The Rapport system has a "store-and-forward" function that shares sketches and drawings in allows participants to save meetings so other people can see them. An engineering team, for example, might brainstorm on a design, then forward a portion of the discussion across the country to people in marketing, who could add their comments and return the meeting file to the engineers.

1.9.8 Pandora

This is an experimental groupware system at the Olivetti Research Laboratory in Cambridge, England. When researchers get to work, they clip on an electronic badge that links them to Pandora, the laboratory's experimental video and audio communication system.

The badges emit infrared signals that allow other research engineers to find each other whenever they want to chat. Once paged, a researcher can sit at the nearest computer terminal and begin to talk to up to five people, whose faces show up in different screen windows.

Pandora also offers a "video news server" that allows users to see recorded BBC news and weather reports by clicking an icon on the computer screen. Researchers can also send video mail with the click of a button.

1.9.9 TeamWorkStation

Ishii and Miyaki (1991), of the Human Interface Laboratories of Japan's NTT, say this mixes, on a workstation display, standard applications and live video projections of colleagues and desktop activity.

This system bridges gaps between the desktop, the personal computer, and telecommunications. The metaphor behind it is the "open shared workspace": workgroup members should be able to bring a wide variety of tools, both old and new, to a cooperative work session and use them simultaneously.

This principle led researchers to choose video as the basic system medium. At the heart of each workstation is a Macintosh computer with two screens, one for individual work and the other for shared work. The audio-visual link is provided by a speaker phone and two miniature video cameras - one camera for faces and one, mounted on a flexible desk lamp, to capture the desktop and the user's hand gestures.

Two to four people can work together with TeamWorkStation, seeing each other in the shared screen window. It is reported that psychologists have found that in face-to-face talks, only about 7 per cent of meaning is conveyed by words, while 38 per cent is conveyed by intonation, and 55 per cent through visual cues. A Wharton School of Business study found that video increased information retention among participants by 50 per cent and accelerated buying decisions by 72 per cent.

1.9.10 Media Space

Xerox PARC developed this system specifically for collaboration in design work. It eliminates the shared computer applications possible on Rapport and TeamWorkStation in favour of video alone, but the video is linked via computer workstations.

With Media Space, design is seen less as a technical activity than a social activity, so video is the best communication medium.

This system links 25 or 30 offices through workstations outfitted with video cameras and monitors. Although the cameras are always on, they face in whatever direction the users elect to point them. Half a dozen people can see each other at once. Media Space has been used successfully within the Xerox PARC lab in Palo Alto, California and between researchers at Palo Alto and another Xerox lab in Portland, Oregon.

Related to this is a system called Videodraw that allows designers to sketch together while seeing each other over the Media Space system. According to Brittan, "Drawing directly on a monitor reproduces the familiar experience of putting pen to paper".

1.9.11 Electronic Cafe International

This is basically a groupware system for artistic collaboration and performance.

Electronic Cafe International (ECI), based in Santa Monica, California, links sixty locations throughout the world, using video and computers as an interactive communications medium to pioneer virtual space.

In ECI, people from different locations are electronically mixed, using satellite linkages, into the same real-time virtual space. The ECI has sponsored dance projects, "Earth Day Global Link '90", and other collaborative creative initiatives that include connections and real-time teleperformances by participants across the globe. The ECI is event-driven; arts groups are encouraged to produce events.

1.9.12 TalkShow

FutureLabs' TalkShow allows screens to be captured and distributed, and allows use of OLE to link to graphic or text objects. It runs over any NetBIOS network, and relies on peer-to-peer arrangements, which eats into memory on each station. It does not support the sharing of a running application. The number of participants is not limited, and users can annotate in text and graphics in different colours.

Rash (1994) says this system is good for free-flowing, unstructured discussions.

1.9.13 DeskTop Conferencing

Fujitsu's DeskTop Conferencing product runs over a Novell NetWare LAN, and allows the control station to echo the screens of programs as they are used, and allow remote control of someone else's computer (Rash 1994). It is advanced in not requiring a screen capture operation, and is basically a server-based whiteboard product that supports drawing with the mouse on the shared images (but not keyboard operation), and allows advance preparation of images using a flipchart utility.

Rash (1994) says that, because of its structured approach to meetings, this is a recommended solution for formal presentations with a strong meeting chair. It supports a maximum of 8 users per conference; users can request control, which the chair can allow or deny; there is a dialogue announcing requests to join the conference; users annotate in different colours, or send private notes or whole files by e-mail.

1.9.14 TeamSync

GlobalStream's TeamSync has no whiteboard, but supports the insertion of graphics into a text-based conferencing system. Rash (1994) says that if requirements include having a transcript of the proceedings of a conference, TeamSync is to be preferred: this approach also allows time-independent conferencing, since late participants can see a rerun of the proceedings to date.

2. Reflections on Requirements

User's needs were the driving force for the MMTCA project. Because of the involvement of two user organisations – BDC (a Spanish bank) and ISL (a German shipping institute) – a kind of cooperative application scenario that happens commonly in their business situations has been identified:

A manager wants to set up arrangements or to delegate tasks involving cooperation between people using standard commercial software tools for cooperation; main concerns include: the cooperation can be in a synchronous or an asynchronous manner; the time span of a cooperation can be short (e.g. up to an hour) or long (e.g. for several days or months); the sequence of task-executing can be designed; and the final product of a cooperation can be a document.

Since there are no CSCW products that can satisfy all of these points, MMTCA has been developed to address the needs of this kind of user.

2.1 What Cooperation is to be Supported?

From the point of view of the last chapter, it may well seem that much of the existing work on CSCW has been misdirected. Many of the writers agree that it is best to take existing procedures and support them, rather than to devise completely new ways of working that add further barriers to user acceptance of the solutions proposed.

From the point of view of the last chapter, computer support for cooperation is best provided where computer support is already familiar. Word processors, spreadsheets, and simple office tools such as electronic mail, scheduling, task delegation are all widely in use. Increasingly environments integrating such tools (e.g. WordPerfect Office) support multimedia documents. What is lacking in such systems is the notion of standard process: each step in what may be a routine matter (such as sending a form for countersignature) has to be individually requested.

Approval and acceptance of terms: Many forms of cooperation amount to approval of some standard request (e.g. for holidays, of expenditure). Computers (and integrated office environments) are often used for the independent operations of composing, transmitting and printing the associated documents. It would be attractive to have end-user tools for establishing routine operations of this sort.

Meetings: At present, for example, many people prepare discussion papers for a meeting on personal computers, and print them to circulate to meeting participants. They could be sent by electronic mail, but in any case, eventually a discussion will take place, in a meeting or on the telephone, where each participant has a copy of the discussion paper in front of them, possibly by viewing it on their desktop computer. It would be attractive to coordinate the displays of the personal computers so that they can point to things, and watch alterations as they are made, as if they were sitting together at the one workstation.

Some of the previous work envisaged converting asynchronous, independent computer supported mechanisms such as editing a document, into multiuser editing. From the point of view of MMTCA, this does not seem to be a useful thing to do. It is much more natural for portions of the document to be assigned to various authors to write, and then be edited together, rather than simply letting all the co-authors loose to make random alterations on random parts of the document. Once a reasonable draft is available, a meeting (real or virtual) can agree further or final modifications to the draft, preparing for the next stages of the process. *Synchronous* cooperative work is inevitably intrusive to a greater or lesser extent, that is, noticeably different from asynchronous work where people can work separately on their contribution. Support for synchronous working should, from this point of view, only be provided where meetings would otherwise be essential.

Some of the previous work implied the provision of special high-technology facilities, for example, special-purpose videoconferencing rooms, or special meeting rooms with computer support. This seems to miss the essential requirements, implicit in the above discussion, that

- the technological support must be familiar, and reflect as far as possible the ordinary working environment. This would prohibit the use of software only found in such a special facility.
- the technology should aim, as does the telephone, to allow groups to carry out their common activities from their desktop.

Such research, however, is understandable when it is considered that adequate desktop equipment was not then available, and is only now becoming feasible.

2.2 Communicate, Cooperate, Coordinate

In this section, the main technical areas related to, and requirements for, a groupwork-oriented computing system are discussed. To support group interaction, three key areas should be catered for – communication, cooperation, and coordination (Ellis et al 1991).

Computer-based or computer-mediated communication, such as electronic mail, is not fully integrated with other forms of communication. The primarily asynchronous, text-based world of electronic mail and bulletin boards exists separately from the synchronous world of telephone and face-to-face conversation. While applications such as voice mail or talk programs blur this distinction somewhat, there are still gaps between the asynchronous and the synchronous worlds. For example, a document cannot be transferred between two arbitrary phone numbers; and it is uncommon to organise a telephone conversation from a workstation. Integrating telecommunications and computer processing technologies will help bridge these gaps.

Similar to communication, cooperation is a cornerstone of group activity. Effective cooperation demands that people share information. Current information systems – database systems in particular – go to great lengths to insulate users from each other. As an example, consider two designers working with a CAD database. Seldom are they able to simultaneously modify different parts of the same object and be aware of each other's changes; rather, they must check the object in and out and tell each other what they have done. Many tasks require an even finer granularity of sharing. What is needed are shared environments that unobtrusively offer up-to-date group context and explicit notification of each user's actions when appropriate.

The effectiveness of communication and cooperation can be enhanced if a group's activities are coordinated. Without coordination, for example, a team of programmers or writers will often engage in conflicting or repetitive actions. Coordination can be viewed as an activity in itself, as a necessary overhead when several parties are performing a task. While current database applications contribute somewhat to the coordination of groups – by providing multiple access to shared objects – most software tools offer only a single-user perspective and thus do little to assist this important function.

On the basis of these three key areas which should be catered for to support collaborative processes and the problems that have been described in the previous section, the main requirements for groupwork-oriented computing systems are discussed below:

- The system should provide mechanisms to facilitate communications among users. A multimedia approach is preferable.
- The system should be able to build an environment under which users are able to carry out collaborative activities, synchronously or asynchronously.

- The system should provide a mechanism to integrate existing single-user tools. By integrating the existing tools, it is meant that in order to ensure the appearance and configuration of shared tools is the same on all participants' displays, the tools' interfaces should be identically customised.
- The system should perform routing of work to individuals based on relationships between units of work. It should allow users to access and perform the work that they should do, by providing an "intray-list" that contains work in progress as well as new work to be performed.
- When necessary, the system should allow for human involvement in determining what sequence of system actions is required to perform tasks. On the other hand, automatically executing tasks should be accommodated as well, where the system actions can be decided in advance and carried out without human intervention.
- The system should provide both programming and run-time support mechanisms for organisers of collaborative processes in instantiating and starting a collaborative process, as well as viewing the structure of a process.
- The system should support monitoring of an on-going process. The progress of work in each process should be recorded. It should be able to generate reports on the status of all activities. This measurement enables a feedback loop whereby an organisation can improve its processes.
- The system should be open, in the sense of being based on industry standards for operating systems, networks, file systems, databases, and window system services; and users being able to build their own customised collaborative applications. It should operate in distributed environments.

2.3 Workflow Management Software

In the last chapter, the concept of workflow in cooperative work was introduced. In many application areas, there are legal or security requirements that procedures should be followed rigorously, for auditing, insurance or safety purposes, and in these areas, an important role for computer support is to provide this kind of guarantee: by having the computer system enforce the procedure and/or record what is done. If the computer system is enforcing adherence to the procedure, then one way of doing this is to make documents accessible only via a controlled distribution system, with no independent access to the documents involved.

Workflow management software is a proactive computer system that manages the flow of work among participants, according to a defined procedure consisting of a number of tasks. It coordinates user and system participants, together with the appropriate data resources, which may be accessible directly or off-line, to achieve defined objectives. Such coordination involves passing tasks from participant to participant in correct sequence, ensuring that all fulfil their required contributions.

In other application areas, computer support is seen more as helpful advice: participants are advised of tasks they should be doing, but they can examine or work on other things whenever they have time. This type of support can be provided by making documents available via a network file system, and seeing the computer support mechanisms as providing reminders rather than dictating what must be done.

In either case, workflow software allows a user to construct a script, which defines the business process for which the system is to be used. This script then controls the business process either in the strong or weak sense considered earlier. In order to develop the script, the user needs first to model the business process and input this to a workflow procedure set-up facility. In the MMTCA project there is a graphical method of setting up procedures, allowing the programmer to display procedures in a "flow diagram" form as the procedure is built.

The software used in workflow systems (Ovum, 1993) has evolved through three stages:

1. from a customised program, written in a base language, such as C to a given business specification and for a specific platform;
2. through rigid application-specific frameworks;
3. to flexible workflow scripting languages that can be packaged for most general office applications and are compatible with most platforms.

It is only now, in the third stage, that workflow is emerging as a significant element of the software market. This trend may be attributed to two main factors:

- a move to open systems, typically UNIX systems
- a move to right-size computer systems.

Many organisations already have in place the necessary workstation and LAN infrastructure to support workflow. Most of these use the PC with MS-DOS and Windows, so that most workflow products are designed for this platform.

Workflow management is a relatively novel activity, so there are no generally accepted steps to follow. However, the following phases are readily identified:

- **Creating the procedure:** This is the most important phase of workflow management. It includes defining the tasks which make up a procedure, setting up relationships among tasks, entering information related to the actions which will be carried out at each task and the users who are responsible for each one.
- **Managing the procedure:** This phase of workflow management is an ongoing process, which begins once a procedure is downloaded to the server. The functionality that should be present consists of updating and/or deleting existing procedures, changing the status of procedures, etc.

- **Producing reports on procedures:** In this phase, the system presents to the user information on all procedures present in the server.

In the next chapter it will be seen that MMTCA's approach supports the whole spectrum of possibilities in this area.

2.4 An example: Cooperative Engineering Design

In engineering work, cooperation occurs between designers working in the same project, consultation with the chief designer, design reviews, training, etc. This case represents an extreme where cooperation needs to be supported but procedures are kept relatively informal.

In cooperation between designers working on the same project there is a need for exchange of ideas on specific problems arising during the design process such as common reference to design specifications, and control of the interfaces between parts of a complex design designed by different co-designers. Cooperating designers can make use of advice and assistance from an expert or consultant such as the chief designer on the specific design they are working on. In general, there might be a number of experts, perhaps one for each technical topic.

Design reviews are an inherently cooperative procedure. During a review, a group of designers reviews a specific design at different stages of the design process, and notably before its release for the prototyping phase. The review process addresses the verification and validation of the results of the design process. It includes the identification of possible errors in the design and deviations from the given specifications and requirements.

A cooperative design environment could also be used for training purposes.

Each member of a cooperating group of designers needs to communicate and share tools and data with any or all of the other members at various times. Cooperative design activities are expected to be dominated by shared drawing, perhaps by shared editing of technical documents, and on the telephone or voice in an enhanced video conference. The designers may all also need to access specifications from the shared database. These specific cooperative operations are supported by such processes as cooperative work, messaging, access to the database and data exchange.

Design procedures also require communication with the providers of CAD requirements and specifications, who may be situated outside the company environment. Requirements are often initially delivered to the CAD project members as a document, but these requirements almost always need to be supplemented and elucidated continuously by personal contact or, with sufficient computer support, through computer conferencing. At the end of the design process communication is necessary with the same (usually) people for the delivery of the final product, which then includes CAD drawings and associated documentation.

Since cooperative design activity is less structured than operations in a bank, monitoring of cooperative design activity requires additional support. The methods, rules and standards being followed by a design team must be continuously followed up by the person coordinating the work (project leader) during the progress of the work. Timing problems according to delivery deadlines must be continuously updated and coordination of the work of members of the design team must be assured.

Agreement on design choices between co-designers working on different parts of the same complex object is a prerequisite for the completion of a complex design without any adaptation problem.

2.5 Cooperative Interaction

In the previous chapter, the question was considered whether new, collaboration aware, applications should be developed to support cooperation, or existing single-user (collaboration transparent) applications be used? Besides the implicit familiarity and abundance of single-user applications, the development time needed to create new collaborative applications puts this approach at a disadvantage. It could also be argued that CSCW work should concentrate on promoting cooperation, not in reinventing cooperative versions of existing applications.

To sharpen ideas, consider the example of cooperative engineering design introduced in the last chapter. In cooperative design three modes of computer-supported cooperation can be envisaged:

- In *Tele-screen mode*, the information within a computer, produced by a single user, may be shown to remote users in a loosely coupled collaboration.
- In *Tele-point mode*, users may share individual workspaces and see or point to those.
- In *Computer-sharing mode*, remote users may collaborate by obtaining full control, through their input media (keyboard, mouse, etc) of the shared workspace.

MMTCA provides this last, most advanced form of cooperation; and with the same standard applications that users are accustomed to using. However, it is reasonable to consider that users might find it more suitable to choose the cooperation mode that they wish to use. For example,

- suppose user A starts to explain his or her drawing to user B using the tele-screen mode.

- if B wants to point to, or mark a part of the drawing to ask a question, the users can move to the tele-point mode and user B can point to the part of A's drawing using his own pointer (i.e. mouse).
- if B felt it was necessary to change a part of the drawing directly, and if A agreed, they could move to the computer-sharing mode.

Users in a cooperative session will be aware that they are operating in this unusual mode, and will generally need to consciously limit themselves to actions that are likely to have the same validity at each participating node. For example, if cooperation extends across timezones, it is not straightforward to insert a timestamp in a document in a cooperative session.

In a cooperative environment the concept of the floor holder is introduced. A floor holder has the right to manipulate shared windows. Four floor passing modes can be identified:

- *Designation mode*, in which the chairperson selects the next floor holder;
- *Button mode*, where a floor holder designates the next floor holder
- *First come first served mode*, in which the floor is passed in the order of the floor request queue;
- *Free* mode, in which all the participants can apparently simultaneously manipulate the shared window.

During cooperative interaction, the user might be able to use the following types of windows:

(a) A *Cooperative Session Management Window* could show menus to enable the user to define or modify the cooperative environment, convening participants, requesting to join an ongoing session, and setting options. It should also enable the participant to request the floor, to handle the participant's own departure, to permit other participants to leave, and allow external services to be started up.

In addition, the window could show status information such as who is the floor holder and has the right to manipulate shared windows, the duration of the cooperative session, the present time, the chairperson's name and the floor passing mode.

(b) The *Shared or Group Windows* could appear on the display surfaces of all participants in the session, and are connected. A shared window is the space where shareable documents may be co-edited by the participants in a cooperative session. This means that the drawings and documents on the shared windows would be shared by all the participants and all the modifications to the drawings and documents made by a floor holder are transmitted to all the participants instantly, based on a What You See Is What I See (WYSIWIS) principle.

(c) *Personal windows* would be private to a participant: their data are not seen by other participants in the session. Personal windows are useful for taking private notes during a session, or for loading and editing personal drawings or documents. More than one shared or personal windows may be open simultaneously if needed. A participant should be able to view and handle, for example,

CAD drawings in shared windows and in his personal windows at the same time, and cut out a portion of a drawing and paste it to another drawing.

Participants can access databases when they need information for reference purposes during a cooperative session. The retrieved information can be cut out and pasted onto drawings on shared windows and personal windows.

Participants may wish to change positions and sizes of shared windows, personal windows, and the video window (if it exists) on their own workstation screen as they wish, while having the contents of shared windows the same as that of other participants. This feature allows participants to do other things, such as preparing drawings and accessing databases personally, wile attending a cooperative session.

Two aspects of this functionality are not fully supported by MMTCA at present. Many applications are single-instance applications and so are either shared or private but not both; and the clipboard is not shared at present, so that cutting from a private window and pasting into a shared window is not supported. The shared window can be moved or resized by the floor holder, and this in practice conflicts with private windows.

(d) *Mail or videoconference windows.* These and other external services should be available to a participant while attending a cooperative session.

2.6 Shared-Input versus Shared-Output

Two kinds of architecture can be adopted using available single-user tools to implement desktop conferencing systems (Lauwers et al 1990); a centralised architecture and a replicated architecture.

The centralised architecture, where only one copy of each single-user tool executes, is shown in Figure 2.1. The conference agent (CA) receives input from one site (i.e. the current floor-holder site) and forwards it to the tools; at the same time, the CA distributes output to all conference sites for display, including the local window system. Since it is the output of the tool that is shared by all sites of a conference, such a system is called a shared-output desktop conferencing system.

The replicated architecture is shown in Figure 2.2. In this case, a copy of the tool runs at every site in the conference. Under a floor-control policy, input is generated at one of the conference sites (i.e. the current floor-holder site) and is distributed to all copies of that tool. The output from each copy only appears locally. Because all copies have the same input, their states remain synchronised, generating identical displays at each conference site. Such a system is called a shared-input desktop conferencing system.

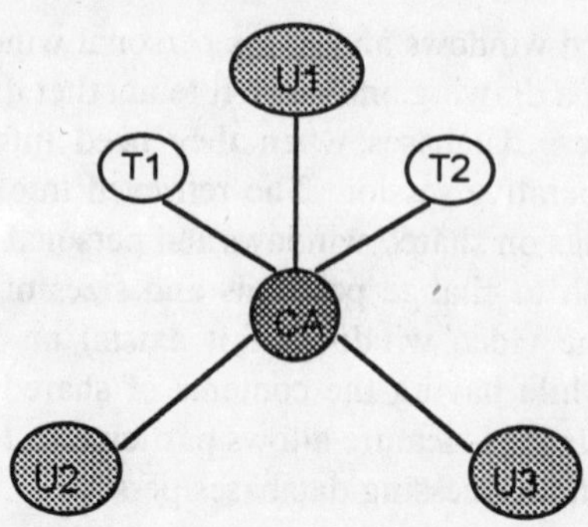

Fig 2.1. The shared-output architecture

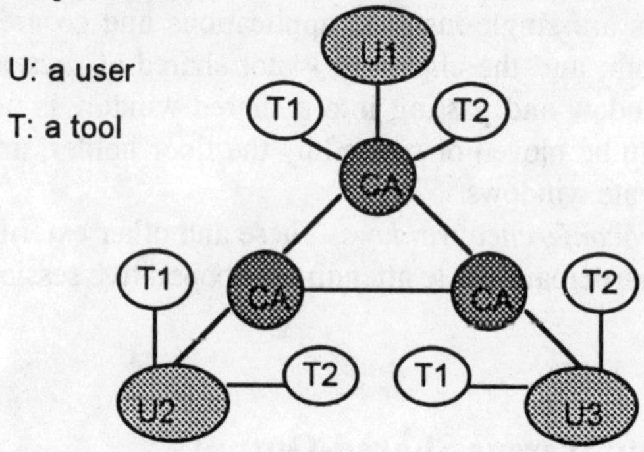

Fig 2.2. The shared-input architecture

Table 2.1. Shared-Input architecture

Advantages	Disadvantages
• Lower bandwidth (only input must be distributed)	• Hard to maintain consistency (input event loss and misordering, different tool initial states, nondeterminism, and latecomers to an on-going conference)
• Better response time (interacting with single-user tools locally)	• More tool licences (multiple copies of one single-user tool)
• Versatility (work under either kernel- based or server-based window systems)	• More memory space used (multiple copies of single-user tools and the files those tools work on)
• Capable of easy extension (just integrate additional single-user tools into conferencing systems)	• Hard to implement (need more complicated designs; e.g. tackling event loss, misordering, etc.)

In terms of performance, the shared-input approach is the winner, but sometimes special application contexts may contribute to a decision as to which approach to adopt. In a 10 Mbit/s Ethernet, it can be practical to use the shared-output approach to implement a desktop conferencing system with two or three participants provided there is only limited use of images or graphics. In this case, performance related to traffic and response time can be acceptable, since the number of participants is small, data is transmitted locally and the throughput of the Ethernet is competitive. However, things would get worse if such an approach were adopted across WANs. Under WAN environments, performance related to traffic volume and response time becomes so vital that a shared-input approach should be used instead. Therefore, we ought not simply to conclude that one of the two approaches is absolutely better than the other, since that may depend on particular application contexts. For MMTCA, one of the design issues is that the developed toolbox is expected to be used in a distributed manner (e.g. under WAN environments), and the multimedia aspect is important; hence, the shared-input approach has been adopted, although it is the more difficult to implement (Lauwers et al 1990).

2.7 Lightweight or Heavyweight Cooperation?

This is a controversial area in the literature. MMConf allows unplanned (lightweight) conferences 'analogous to a quick phone call' to take place (Crowley et al. 1990). Although such collaborations undoubtedly have their uses, without a structured (heavyweight) model for cooperation, group collaboration is unlikely to lead to the production of coherent - and useful - target products (Jeffay et al. 1992).

Another consideration is a technical one: for any desktop conferencing system to work, the systems must be carefully configured to match sufficiently well for similar displays to be possible on the participating machines. In the case of shared-application operation, the display characteristics must match: similar screen resolution, number of colour planes, and fonts. For shared-input operation, similar versions of the software must exist, with similar templates and customisation (MMTCA can arrange for these to be downloaded when required through operation of the tool profile concept). In either case the keyboards and mice must be compatible.

Nevertheless, it is reasonable to consider that in a department where these conditions are met, so that all desktop machines have a similar configuration, ad hoc cooperative sessions might be very attractive. For this reason, in MMTCA the concept of the ready-to-run cooperative session has been added, whereby any "organiser" can set up a cooperative session and specify dynamically not only the participants but also the documents and applications involved.

2.8 Conference Awareness

Stefik et al (1987) invented the concept of What You See Is What I See or WYSIWIS, which they pronounce as "whizzy whizz". They noted that the advantages of WYSIWIS are a strong sense of shared context (e.g. people can refer to something by position) and simple implementation, but felt that its major disadvantage is that it can be inflexible. In their experience users often wanted independent control over such details as window placement and size, and might require customised information within the window. They suggested that WYSIWIS can be relaxed along four key dimensions: display space (the display objects to which WYSIWIS is applied), time of display (when displays are synchronised), subgroup population (the set of participants involved or affected), and congruence of view (the visual congruence of displayed information).

However, Stefik et al were developing a multiuser system (CoLab) where the level of cooperation was quite low. Basically each user was independently editing part of a shared document, and while it was therefore important to be kept up-to-date with changes being made concurrently by other users, it is not surprising that they found it necessary to provide concurrency control so that two users could not be simultaneously editing the same piece of text, and to consider issues such as distraction where updates to other parts of the screen could distract someone while editing their piece of text. Other research groups added "clouds" to indicate parts of the document that were locked for other users to update.

From the viewpoint of this project, co-authorship of this kind is like writing a document in a committee meeting. For anything other than small changes, it is always better for people to go away and come back with draft sections that can be discussed and integrated in a meeting. Sharing or concurrency control should be provided to cope with accidents where more than one person is trying to modify the same document: these are really failures of management, since the work should be allocated so that participants do not tread on each other's toes.

Ellis (1991) gives the following example: In a single user system the contextual information plays a key part in the interaction. For example, if a user wants to delete some text the following actions might be performed:

1. The user selects the text to be deleted
2. The system inverts the text to show that it has been deleted
3. The user selects the "delete" option from one of the menus
4. The system displays a window which says "Delete Text – Y/N"
5. The user selects "Y"
6. The system deletes the selected text

On the face of it this seems very straightforward, but the second user will get no feedback about the actions of the first user until the text is deleted. The second user is not party to events one to five. If every user sharing the application is informed of all the actions of the other users then users may be quickly distracted by all this additional, and largely inappropriate, information. In some cases it is possible that adding multimedia communications to the system might overcome this problem as users often tend to verbalise their actions as they are performing a task. For example, users frequently thought that resizing or iconifying a shared window would produce the same result on the other users' workstations (indeed if we were strictly obeying the rules of WYSIWIS then they would!)

In the next chapter it will be seen that MMTCA keeps to a very strict WYSIWIS paradigm during cooperative sessions, but avoids many of these pitfalls. In the first place, only one user at a time (the floor holder) can modify the document, and all participants can see the mouse movements and feedback while this is happening. Secondly, in MMTCA the shared window can only be iconified by the floorholder, and then of course it has the same effect on all screens.

Such close interaction only makes sense during a negotiation session or similar conference, and usually accompanies a telephone conversation (or videoconference). Interaction between people generally involves the use of invaluable visual and audible clues to what is being discussed. It is natural then to assume that successful cooperation of geographically distributed users can be promoted by the provision of shared perception (i.e. videoconferencing) applications.

3. The MMTCA Approach

Three of the key areas in CSCW applications are the concepts of *communication, collaboration and coordination* (Ellis et al 1991). As a CSCW product, MMTCA necessarily provides for all three areas. Collaboration in MMTCA is provided through dynamic control, especially in a Cooperative Session (CS) – i.e. a synchronous task. MMTCA provides implicit communication through the WYSIWIS aspect of a CS, and its feedback on which users are currently logged in, updates on task state changes in user intrays, and participants/chair/floorholder in a CS. Explicit communication facilities are provided by the optional videoconference and other external services that can be integrated into the MMTCA environment.

MMTCA provides coordination through its Procedure-Task-Action (PTA) model for a work process. This gives a structured hierarchy to the process. Goals in the process are provided by the production of a *metadocument*, which is the running of an instance of a procedure, with the consequent production of a set of *documents* for that procedure instance. Work in the procedure instance is carried out by *participants*, the workflow between *tasks* is controlled by *links*, and can be controlled and altered in a particular procedure instance by the link activations, and also by the use of *variables*.

The following lists main differences between MMTCA and other related work.

- Many desktop conferencing systems (Crowley et al 1990, Lantz 1986, Stefik et al 1987) cannot support a workflow control mechanism, while MMTCA can.
- Although workflow mechanisms are also supported by some systems (Dwight 1991), our system provides users with a collaborative environment, in which they can select their favourite single-user tools (theoretically no limitation to the number of tools selected), while those systems just support one single-user tool (image management or engineering product data management, etc.).
- Some "office procedure" systems (Sarin et al 1991) provide functionality which overlaps with our system (i.e. they can support workflow control, multiple single-user tools, etc.); MMTCA can support synchronous collaborative applications as well as asynchronous ones, while those systems can only support asynchronous applications. To support synchronous collaborative

applications through the shared-input approach is more difficult (Lauwers et al 1990) than to just support asynchronous ones.
- Both our system and some "office procedure" systems (Zisman 1977, Ellis and Bernal 1982) have similar graph-based tools to describe sequencing dependencies among tasks in a cooperative process; our system can modify the structure of a process dynamically, while other systems cannot.
- A creative involvement of potential end users in design process is essential. A banking and a shipping company have participated throughout the development of MMTCA, in order to provide user input. It has been noted elsewhere that insufficient or non involvement of end users in the design process may be the reason why there are relatively few successful (CSCW) products (Gronbaek et al 1993).

Apart from shipping and banking, the system can cater for various applications which are group-work-oriented, such as distance learning.

Among the five features listed above, the workflow mechanism and the ability of catering for cooperation synchronously as well as asynchronously are the two most distinctive features of MMTCA. They have been identified by other CSCW researchers (Marca and Bock, 1992) as two important features which current CSCW systems ought to support. The year 1994 witnesses several trends in computing and communication technology: the continuing popularity of personal computers and Microsoft's Windows operating system, the growing importance of CSCW, and the availability of powerful networks (both LANs and WANs). These trends lead us to believe that MMTCA will become more important over the coming years.

Our experience with MMTCA shows that there is a great potential in using available computing technology to support collaborative activities, both locally and remotely.

3.1 Organising Work to be Done

MMTCA assumes that the manager is not a computer programmer, but has a clear concept of how the work is to be organised into *tasks*, and the software packages (word processors, spreadsheets etc) that participants might use on their PCs in order to carry out the work.

What the manager does is to set up one or more administrative *procedures*, for example, for appointing staff, or negotiating a sale. Such a procedure will often be used many times (for example, with different posts or customers), and each time it is used a set of documents will be involved, generated by the tasks of the procedure, or standard forms or reference material.

The set of documents corresponding to such a use of a procedure is called in MMTCA a *metadocument*. Each metadocument corresponds to an *instance* of a procedure. The manager may assign the responsibility of initiating (instantiating) a procedure to a particular individual or group, and may specify responsibility for the various tasks in the procedure in more or less detail.

The manager carrying out this role is called the *procedure designer* in the rest of this book. The tool in MMTCA to design procedures is called ViEW: Visual Editor for Workflow, and this is a powerful icon-based interface for carrying out all of the above steps.

There are three further tools provided in MMTCA to help organise the work to be done. These are

- an administration tool for assigning permission to use MMTCA in various ways, and for defining groups of people;
- a metadocument browser, for examining the current state of running or completed procedures and instances;
- a tool profile editor for integrating new tools into the environment: this basically declares to MMTCA what initialisation files the tool uses.

3.2 The Procedure Task Action Model

The MMTCA approach to workflow is based closely on two approaches from the literature, and introduced in Chapter 1: those of Ould (1992) and Christie (1993). It is seen as a simple and effective mechanism for modelling group processes based on concepts that are immediately meaningful to those involved in them. Both Ould and Christie focus on Roles and Activities. In MMTCA however it has been found useful to consider activity in a structured way. Procedures are the largest kind of activity in MMTCA, corresponding to an entire business process; Actions the smallest; while Tasks are intermediate and identified by two properties: (a) tasks cannot be resumed, only restarted from the beginning; and (b) tasks are assigned to a group of people (often just one person) and documents are distributed for tasks to be performed.

Procedures are made up of tasks, and tasks of actions. Thus the PTA model is "*action-driven*": it is through *actions* that actual work is carried out. This model consists of three components:

Action: This is the most elementary concept. *Actions* may be performed by individual users or groups. They are equivalent to program activation (e.g. use word processor to write a letter, use a database program to find a customer's record, use a CAD program to draw a machine part, etc.). Each *action* should be regarded as a single "unit of work" with clearly defined inputs and outputs.

Task: *Tasks* are provided to introduce order to the *actions* of an individual user or a group of users. *Tasks* can be regarded as mini-programs which specify how a set of *actions* should be carried out by a user or a group responsible.

Procedure: This is the most high level concept and corresponds to a "project" in project management terms. *Procedures* are provided to introduce order to *tasks* carried out by individual users or groups of users. *Procedures* can – exactly as in the case of *tasks* – be regarded as mini-programs which specify how *tasks* are to be carried out by the individuals or groups responsible. For example, in the context of a *procedure*, the time sequence of *tasks*, their inter-dependencies in terms of *documents* (e.g., *task A* produces *document A1*, which is required input for *task B*, which produces *document B1*), etc. should be specified. In the context of a *procedure* we are able to specify loops of *tasks*, alternative paths, etc.

The PTA model forms a comprehensive representation of how people carry out their work in a modern organisation environment, and provides obvious ways to cater for the three key areas of communication, cooperation and co-ordination. It can support collaborative activities in a synchronous or asynchronous manner.

The level at which a synchronous or asynchronous cooperation should be carried out is that of *tasks*. *Procedures* are not appropriate because they are composed of activities (i.e. *tasks*) which usually are not carried out at the same time. On the other hand a single *action* is too low level a concept. The activity described by a single *action* is not rich enough to involve a group of people. Therefore, it is *tasks* that should be performed either synchronously or asynchronously.

In the case of asynchronous cooperation no special provisions have to be made. The *task* will be performed by a single user in a manner quite similar to that of normal PC usage. The only difference will be that MMTCA will guide the user as to what programs to load and which files to use, according to the *task's* specification.

For synchronous cooperation, instead of a single user, a group of users will carry out the *task*. They will all be running the same single-user tools (as specified by the *task*), viewing the same *documents*, and will be aware in real-time of each other's actions.

The node software runs on top of Microsoft Windows and the server runs under Unix. The tools shared in a synchronous task are Microsoft Windows single-user tools. Since Windows provides a multitasking environment, the user is free to activate other single-user tools along with MMTCA and those single-user tools which MMTCA activates.

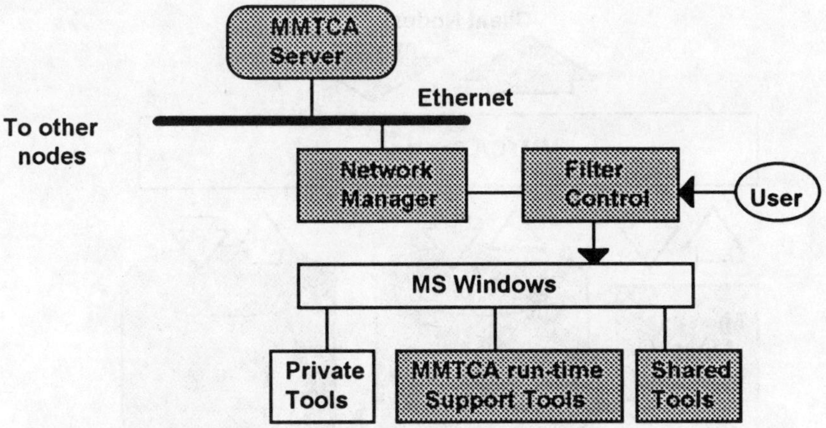

Fig. 3.1. The MMTCA system architecture.

3.3 MMTCA Architecture

MMTCA is implemented on a node-server architecture. Services are presented to users through graphical user interfaces. During the programming phase, users at nodes design cooperative *procedures*. When the designs are complete, the *procedure* definitions are sent to the MMTCA database for storage. During the run time phase, nodes offer users an environment appropriate for carrying out cooperative work. Fig. 3.1 shows the MMTCA system architecture.

MMTCA uses a client-server architecture to implement its information-sharing environment (see section 10.1). The server provides the shared workspace which client nodes access. Nodes do not communicate directly with each other, only through the server.

The MMTCA server currently runs on a Unix machine. It implements a Document Store in the file system, and uses a choice of SQL products for the database (Oracle, Informix or Ingres). Access to these is through the server process, which also implements a Message Manager module to provide information and control message distribution between nodes.

The MMTCA node software provides a number of tools and services for presenting the shared workspace to the user, and integrating their single-user applications into the workspace. The node software runs on a PC, under Microsoft Windows.

The five information categories identified earlier are catered for by the different architectural elements of the MMTCA system:

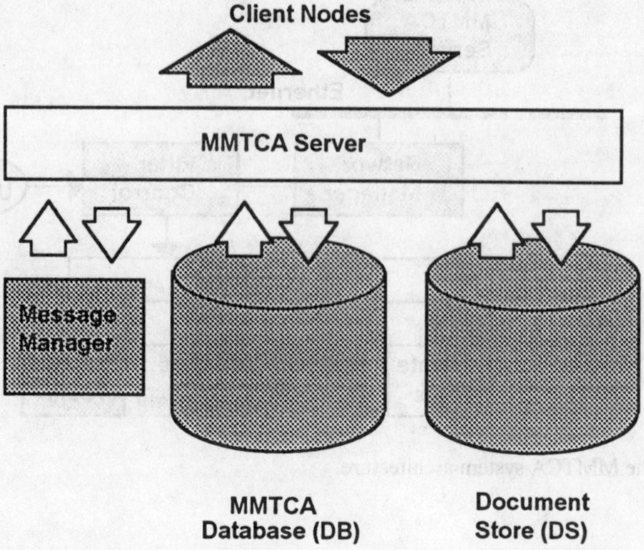

Fig. 3.2. Information in the MMTCA Architecture

- *System Definitions* - these are held in the database.
- *Procedure Definitions* - these are held in the database, and the document store is used for holding documents from the procedure definition.
- *Procedure Instances* - these are metadocuments held in the database, and the document store is used for holding actual procedure instance documents.
- *Shared Awareness* - this is produced by a combination of transient database information, and the MMTCA server's Message Manager, which incorporates the Cooperative Session Controller and other message management functions.
- *Dynamic Control* - this is produced by a combination of transient database information, and the MMTCA server's Message Manager, which incorporates the Cooperative Session Controller and other message management functions.

3.4 User Tools and Services

The MMTCA node software has a Network Manager (NM) module to manage its communication with the server. This communication is provided to applications as a number of MMTCA services which can be used to access information in the shared workspace.

- *Login* – allows users to login and logout of the MMTCA server. It registers the user and node as active in the shared workspace.

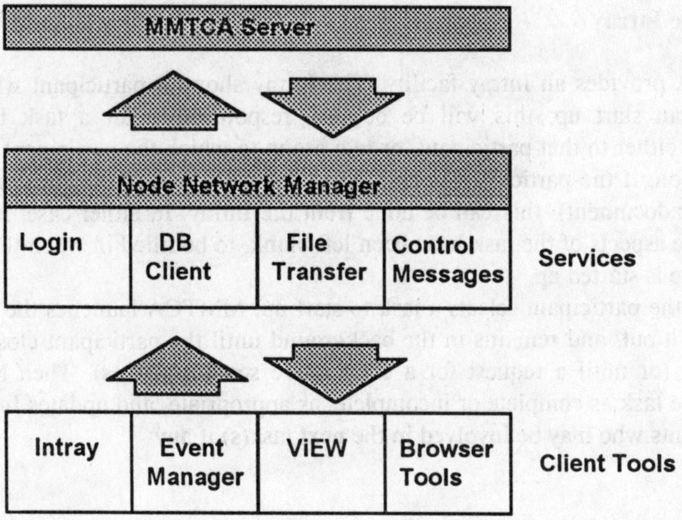

Fig. 3.3. MMTCA Node Services and Tools

- *DB Client* – provides access to the MMTCA database.
- *File Transfer* – provides access to the document store for retrieval and storage of documents.
- *Control Messages* – provides access to sending and receiving shared awareness information, and dynamic control of user activities in the shared workspace.

These services are provided for the use of MMTCA client tools on the node. They could also be used to integrate existing applications (using macro languages, DDE, etc.) and new collaboration-aware applications (using the MMTCA API).

3.5 Carrying out the Tasks

The user will be conscious of MMTCA's presence in two ways:

- through use of the Intray, and
- during cooperative sessions.

3.5.1 The Intray

MMTCA provides an Intray facility. The Intray shows a participant what tasks he/she can start up: this will be because responsibility for a task has been assigned either to that participant, or to a group to which the participant belongs. In addition, if the participant is entitled to initiate a procedure (thus creating a new metadocument), this can be done from the intray. In either case, it may be that some aspects of the task have been left blank, to be filled in when the task or procedure is started up.

When the participant selects a task to start up, MMTCA launches the tools for carrying it out, and remains in the background until the participant closes down the tools (or until a request for a cooperative session arrives). Then MMTCA marks the task as complete or incomplete, as appropriate, and updates Intrays for participants who may be involved in the next task(s) if any.

3.5.2 Cooperative Sessions

A Cooperative Session (CS) can be regarded as a synchronous, real-time cooperation Groupware activity, that is, a simultaneous activity which involves communication, collaboration and coordination within a whole group of users. It arises from a combination of two important abstractions introduced in the area of computer-supported synchronous cooperation among distributed users: WYSIWIS (What You See Is What I See) and Rooms.

Within the MMTCA application, a cooperative session is defined at the task level. A whole group of users will carry out the task in a synchronous cooperative manner. A Cooperative Session Manager will take care that all users participating in the cooperative session are kept in synchronisation, and that whatever happens in one user's screen appears on the screens of all other users (i.e. they will all be running exactly the same applications, seeing the same documents, and will be aware at real-time of each other's actions, such as mouse movement, data entry via the keyboard, etc.).

It should be noted that what users are supposed to be doing during the session (i.e. applications to run and documents to open) is fully specified at the action level of the task's specification.

- *Chairman*: A user with special privileges in the CS. It provides for a centralised control point which is useful to ensure that the session will result into something meaningful. Among his/her responsibilities are to activate the session, decide to end it, save its results if s/he believes that they are worth saving, control the floor policy, etc.
- *CS Space-Time*: all documents that are handled during a CS with the modifications that have been incurred upon them during the CS. The CS space-time at time zero (i.e. beginning of the CS) denotes the initial state(s) of all documents.

- *Floor Token*: a conceptual mechanism for floor passing control. The current owner of the Floor Token has the floor control. It is the scheme employed to allow for multi-user access to the system.
- *Floor Holder / Floor Owner*: the user that holds the Floor Token at a certain moment. In a Cooperation scheme a user will have to take hold of the floor-token in order to be able to act in the shared environment. As long as s/he does not hold it, s/he is a passive observer. The Floor Owner is for the time being the master of the CS, s/he can generate application events. These events will be dispatched by the server to the rest of the nodes (Slave nodes), which just reproduce the events.
- **Floor Policy**: specifies the protocol used for floor exchange between users. It could be established during the programming phase (by default) or decided during the procedure instantiation. Two main floor policies are distinguished:
  - *Designation Floor Policy*: floor exchange is conducted by a user (chairman or floor holder).
  - *Queue-Managed Floor Policy*: floor exchange is conducted by the server, which queues all requests to grab the floor received from the users.
- *Cooperation Policy*: describes the cooperative characteristics of the session such as: the minimal number of participants to start the session, whether the session is a Closed or Open Meeting, etc.

When a cooperative session is selected, the participant who starts it up becomes the chairman, and MMTCA pops up a dialogue box on all potential participants to ask them to join the session. If the people joining the session meet any conditions laid down in the procedure, the task starts up in a cooperative mode.

All participants then see the same shared windows (in addition to any windows that were operating before the session started). At any time, one of the participants holds the floor. Any keystroke or pointer gesture by the floor holder in one of the shared windows is also shown on the other participants' screens, and the other participants cannot act on the shared windows: but they can use the mouse or keyboard in windows that do not form part of the session.

During a cooperative session a small icon on screen informs participants whether or not they have the floor, and whether any other people have requested it.

This is how MMTCA supports work, using standard tools and facilities on personal computers.

3.5.3 Starting a Cooperative Session

A Cooperative Session is initiated as a result of the activation of a synchronous task and it may be initiated only by the CS chairman. One or more roles specified at procedure definition time can initiate the CS. If several, the first one who starts the CS task would be the chairman.

When the CS chairman requests to activate a task that corresponds to a CS, s/he may alter any characteristics of the CS that are given by default, such as:

- Registration Deadline
- Floor Policy
- Cooperation Policy
- Type of Meeting (Open /Closed)

The chairman can also instantiate new participants or remove some of the existing ones.

3.5.4 Joining a Cooperative Session

The Chair may grant permission to a newcomer to join an on-going CS that has been defined as an Open meeting. Any user who is a potential participant in the CS can join the session.

A user expresses his/her interest in joining an on-going CS by selecting the task in his/her Intray. This provokes that a *CSJoin* task control message is sent to the server. The server then forwards this message to the CS Chairman. The Chairman may decide either to allow or not the joining of the new user, but first, s/he becomes the current floor owner by issuing a *CSGrabFloor* floor control message.

If the chairman chooses to ignore the join request, s/he sends a *CSJoin* message with a negative answer to the requester and nothing else happens.

Otherwise, if the chairman decides to allow the user to joins the on-going CS, the following things occur:

- events propagation is stopped,
- participants are notified of the temporary task suspension due to a new participant who wants to join,
- the system pauses the session, updating the CS Space, so that the CS can be re-started later on with the new set of users and documents.
- CS execution is automatically resumed with all the participating users plus the newcomer.

In this way, when the CS execution resumes, all the applications running on all participants' nodes are at the same position.

3.5.5 Stopping a Cooperative Session

Only the chairman may decide to stop an on-going CS. There are some common situations in which the chairman may decide to stop a running CS:

- the task is already finished,
- the task is suspended,
- the chairman wants to leave the session,

- some participants, whose presence is essential for the session, have left the session,
- the last participant has left the session,
- a new user wants to join the session.

In a *Closed meeting*, it is possible to determine the minimum number of participants that are necessary to keep on running the CS, that is, their presence is essential in all CS time execution. If a participant leaves the session and there aren't enough participants to continue with the CS, the chairman will be informed, so that he can decide whether to finish the CS or not.

3.5.6 Stand Alone Cooperative Session Definition

A Cooperative Session (CS) can be regarded as a synchronous, real-time cooperative Groupware activity, that is, a simultaneous activity which involves communication, collaboration and coordination within a whole group of users.

A Cooperative Session Manager will take care that all users participating in the cooperative session are kept in synchronisation, and that whatever happens in one user's screen appears on the screens of all other users (i.e. they will all be running exactly the same applications, seeing the same documents, and will be aware at real-time of each other's actions, such as mouse movement, data entry through the keyboard, etc.).

Within the MMTCA Toolbox, a cooperative session is defined at the task level and it is integrated within a procedure. A whole group of users will carry out the task in a synchronous cooperative manner. It should be noted that what users are supposed to be doing during the session (i.e. applications to run and documents to open) is fully specified at the action level of the task's specification.

Moreover, the MMTCA Toolbox will provide a special type of Cooperative Session, called *Stand Alone Cooperative Session*, which allows any MMTCA user to define or start a Cooperative Session at any time without having to fulfil all the requirements imposed by the Workflow management implemented within the MMTCA Toolbox. So, users can define a CS in a short way without having to worry about procedures, tasks or actions. The MMTCA system hides all the Workflow implementation from the user. A Stand Alone CS could be considered as a special kind of procedure in the sense that the user can define a generic CS procedure that can be later instantiated to specific CS metadocuments.

3.6 Procedures and Metadocuments

This section considers the various types of objects and entities that exist in the database of the MMTCA user. Structures used only in the management of the

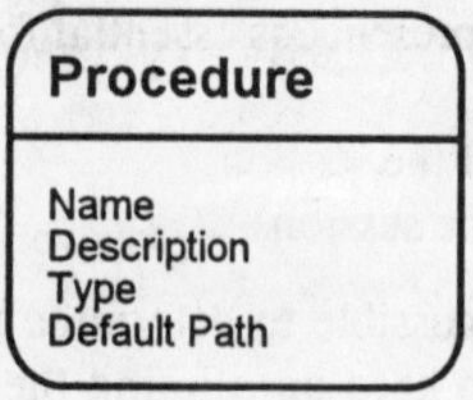

Fig. 3.4. The Procedure Object

MMTCA system will be described elsewhere. What is discussed here are those entities designed and placed in the database by users, either during procedure definition (for example, using ViEW), or when carrying out tasks defined in such procedures (at "run-time"). This section may be skipped at a first reading: it is important for a full understanding of the MMTCA approach, but this depth of understanding is not needed for using MMTCA.

3.6.1 Procedures

A procedure is a job that may be broken up into tasks. These tasks will be performed in some sort of order, that is, certain tasks will be completed before others will start. Users familiar with Activity Networks, PERT charts or similar workflow scheduling tools will already be familiar with many of the concepts involved. A procedure has a starting point and a finishing point. To proceed from the start to the end, the required paths through the Activity Network must be followed.

Activity networks and PERT charts are used in most cases to describe details of particular workflows. However, in a procedure, we wish to describe more gen-

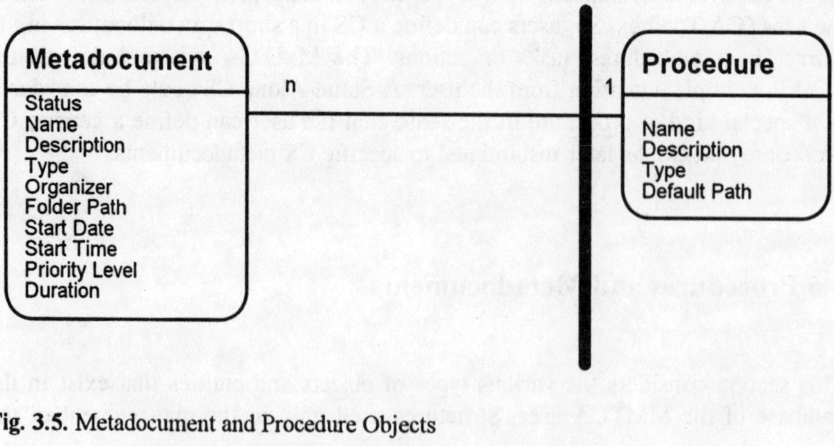

Fig. 3.5. Metadocument and Procedure Objects

eralised information of potential workflows that may be followed for particular instances of a procedure. Thus the activity network for a procedure may have loops and optional branches. So now we have an idea of a procedure. It is a set of tasks with a defined start and end point, and some indication of the permissible order in which the tasks may be performed.

3.6.2 Metadocuments

If we consider a procedure is a generalised set of tasks specifying the order in which tasks may be performed, then a Metadocument is an instance of a particular procedure, in which instances of the tasks of the procedure are performed in a particular order that conforms to the constraints on the workflow specified for this procedure. Thus the procedure acts as a template for the metadocument, and for any one procedure there may be many different metadocuments, each of which instantiates the generic objects of the procedure within the constraints defined for the procedure. (In diagrams such as the one above, the thick black line is used to separate information related to the procedure (and so applicable to all corresponding metadocuments) and information related to a single metadocument.)

So far only the Task objects have been introduced, though it may be deduced from the above description that there are Link objects or entities which are used to define the potential or actual workflows. In the rest of this chapter, other objects and entities will be introduced. In all cases, the procedure objects describe generic information applying to all metadocuments based on the procedure, while the metadocument objects describe information that is particular to the metadocument and may differ in other metadocuments that are based on the same procedure.

3.6.3 A Quick Look at the Other Object Classes

We have already come across Procedures, Metadocuments, Tasks and Links. There are many other classes of objects that the user may manipulate within the MMTCA system. There are Applications and Documents, Users and User Groups, Actions and Participants, Variables, Tool Profiles and others that we may meet later.

All these classes of objects have a particular role to play within the MMTCA system. Some of the classes may be divided into subclasses. As far as possible, the classes have been given sensible names. There remain some difficulties, however; for example, if we have users and user groups, what is a participant? Why do we need user objects if we have participant objects?

For this reason among others, the precise role of these classes and their instances will be set out in this chapter.

Tasks, Actions, Applications and Documents: A task is composed of Actions which occur in a given sequence. An Action will involve the running of one or more applications concurrently. For any Application there may be appended Documents, which are data files to be processed in some manner by that application.

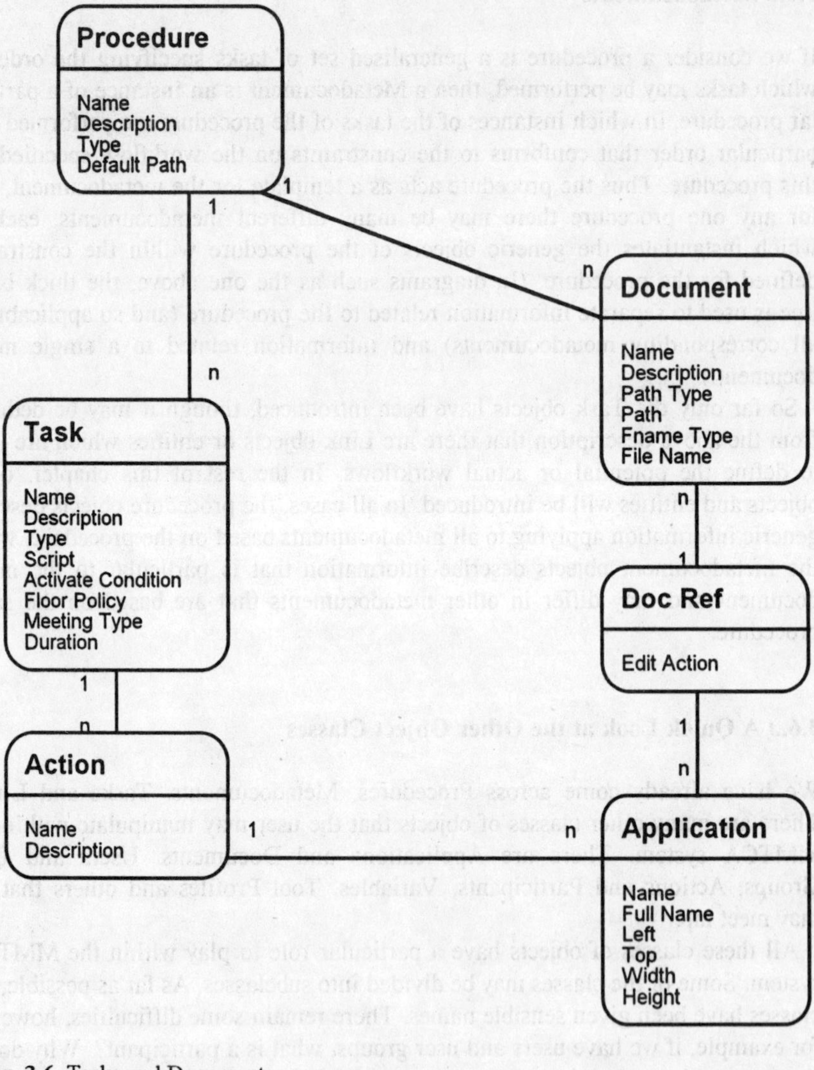

Fig. 3.6. Tasks and Documents

It may be hard to envisage the difference between the generic task of the procedure and its instance in the metadocument; the same may be said for actions, and possibly also applications. However, when we consider documents, the difference becomes real for most people. Let us take a simple example. In a given procedure we may have a document called an Invoice that is created by an application called the Invoicer. In a given metadocument, this Invoice document will have the details for a particular customer and a particular order, and may be represented by a particular piece of paper at some stage.

Participants, User Groups and Users: Participants and Users represent two different ways of looking at the people involved in a given system. The User object represents an individual person. This person will have a name, an address, a place of work and many other attributes. Few of these attributes are of interest to the MMTCA system. The user may belong to one or more User Groups, which are described later on.

The Participant object represents a generic person, somebody that will perform a particular role with respect to a procedure, metadocument or a part of either. It is rarely useful to specify that a particular person must act a particular role for all instances of a given procedure. In even the most constrained circumstances it is useful to allow for change.

Let us consider an example. Suppose we specify in a given procedure that Mr. Smith has to sign this document. This may be quite reasonable when the procedure is specified, since Mr. Smith is the bank manager, and nobody else can sign the document. What we really mean is that nobody else but the bank manager can sign the document; we do not want to redesign the procedure if Mr. McDonald takes over as the bank manager.

3.6.4 A Closer Look

Now we have an approximate idea of the objects and entities involved in the MMTCA database that are of direct interest to either the user of the system or to procedure designers. In a well-designed system, the naive end user will need to know none of this. All the naive user needs to know is how to do the job with the software he or she will normally use to do the job, together with a few details of floor policy when asked to join in a cooperative session, and a few details on selection of tasks from the MMTCA intray. These aspects will be covered in other chapters.

For the procedure designer, however, it is quite important that a good understanding of the precise meanings of the various objects and entities concerned in procedures and metadocuments is established. This will enable the designer to translate a good and clean abstract design of a procedure into a good and clean implementation of the procedure.

There will of course be constraints on what it is possible to implement, as is the case for all design situations. However, designers are accustomed to working within similar constraints if their output is to be of any real use. Our primary purpose here is to give the designer of procedures a firm basis toward which he or she can tailor the designs. It must also be said that the constraints imposed are usually for sensible reasons, and an attempt has been made to provide the procedure designer with the most flexible toolkit without unduly compromising the cleanliness of the design system.

The following descriptions assume synchronous, i.e. cooperative, operation. The requirements for asynchronous operation are considerably less demanding.

The Application Object: The purpose of the application object is to represent an actual executable program that is expected to be used at some stage during a given task. The object stores information on the name of the application, and where the executable file is to be found on the client node. Information may also be stored on the position this application is to occupy on the desktop on the client node. The application object relates only to a single action within a single task. Though the same application is likely to be used elsewhere, these other invocations are represented by a separate instance of the application object

The server node is the machine where the database is kept, together with the data files being used in current metadocuments. Typically, this is a Unix machine with none of the users working directly upon it. The client nodes are the machines where the users are actually working. These are in communication with the server, and receive the relevant data and session control information from it. The server is also responsible for distribution of input events during cooperative sessions. These aspects will be covered in other chapters.

The requirements for integrity during a cooperative session demand software that reacts to the single stream of input events in an identical fashion. Thus the software should be identical on all nodes in order that responses to a requested function are identical, also the position of the desktop and the application on the desktop should be identical on all nodes so that a given position-dependent (i.e. pointer device) input event generates a request for the same function on all nodes in the cooperative session. Again, these aspects will be covered in other chapters, and it is sufficient to note here that the application object stores the information needed to ensure the required behaviour.

There is no metadocument specific data attached directly to the application object. It would not normally be of use to specify different executables to be used for a particular metadocument, and the position of the application on the desktop may normally be altered as required by the floor holder. Since this operation is achieved by one or more input events, the result is identical on all cooperating nodes.

The Tool Profile Object: A given application object may have tool profile objects associated with it. Certain applications may need no tool profile objects, while others may need several. The concept of a tool profile object arises as a result of the ability to tailor many modern applications for individual users. This is done typically both to retain user-specified preferences and reload them in future invocations of the application, and also to retain information about work in progress.

The names and numbers of these profile files are application dependent and beyond the control of the MMTCA system. It is, however, possible for the MMTCA system to control the contents of these files. This is achieved during cooperative sessions by copying existing profile files to backup and bringing new versions of the file from the server. The backup files are replaced at the end of the session. By this operation the MMTCA system ensures that applications on all nodes receive the same tailoring information, and will thus behave in the same way if all else is equal.

The tool profile object is the system object which keeps the information to enable this operation to be performed. All potential profile files for a given application should be represented by a tool profile object for that application in the procedure. This object holds information on the file name, the path where it is held on the client node and the path where it is held on the server. This information is all by default, and may be overridden in a given metadocument. There is also some indication of those cases in which the profile file is essential. For certain jobs not all the profile files may be needed. Document template files, for example, may not be needed where there is no need to create new documents.

For a given application, all essential profile files must have a related object in the metadocument. There may also be objects representing optional profile files if they are considered relevant in the context of a particular metadocument. Commonly, these objects will take the default values from the related procedure

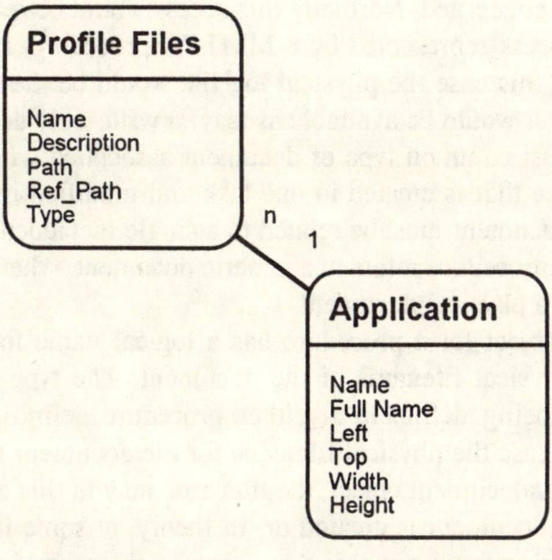

Fig. 3.7. Tool Profile and Application

object, but they may be overridden at the time of metadocument instantiation. Facilities may be provided to edit these objects at a later date, up to the start of the task concerned. Since file transfer of profile files is done on a per-task basis, this is the latest time at which editing of the data can be permitted. Unlike data files, profile files cannot be transferred in advance of the task.

The Document Object: Most people will already be familiar with the concept of a document. The MMTCA usage of the concept is not likely to differ much, but should still be explicitly stated. In the broadest sense, a document is a file that will be used as data for an application. In the context of MMTCA, there are many aspects to be considered. Documents may be created or deleted, and be presented with read only, write only or read and write permission. They may be essential or optional for a given task. We also need to consider client - server issues and procedure or metadocument issues.

The document may be associated with more than one task in a procedure. It is feasible that the document may associate with more than one physical application. Consider source code, for example. It may associate with an editor at one stage, and with a compiler at some later stage. Thus there is a potential many to many relationship between document objects and application objects. This relationship is represented by the Document Reference object, which shall shortly be described.

Document objects are specific to a particular procedure, though there is no reason to prevent a document object from a different procedure referring to the same physical document, wherever such sharing of documents would be appropriate.

Let us consider a few examples of real documents that may need to be represented. Suppose the workplace has an on-line manual for a system. There may be several procedures where it would be useful to have the manual available during certain tasks. The physical document would be the same for all metadocuments in all the procedures concerned. Normally this access would be read-only.

For a given process represented by a MMTCA procedure, there may be a log file associated. In this case the physical log file would be the same for all metadocuments, where it would be available as (say) a write-only document.

Probably the most common type of document associated with MMTCA procedures would be one that is created in one task and modified in subsequent tasks. Such a physical document must be related to a single metadocument, and any reference to it in the procedure refers to a generic document, where the object acts as a place holder for a physical document.

The document object for a procedure has a logical name for the document in addition to the physical filename of the document. The type of the filename is also recorded as being definable at either procedure definition time or at run time. In the latter case the physical filename for the document may be null. In the corresponding metadocument object, the filename may in this case be instantiated either as the metadocument is created or, in theory, at some later time up to the start of the first task referring to this document. In the case of document creation, the filename may potentially be instantiated even later. However, the design of the underlying MMTCA database currently requires these fields to be instantiated at the time of creation of the metadocument.

In the special case of a document with an associated Document List Variable object, described later, the filename is not relevant.

There is also a path associated with the document object. For the procedure, this may be one of three types. In the case of a path recorded as define time, the path should be recorded with the document object for the procedure. Other path type options are inherit path, whereby the folder path defined for the metadocument is inherited for metadocument instances of the document object; and run time path, whereby the path is defined explicitly as the metadocument is instantiated, as in the equivalent case of the filename.

Each document object in the metadocument will inherit some information from the corresponding object in the procedure. It will also have a single physical document associated with it for at least part of its life cycle (unless there is an associated document list variable). There is information held in the document object relating to this physical document.

The reference path for the document is the directory on the server where the reference copy of the shared file resides. This directory is created automatically at procedure instantiation, i.e. metadocument creation. The reference path information is recorded automatically into all document objects for the metadocument at this time. Depending on circumstances, the filename and path for the file on the client node may either be recorded explicitly at procedure instantiation time or be inherited from the related document object for the procedure.

Other information held in the document object is used to manage concurrent access to the document. The status of the document may be recorded as one of three states; not yet created, up to date, or locked during modification. In the latter case, the identity of the locking task and action will be recorded. This information is required since a document may be shared between tasks which are potentially concurrent.

It is important to note that the MMTCA system does not make allowances for managing the sharing of physical documents between procedures or metadocuments. Normally these will be stable documents which will not be modified, but MMTCA implements no mechanism to prevent conflicting updates attempted in tasks belonging to separate metadocuments. What happens in reality is that modifications are made to different copies of the original physical document, so the potential for recovery remains.

As we have seen, document objects are quite complex. A quick summary may be in order. The procedure holds information about generic logical documents, which may as in the case of, say, reference manuals, be instantiated. The metadocument holds information about those physical documents which instantiate the logical documents for this metadocument. This information may be inherited from the procedure or instantiated explicitly for the metadocument as it is created. Conflicting updates from within the same metadocument are prevented.

The Document Reference Object: As has been noted earlier, there is a potential many-to-many relationship between document objects and application objects. The document reference object serves two purposes. It explicitly associates a procedure document with an application object, and it also records the type of edit action that is performed on the document by this particular application.

There are currently four classes of edit action that are supported: creation, consultation, modification and deletion. This information is used when determining where file transfer should occur and in determining when the server copy should be locked against conflicting modifications.

If the document reference object is not instantiated in the metadocument, all information is inherited unchanged.

The Variable Object: A variable object has two aspects of significance, its existence and its value. This may be said for all objects to some degree, but whereas for most other classes of object action is taken only if the object exists; for vari-

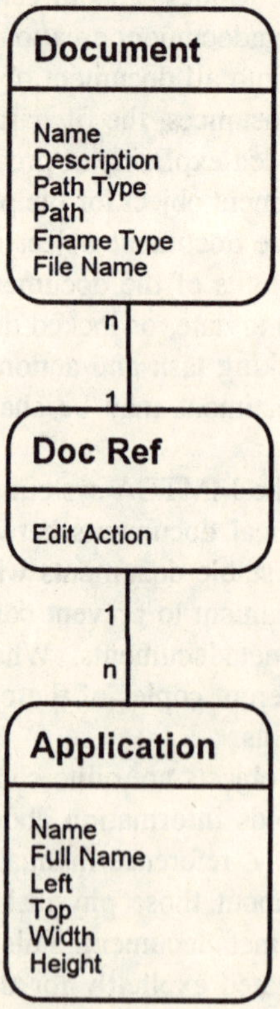

Fig. 3.8. Documents and Applications

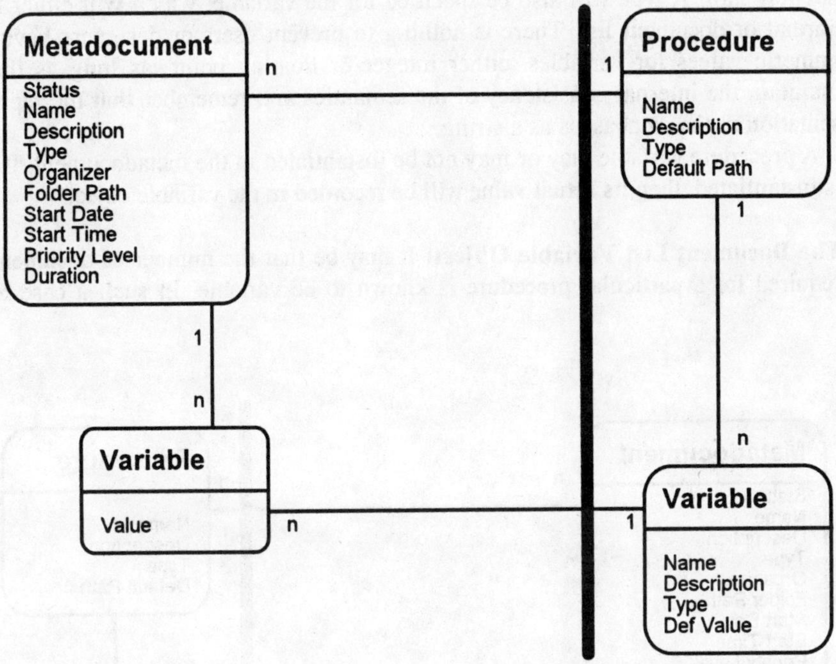

Fig. 3.9. The Variable Object

able objects, in certain cases action may be taken explicitly if the object does not exist.

There are currently only two cases where variables are used by the MMTCA system, but they are provided in order that they may be used as required. The document list variable is one of the existing cases, and is described in the following section. Variables are also used in Variable Mediated Links. This is a particular feature enabling conditional branches during calculation of workflow. A particular link may be created if a given variable exists, thereafter further links may be created dependent on the existence or otherwise of the variable mediated link, until the rescheduling of the workflow is complete. More detail will be given in the discussion of Link objects.

Note that the significant feature is the presence or absence of the variable object, and not its value. The reason for this is that the workflow rescheduling algorithm is of necessity generalised, and cannot take into account the semantics of particular values associated with variables. The semantics of the value cannot be known until a particular procedure is designed, thus any behaviour dependent on the value must be procedure specific.

For a procedure variable, the name and default value of the variable may be specified. The default value will be a character string of up to 250 characters, possibly null. A type will also be specified for the variable, which will either be normal or document list. There is nothing to prevent users or designers having numeric values for variables, either integer or floating point, as long as they maintain the internal consistency of the semantics and remember that the representation in the database is as a string.

A procedure variable may or may not be instantiated in the metadocument. If it is instantiated, then its actual value will be recorded in the variable object.

The Document List Variable Object: It may be that the number of documents required for a particular procedure is known to be variable. In such a case for

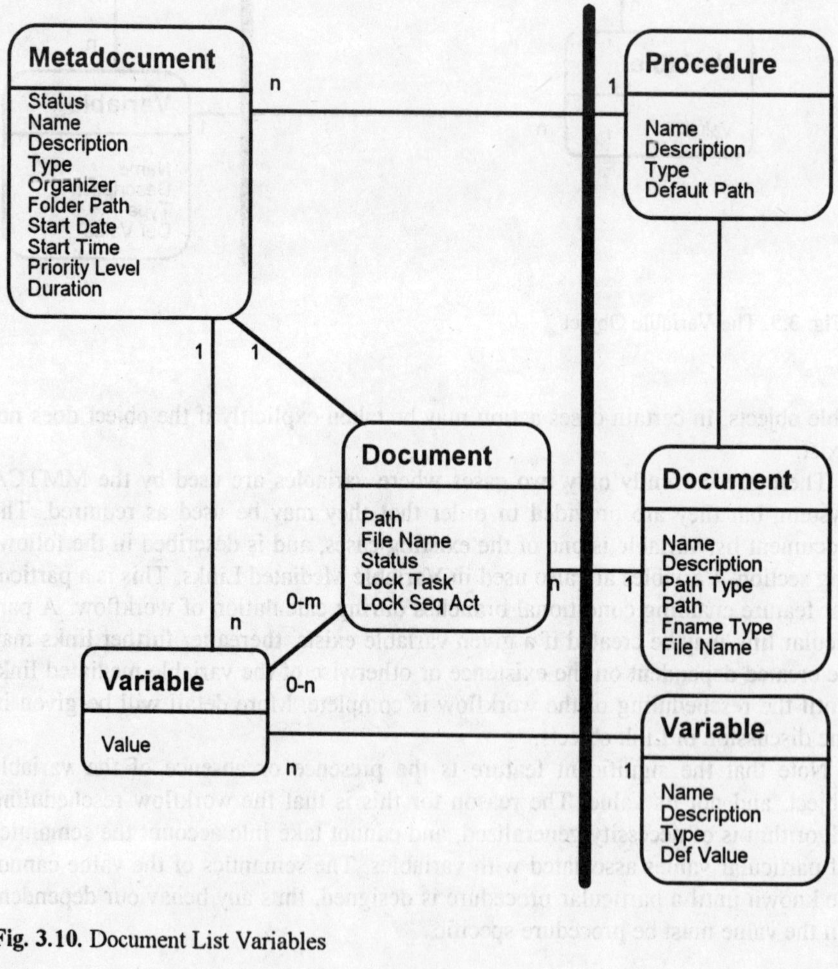

Fig. 3.10. Document List Variables

each logical document concerned there may be a list of zero or more physical documents. With the exception of the filename, all other details pertaining to the documents in the list must be identical for this solution to be used.

In the document object for the procedure, there may be a variable identified to hold such a document list. Each metadocument based on this procedure should have an instance of the variable object corresponding to the procedure variable object identified in the procedure document object. The value of this metadocument variable will be a list of zero or more filenames.

The physical representation of the document list in the database should not concern us here, and may be subject to change. However, since it may impose real constraints on the procedure designer, it may be said that the current representation is a string of up to 250 characters comprising the filenames separated by semicolons. Thus there should be no problems in internal representation until the list of filenames exceeds the low twenties, assuming standard MS-DOS filename limitations.

The Action Object: The action object is the smallest unit of concurrency, and the smallest unit of workflow. An action is one of a sequence of actions defined for a given task, and acts as a holder for a set of applications which will execute concurrently on all the nodes involved in the particular task. Action objects are not instantiated for metadocuments since all information is either inherited from the procedure or held in the component objects.

An action object cannot figure in the rescheduling of workflow algorithm, but there will be a single thread sequence of one or more consecutive actions within a task. The description of the task object will cover this in more detail.

The User Object: The user object is one of two administrative objects that will be described here. Others may be of interest in other chapters, but are not of interest to the user's view of the system and do not figure during design of procedures.

The user object holds minimal information about a particular person who may interact in some capacity as a user of the MMTCA system. The information held includes the name by which the user is known to the system, the name by which the user is known to other users, the user's authentication information, the authorisation level due to this user, and the node at which the user usually works.

The primary purpose of the user object is to link an individual in a secure manner to the jobs and tools that he or she needs. When a user logs in to MMTCA, all the tasks awaiting his attention appear in his intray. If a user attempts to initiate a particular operation in the MMTCA system, then her user object may be accessed to ascertain whether she holds the appropriate authorisation to initiate this operation. However, of greater interest here is the use of the user object to nominate people that may act in a particular role as participants in a given metadocument, and thereby determine which tasks should appear in the user's intray.

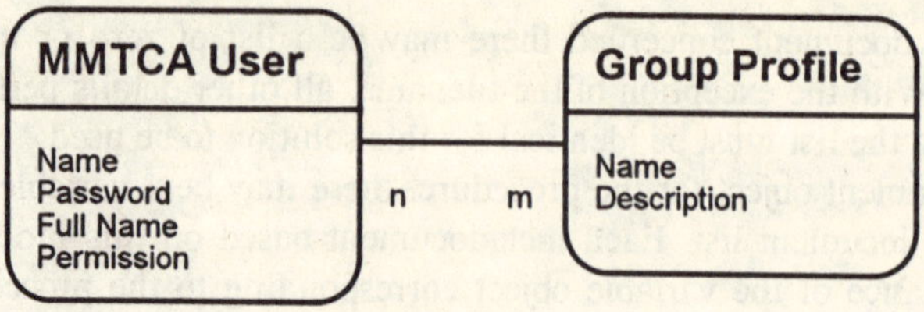

Fig. 3.11. Users and Groups

The current options for permission levels are administrator, programmer, organiser and user. Broadly speaking, the administrator may alter administrative objects in the MMTCA system, the programmer may design new procedures, the organiser may instantiate procedures and start the resultant metadocuments, and the user may start tasks that appear in his or her intray. For full details on what is possible, see the following chapter.

The User Group Object: The user group is a named container for a list of user objects. In addition to the specific roles with respect to the MMTCA system that are defined within the permission levels for the user objects, users will have some place in the company or other organisation employing the MMTCA toolbox. Generally, the position they hold will affect the roles in which they may participate in a given procedure. The user group object permits the collection of users into groups, any of which may be selected as a potential participant in a particular role for a given procedure instance.

Clearly, there is potential for there to be a many to many relationship between users and user groups. This linkage is made by a simple relation within the database, which holds no additional information.

The Participant Object – a First Look: As a procedure is designed, it will become clear that various people will be involved in the procedure in various roles. It is frequently possible at this stage to give readily meaningful names to these roles. Two approaches toward naming roles can be taken. It may be possible to nominate a class of employee who is qualified to act out the role, or alternatively it may be possible to describe what function an individual acting in this role performs with relation to the procedure.

If the former approach were always preferred, it may suffice to nominate a user group immediately, from which the individual user may be chosen at a later date. However, the use of an intermediate object to represent the role allows flexibility of representation and facilitates retention of information as to who actually performs the work in a particular instance of the procedure.

We should know a bit more about task objects and metadocument objects before we look at the participant object in greater detail.

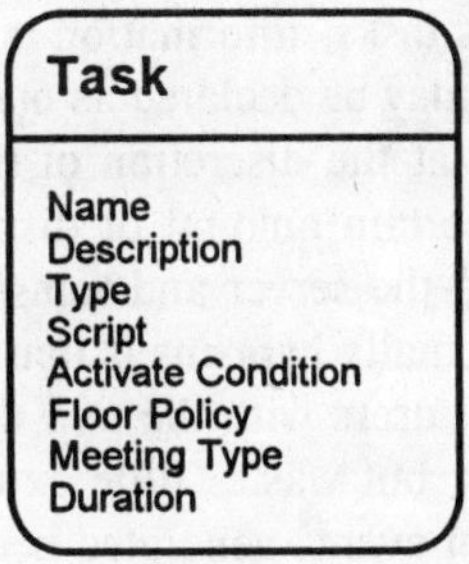

Fig. 3.12. The Task Object

The Task Object: The task object is the smallest unit of programmable workflow, the smallest scope of participant binding, and the unit of cooperative working. In everyday terms, a task object represents a job that is done by one or more participants as a coherent unit of work. It has a set of people, a set of tools and a purpose

In terms of the MMTCA system, a task is a sequence of one or more actions performed by one or more participants. At this stage, it is advisable to mention a further constraint imposed by the MMTCA system. If the task is a cooperative session, i.e. if it involves more than one participant, then there can only be one action contained in the task. Once the single action is completed, the cooperative session terminates.

In the case of Asynchronous tasks, i.e. those tasks explicitly involving only one participant, once one action terminates, then another action is automatically started, until all actions for that task are complete.

A task is also the smallest unit of work that can be done in one session. A task may be left incomplete, whereby the work to date is saved or optionally discarded, and the task is restored into the intray of those users concerned. When a task is restarted, it restarts from the beginning.

Since so much of the work done by the MMTCA is centred round the task object, we shall take a separate look at the Intray Task object later. This section will cover most aspects of metadocument instances of task objects.

A task object for the procedure holds the generic information that has been designed into the task. A task may be defined as either asynchronous or synchronous. Synchronous tasks require cooperative working between at least two users, and thus require more information to be defined and held for the task.

All tasks have a name and a script. The script is a batch file created as the procedure is designed, which runs on the client node where the task was started. In the case of synchronous tasks, the events of interest generated on this node will be shadowed on the client nodes of the other task participants, it is not necessary to run the script on these other nodes.

All task types may have information about the estimated duration of the task. This is optional, and may provide aid for tools designed to help resource scheduling and critical path analysis.

In the case of synchronous tasks, information is also held on the meeting type and floor policy. A meeting may be declared as open or closed. An open meeting permits participants to join, at the discretion of the chairman, after the session has started. This causes a certain amount of disruption, since at minimum the data files need to be saved to the server and transferred out to the client node of the new participant. What actually happens is that the session is temporarily suspended, then restarted for all users with the new data files. This causes a certain amount of unnecessary work, but wastes little extra time and prevents problems that may occur tracking input events generated between saving the data files and starting the new participant.

The floor policy for a synchronous task may be one of: chairman driven, floor driven, first come first served, or prioritised. A floor policy is required both to prevent the anarchic situation of a meeting where everyone is talking at once, and to ensure that input events occur in the right order. If there is only one source of valid input events at a time there is no need to attempt to merge two or more separate streams.

The Intray Task Object: For each task that is or has been scheduled in a metadocument there is an intray task object. In simple procedures there may, at the completion of the metadocument, be a one to one mapping between intray task objects for the metadocument and task objects for the procedure. However, more complex workflows may be programmed, where there are conditional branches. These may be used to produce loops in the workflow, or merely to select options between non-looping branches. Thus certain tasks in the procedure may never be performed in the metadocument, and other tasks may be performed more than once. A currently active task will also have a chairman and a current floorholder from among the participants.

The intray task object may be in one of five states; scheduled, ready, running, suspended, or terminated. Most of these have the obvious meanings. A task is marked as scheduled when its start time has not been reached but it is otherwise ready to run. A task will be marked as scheduled or ready on creation of the intray task object. The intray task object is created either at procedure instantiation as one of the start tasks of a procedure, or when reschedule of workflow at the end of another metadocument task has enabled the link to the task concerned.

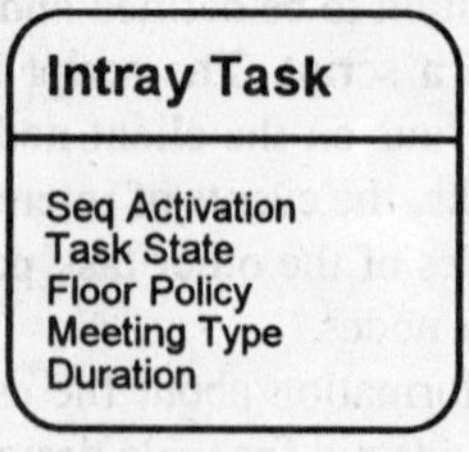

Fig. 3.13. The Intray Task Object

Floor policy and meeting type may be inherited from the relevant task object in the procedure. It is possible, however, for the chairman to override these defaults as the task is started.

The chairman of the task is one of a set of potential chairpersons, which is a subset of the potential participants of the task. By starting the task, the user becomes the actual chairman of the task. Thus task participants who are not members of the set of potential chairpersons cannot start the task.

Currently, there are no circumstances where a change of chairman is permitted as the task is running, however, this may change at some later date. It is possible for a task stopped while incomplete to be restarted with a new chairman. While a task is actually running, the current chairman and the current floorholder are represented by a relation between the intray task object and the user object of the user concerned.

The Participant Object – a closer look: As we have already seen, the participant object is used to denote the generic role of a person with respect to a procedure. In a particular instance of a procedure, these roles are going to be filled by particular people. The participant object is used as the key part of a mechanism that allows the procedure designer sufficient flexibility and expressivity to define

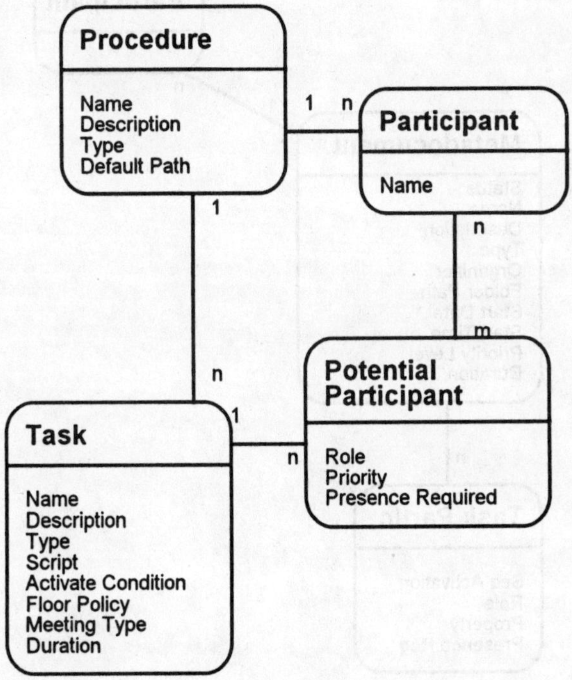

Fig. 3.14. The Participant Object

the requirements of manning a particular procedure. Certain of this flexibility can be passed down to the organiser of a procedure instance or metadocument, while at other times the designer can impose strict constraints to this flexibility.

In theory the procedure designer, working in conjunction with the administrator, can impose absolute constraints on who does what, or can grant absolute freedom. A participant object is constrained by the procedure designer to be bound only to a member of a named user group. The user group, under the control of the administrator, may have from one member to a maximum of all users known to the MMTCA system.

In addition to this flexibility over participants for procedures, the procedure designer may specify for each task which of the participants for the procedure are essential and which are optional. The designer can further nominate a subset of the potential participants for a task as being potential chairpersons. At least one chairman must be nominated for each synchronous task at the time of procedure design. Finally, if the floor policy is 'prioritised', the designer can nominate a priority of high, normal or low to each potential participant of the task.

For asynchronous tasks there cannot be more than one essential participant, since there can only be one user doing the task. In practice, one essential partici-

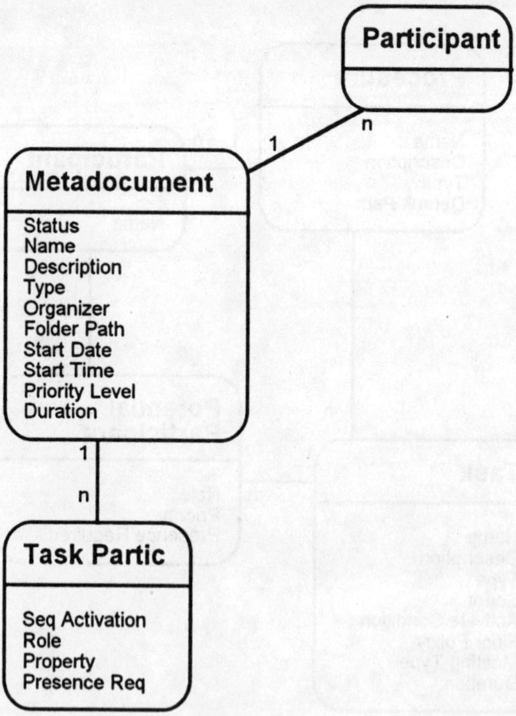

Fig. 3.15. Participants and Metadocuments

pant is nominated at procedure design, though theory also permits multiple optional participants. Again, since there is only one user, the concept of a chairman is meaningless for asynchronous tasks.

For individual metadocuments the participant object needs to record which user is bound to the participant, and for what scope. The currently available scopes of binding are for the duration of the metadocument, or alternatively per task in the procedure. Currently a user bound for the first iteration of a task is bound to that participant for subsequent iterations of that task. This is subject to change. Binding a user to a participant for the metadocument prevents the participant being bound on a per task basis and vice-versa.The role (normal or potential chairman), priority and requirements for presence for a participant in a metadocument task are by default inherited from the procedure task participant details, but may be overridden in the individual metadocument participant object. The priority and role information may be overridden at any time before the start of the task, and optional participants may join when the task is starting. All essential participants must be bound to a user by the time the task starts, and there is a dialogue available to the chairman to make these bindings as he or she requests to start the task.

During the running of a task a note is kept of the actual participant and user bindings of all real participants, since formal participants that are bound to users may be marked as optional for a task, and the user may have opted out of participating.

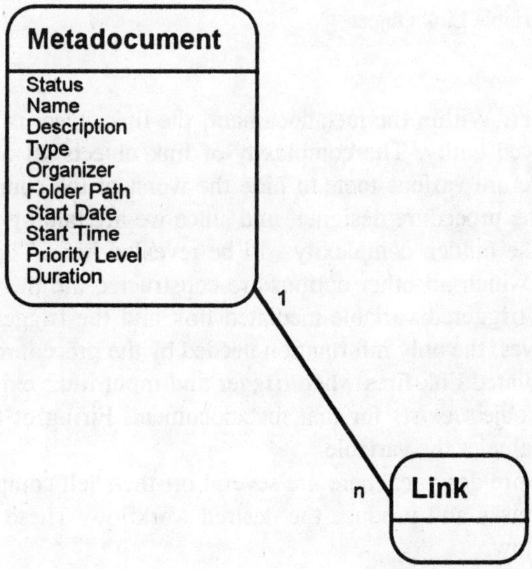

Fig. 3.16. The Link Object

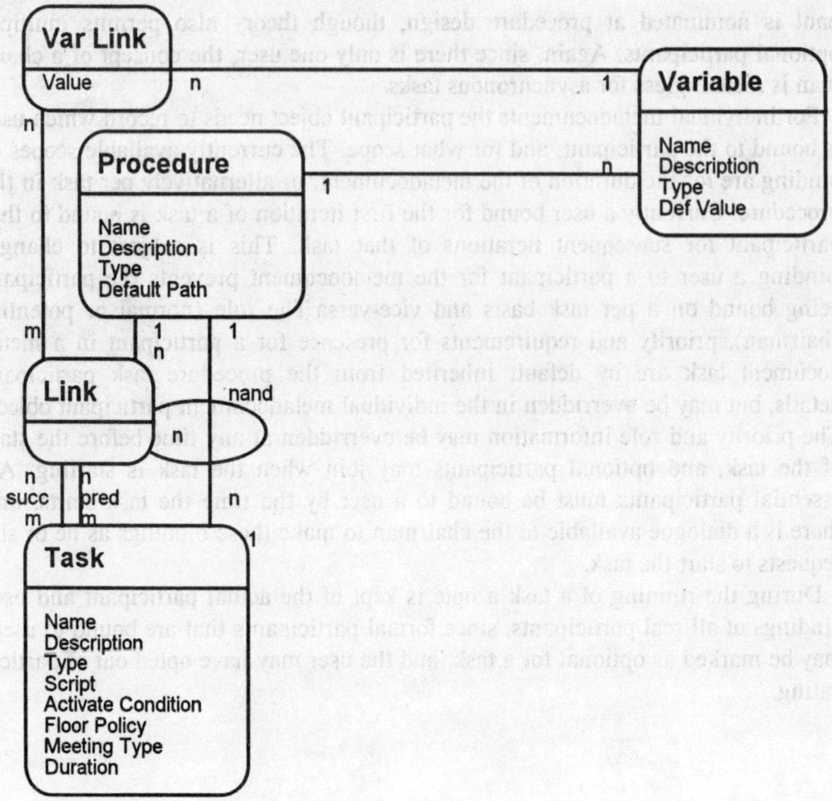

Fig. 3.17. The Variable Link Object

The Link Object: Within the metadocument, the link object is a relatively simple and short-lived entity. The complexity of link objects all occurs within the procedure. There are various tools to hide the worst of the complexity from the user and from the procedure designer, and since we are talking here about these views, little of the hidden complexity will be revealed here. The three primitive link types from which all other options are constructed are the predecessor-successor link, the triggered variable-mediated link and the triggered NAND link. Of these primitives, the only information needed by the procedure designer is that the variable mediated link fires when trigger and input links exist only when the named variable object exists for that metadocument. Firing of the link is independent of the value of the variable.

For the procedure designer there are several off-the-shelf components that may be used to link tasks and produce the desired workflow. These compound links are described below.

The starting task link is a 'flag' that is attached to tasks in a procedure which should be scheduled immediately the procedure is instantiated. There must be at least one starting task in a procedure.

The simple predecessor successor link will schedule one successor task imme-

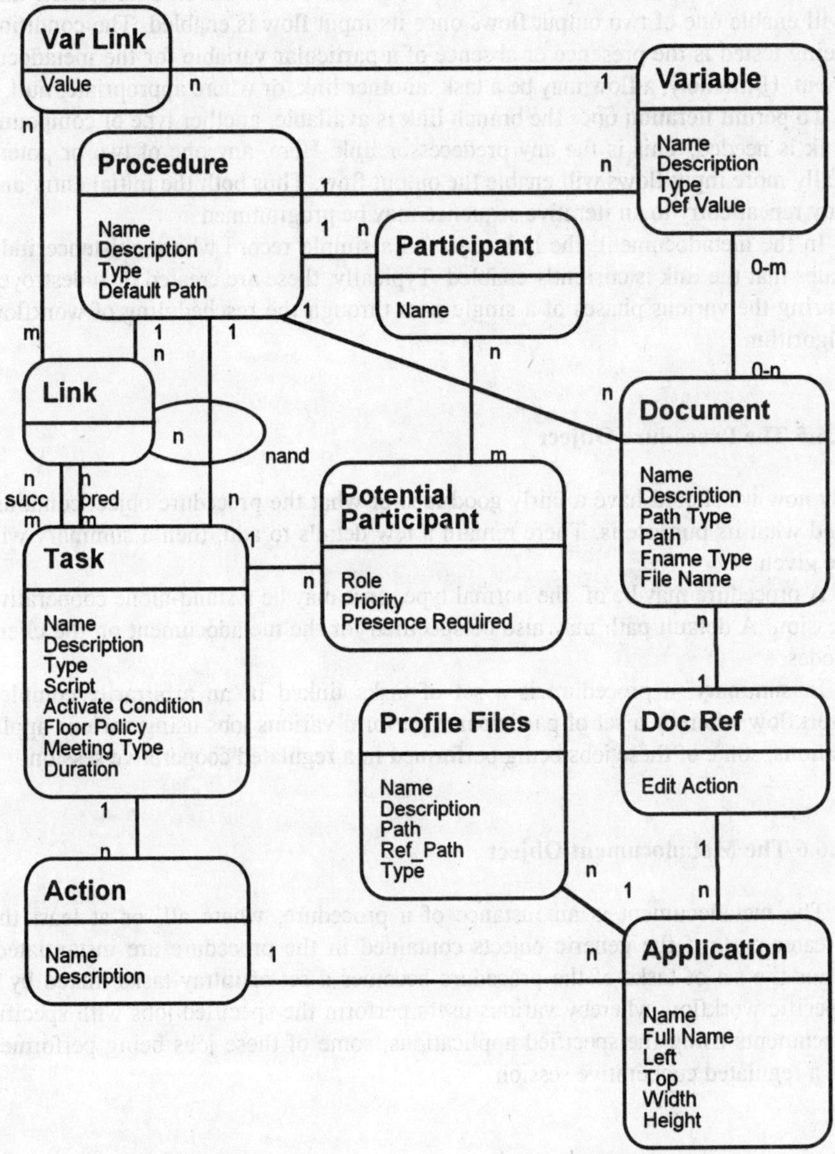

Fig. 3.18. The Procedure Object

diately on completion of the single predecessor task.

The multiple successor link will schedule all its successor tasks immediately on completion of the single predecessor task.

The multiple predecessor task will schedule the one successor task once all the predecessor tasks have been completed. The one successor task is scheduled immediately on completion of the last predecessor task.

The following two compound links are available. The conditional branch link will enable one of two output flows once its input flow is enabled. The condition being tested is the presence or absence of a particular variable for the metadocument. Ultimately, a flow may be a task, another link, or where appropriate, null.

To permit iteration once the branch link is available, another type of compound link is needed. This is the any predecessor link. Here, any one of two or potentially more input flows will enable the output flow. Thus both the initial entry and any repeat entry to an iterative sequence may be programmed.

In the metadocument, the link object is a simple record whose existence indicates that the link is currently enabled. Typically, these are created then destroyed during the various phases of a single pass through the rescheduling of workflow algorithm.

3.6.5 The Procedure Object

By now we should have a fairly good idea of what the procedure object contains, and what its purpose is. There remain a few details to add, then a summary will be given.

A procedure may be of the normal type, or it may be a stand-alone cooperative session. A default path may also be specified for the metadocument on the client nodes.

In summary, a procedure is a set of tasks linked in an arbitrarily complex workflow whereby a set of participants perform various jobs using various applications, some of these jobs being performed in a regulated cooperative session.

3.6.6 The Metadocument Object

The metadocument is an instance of a procedure, where all, or at least the greater part, of the generic objects contained in the procedure are instantiated. Thus the set of tasks of the procedure becomes a set of intray tasks linked by a specific workflow whereby various users perform the specified jobs with specific documents using the specified applications, some of these jobs being performed in a regulated cooperative session.

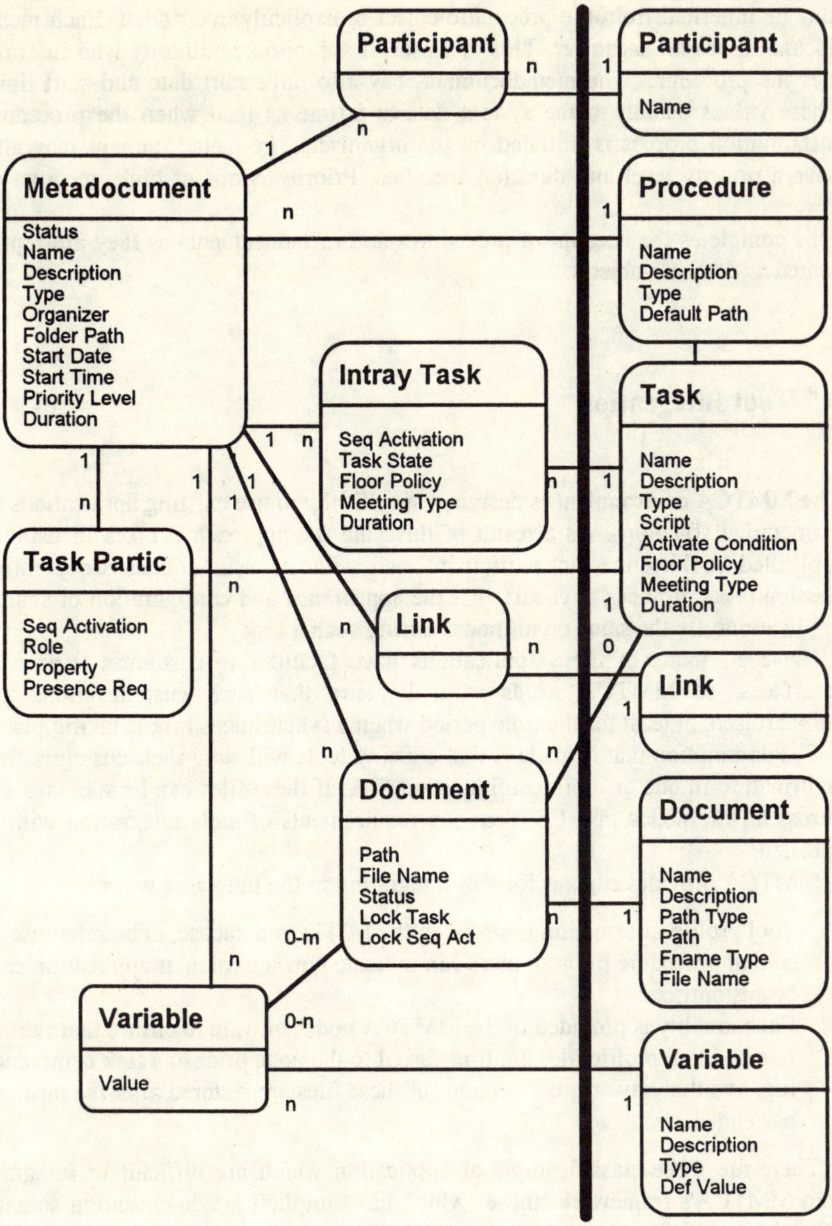

Fig. 3.19. The Metadocument Object

Various attributes of the metadocument object remain to be described. The folder path is a client node directory where the data files are sent by default. This may be inherited from the procedure object or explicitly overridden. Each metadocument has an organiser. This is a user of appropriate authority who instantiates the procedure. The metadocument may also have start date and start time. These values default to the system date and time as read when the procedure instantiation process is initiated by the organiser. The metadocument may also have a priority level and duration specified. Priority is one of high, medium or low.

This completes the account of procedures and metadocuments as they are represented as database objects.

3.7 Tool Integration

The MMTCA environment is designed specifically to use existing applications in cooperative situations. As a result of this, and the approach it takes in using a replicated architecture on participant nodes in its synchronous Cooperative Session tasks, it needs to ensure that the appearance and configuration of shared applications are the same on all nodes during such a task.

However, many of these applications have facilities to customise their user interfaces, so MMTCA needs to make sure that such customisations are standardised, at least for the time period when a synchronous task is taking place.

The assumption that is made is that existing tools will store their customisation information in one or more configuration files. If these files can be standardised across all the nodes in a CS, then the requirements of tools integration will be fulfilled.

MMTCA provides support for tool integration in the following ways:

- Tool profile information is stored in the MMTCA database, to be referenced so that procedure programmers can indicate how a particular application can be customised.
- Functionality is provided in the MMTCA node software to ensure that the relevant tool profile files are transferred to the node prior to a task commencing, and that any original versions of these files are restored after the task has ended.

There are three classifications of application which are difficult to integrate into MMTCA's framework: those which have implicit single-execution semantics; those which make use of dynamic resource; and those which incorporate non-deterministic behaviour.

Examples of applications which have single execution semantics include mailing programs and printing programs. If, during a cooperative session, a memo is mailed, it is feasible to assume that only one copy of the memo should actually be sent. Similar problems may be encountered when selecting the print option from an application during a cooperative session.

Suppose a node is equipped with a microphone. During a CS, the floor holder may wish to add a voice annotation to a document. Although MMTCA easily supports activation of both the local and remote recorder tools, how can we ensure the same voice annotation is transparently distributed.?

3.7.1 Tool Profile Information

The MMTCA mechanism for storing tools integration information is the provision of tool profiles. Procedure programmers are provided with a facility to produce a tool profile template for any given application, which will carry information on the configuration files which that application needs, storage of these files in the MMTCA server, and the various options on how these files may be applied. These Tool Profile Templates (TPT) are produced using the Tool Profile Editor, and stored in the MMTCA database and server file system. The tool profile templates are used to produce actual tool profiles in a procedure design – details of the real configuration files specified in the template are stored for that procedure in the MMTCA database. When the procedure is instantiated, the procedure instance has its own copy of the tool profile data.

From the above it can be seen that there are three levels of tool profile information:

- *Tool Profile Template* (TPT) data – used in the specification of how a tool profile will appear in terms of the logical configuration files it needs, and the actual template configuration files themselves.
- *Procedure level tool profiles* – used in the programming of the procedure, and created from the templates specified in the database. Actual configuration file data stored in the MMTCA server is referenced by the tool profile data in the MMTCA database.
- *Instance level tool profiles* – the actual tool profile data used in an instance of the procedure. This data is based on the procedure level tool profiles, and is created at procedure instantiation time.

3.7.2 Tool Profile File Transfer

When the tool profile needs to be used, i.e. the application is going to be used in a CS, facilities are provided to transfer the tool profile files from the MMTCA server to their destination directories on each of the participating node machines. Any copies of existing files for the tools will be backed up, and then restored after the CS has ended.

Tool profile file transfer facilities are similar in many ways to the ordinary file transfer provided by MMTCA, except the setup and cleanup procedures are different, and the information as to where the files should be transferred to and from is accessed from different tables in the MMTCA database.

Before the files are transferred to a node, any existing copies of these files (i.e. the application's current customisation options on the node) are backed up. The files are then transferred to the node. All nodes in a CS should now have the same customisation options for their shared applications.

After the CS has ended, the node copies of the tool profile files need to be discarded, and the original node versions of these files restored, so that the application customisations on the node will be back to normal.

Part 2: Using MMTCA

From the discussions of the preceding chapters, it will be clear that in MMTCA the purpose is to empower the end-user – the manager or secretary in a business environment – to establish routine processes and/or delegate tasks to members of the group, and then to provide an environment to support carrying them out.

The first stage, of *organising work to be done*, can be seen as consisting of several different activities:

- establishing roles in the group,
- defining the work to be carried out, and assigning them to groups or individuals
- monitoring the resulting activity.

The second stage, where members of the group actually *carry out the resulting tasks*, requires support in the following ways:

- keeping members advised of the arrival of new tasks
- supporting task start-up and taking action on the completion of tasks
- managing cooperative sessions
- enquiring about the status of work.

All of these aspects are discussed in this part of the book.

Screen dumps shown in these chapters are taken from the research prototype version of MMTCA, which used Windows 3.1, and did not use the advanced features of OLE. With the arrival of OLE2 and later versions of Windows, the user interface will be upgraded accordingly, but the facilities offered will be equivalent.

It is expected, in particular, that metadocuments, procedure trays etc will be viewed as containers, so that documents they contain can be activated. It is believed that this document-oriented approach to tasks will soon be more natural to users than the existing application-oriented approach.

Chapter 4 presents the tools associated with organising work to be done: the administration tool for authorising MMTCA users, the ViEW procedure design tool, the metadocument browser, and the tool profile editor.

Chapter 5 discusses the run-time tools, used when carrying out the tasks. This involves the Intray tool and external services, but the various sections of this chapter deal with initiating procedures (creating metadocuments), starting tasks, participating in cooperative sessions, and creating ad-hoc cooperative sessions.

Chapters 6 to 8 outline the three case studies carried out as part of the MMTCA project, in banking, shipping, and manufacture.

4. Organising work to be done

4.1 Authorising MMTCA Users

The MMTCA Administration Tool, from now on called the ADM tool, is aimed to provide the administrator of a MMTCA installation with a set of administration facilities for management of MMTCA nodes and users.

Once a valid user with ADMINISTRATOR permission has logged in to the tool, ADM allows her/him the following administration functions:

- Adding, modifying, or deleting MMTCA nodes
- Adding, modifying or deleting MMTCA user groups
- Adding, modifying or deleting MMTCA users

The ADM tool can be seen as a tool to add, modify or delete records in the tables supporting these three entities.

4.1.1 Login Process

A user invokes ADM from the Windows Program Manager, like any other Windows application – either by double-clicking its icon with the mouse, or through the run dialogue of the Program Manager. Then the user is presented with the Login Dialogue.
The user enters his/her name and password and clicks on the *OK* button[1]. If the user clicks on the *Cancel* button MMTCA exits and the user is returned to the Windows Program Manager. If the user supplied name and password are correct, and the user's permission is `ADMINISTRATOR`, the user is presented with the ADM main window. If the user-supplied information is not valid or s/he does not have the right permission, an error message dialogue is presented to the user, ADM exits and control returns to the Windows Program Manager.

---

[1] An operation such as clicking a dialogue button with the mouse can always be invoked through the keyboard, using standard MS Windows mechanisms.

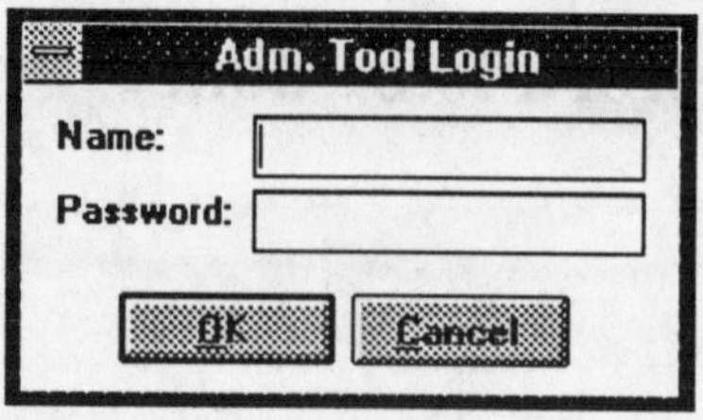

Fig. 4.1. ADM Login Dialogue

Fig. 4.2. ADM Tool Main Window

All the ADM functions are accessed from the menu bar of the ADM main window.

4.1.2 Exit Process

The user exits ADM from the main window menu. The *Exit* menu item is invoked under the *Main* pop-up menu.

4.1.3 Node Editing Process

The user may access this function by selecting the *Nodes...* menu item under the *Node* pop-up menu of the main window. Then the user is presented with the Node Administration window.

The Node Administration window has a database form layout. It presents the details of the currently existing nodes, listed as a set of lines with a scroll bar associated. Each line correspond to an item or record. Each column corresponds to an editable field, which name appears on top of the column (Name, Address, Status, Location).

At this point, the user will be able to inspect the information associated to every item description and modify it. As in other MS Windows applications, Tab and Shift-Tab keys can be used to move forward and back along the fields in a line and between lines. Textual fields are edited in the usual MS Windows way. For

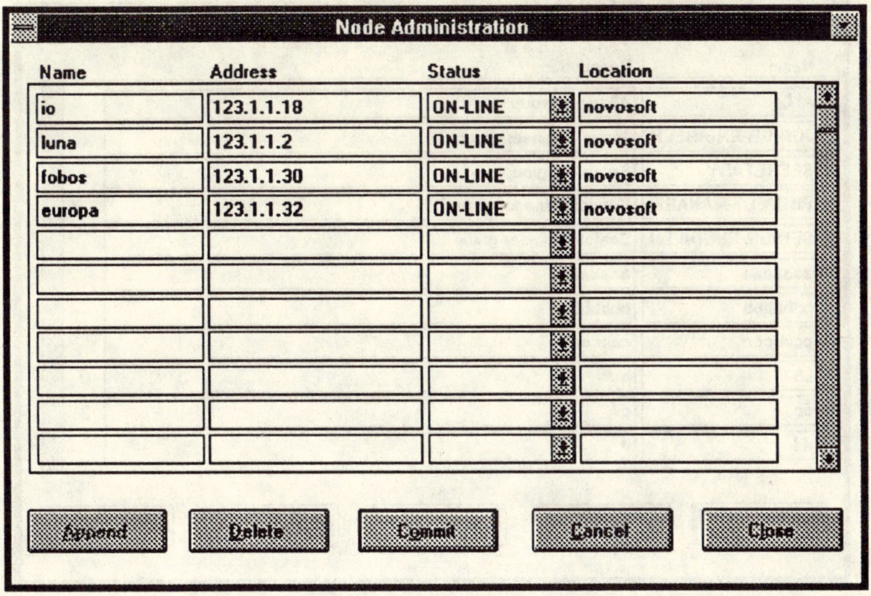

Fig. 4.3. Node Administration Window

the enumerated fields, a combo box is open on clicking in the field or in the contiguous arrow, allowing to choose one of the valid values. The scroll bar can be used to move around the different lines.

S/he also will be able to append new item definitions by inserting information in the fields. If the window is not full of lines, s/he may do it by editing the first empty line. Otherwise, the button *Append* will appear enabled and, when clicking on it, a new empty line will be opened on the bottom for editing.

An existing line or node may be deleted. With the cursor positioned in the selected line, the user click on the *Delete* button and then, after a confirmation, the node is marked as deleted by writing a D at the end of the line.

The modification, insertion and deletion operation may be iterated and they may be applied to different lines. Following the DB approach, all these changes are not actually performed up to the user has clicked on the *Commit* button. The user may cancel all the changes from the last commit by clicking on the *Cancel* button.

To end with the editing of nodes, click on the *Close* button. If there are some changes not committed a message will appear warning about it, allowing to cancel the closing operation.

To keep the database coherent, ADM will control a number of situations: the appearance of all the obligatory fields in a new node definition, the not deletion of nodes where users are currently connected or that appears as default node in a user description, etc.

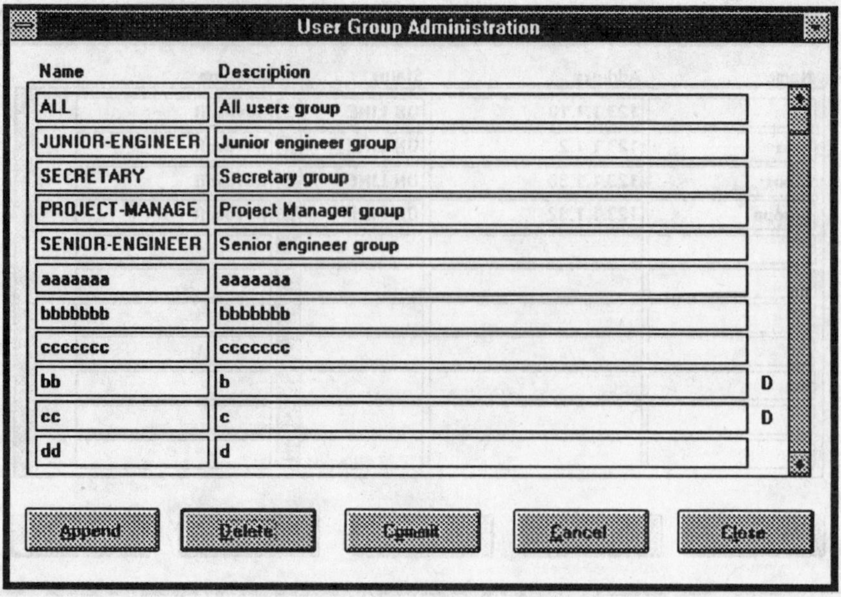

Fig. 4.4. User Group Administration Window

4.1.4 User Group Editing Process

The user may access this function by selecting the *Groups...* menu item under the *User* pop-up menu of the main window. Then the user is presented with the User Group Administration window.

The User Group Administration window has the same lay-out and behaviour than the ones described for the Node Administration window. Two fields are presented for every user group description: Name and Description.

To keep the database coherent, ADM will check for a number of situations: the appearance of all the obligatory fields in a new group definition, the not deletion of groups to which users currently belong, etc.

4.1.5 User Editing Process

The user may access this function by selecting the *Users...* menu item under the *User* pop-up menu of the main window. Then the user is presented with the User Administration window.

The User Administration window has the same lay-out and behaviour than the ones described for the Node Administration window. Six fields are presented for every user description: Name, Password, Full Name, Permission, Default Node

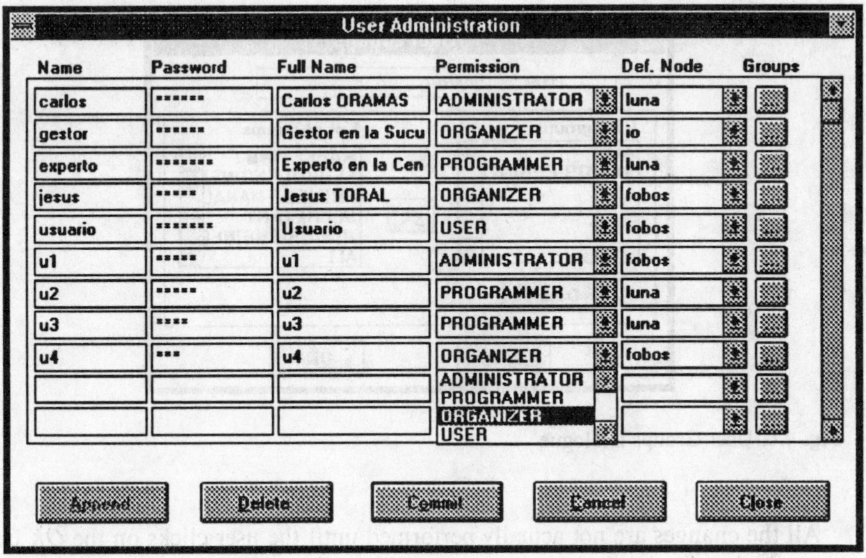

Fig. 4.5. User Administration Window

and Groups. The way of accessing or modifying the first five fields is the usual one. The field Groups is explained later in this section.

The new users are automatically registered in the generic group ALL on committing of the user insertion: MMTCA requires that every user belong to this group.

To keep the database coherent, ADM will check a number of situations: the appearance of all the obligatory fields in a new user definition, the not deletion of users currently logged in or that are involved in active metadocuments, etc.

The field Groups gives information about the group(s) to which a user belongs. Clicking on the groups button, labelled with '..', under the column Groups, activates the User Groups dialogue for this user, provided that there are no changes pending in the User Administration window.

This dialogue presents on top the related user, on the left hand side the list of the groups to which this user belongs to and on the right hand side a list of all the existing groups.

One or more groups names may be selected in the User Groups list to unregister the user on them, by clicking afterwards the *Delete* button under this list. It is not allowed to unregister the user from the ALL group (not checked in this version).

The processed user may be registered in new groups by selecting them in the List of Groups, and then clicking on the 'shift' button, labelled with '<<'.

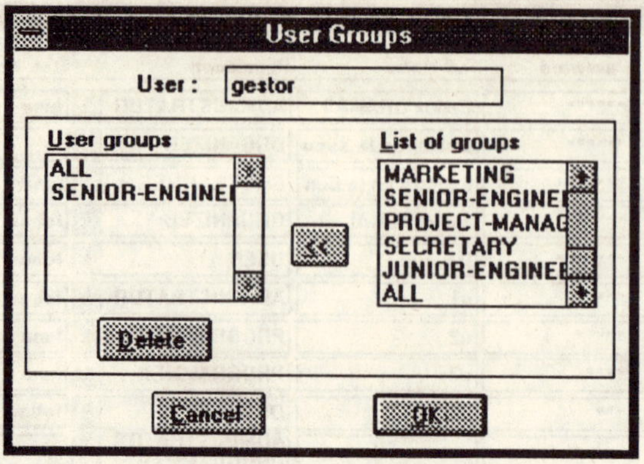

Fig. 4.6. User Groups Dialogue

All the changes are not actually performed until the user clicks on the *OK* button, which commits the changes and closes the User Groups dialogue. The user may cancel all the changes by clicking on the *Cancel* button.

4.2 Procedure Design

This section provides a user-oriented introduction to ViEW (Visual Editor for Workflow). It briefly presents the basics of workflow management in general, and then explains how to use ViEW, in order to create tasks, link them, and enter information about cooperation, participants and actions for each task.

Before we go on we will briefly explain how ViEW fits with the rest of the MMTCA environment.

The purpose of ViEW is to allow users to design cooperative applications. In MMTCA a cooperative application is called a *procedure* and is made up of *tasks* and *actions*. A task is a set of actions which a single user (or group of users in case of a cooperative task) is able to carry out without the need to exchange data with other users. So the boundary between one task and the next one is the point where the user (or group) needs to send or get information to or from other users.

As already noted a task consists of a set of actions. These actions are carried out in sequence, but one can imagine that even a full programming facility might be necessary (with statements for loops, if...then...else, case, etc.). An action is just one, or more, existing applications activated at the same time.

The execution of these cooperative systems is taken care of by the run-time part of MMTCA, which stores all relevant information in a database, that resides on the MMTCA server. Therefore, the design of a cooperative application (i.e. a

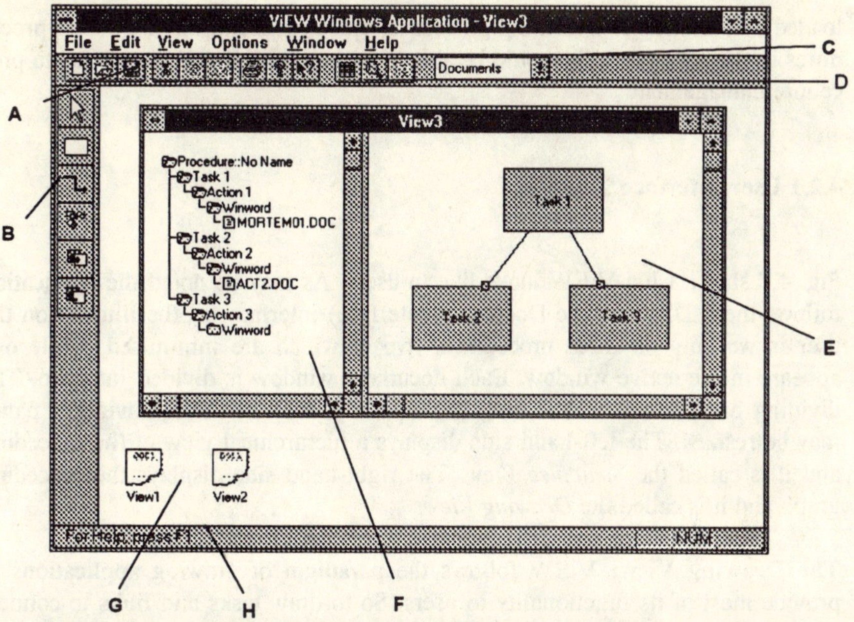

- **A** The standard function toolbar includes buttons for functions such as new, open, save as, cut, copy, paste, print, help and context sensitive help.
- **B** Tool buttons that allow the creation and manipulation of objects: Select tool, Task tool, Simple Link tool, Conditional Link tool, Flip to Front tool, Flip to Back tool.
- **C** Combo box that displays the tree expansion level of the active document.
- **D** Option buttons: show or hide grid, zoom, expand tree-like form of procedure.
- **E** Active drawing view.
- **F** Structure view of the current procedure.
- **G** Iconified procedures.
- **H** The status bar displays to the user messages appropriate to the current action. This feature does not work in the current version of ViEW.

Fig.4.7. The ViEW Editor

procedure) ultimately consists of nothing more than creating or updating these records in the database. The noteworthy point about ViEW is that it provides a graphical interface, which hopefully will render the process of workflow specification more intuitive.

So ViEW creates and downloads the specification of procedures to the MMTCA server. To be complete from a functional specification point of view, the application should also do error checking (before the specification is downloaded), simulation of a running procedure, upload and editing of existing procedures in the server, and it should be able to carry out all functions related to procedure management.

4.2.1 User Interface

Fig. 4.7 shows what ViEW looks like to users. As may be noted the application follows the MDI (Multiple Document Interface) interface. In the illustration the user is working on three procedures, two of which are minimised, while one appears in the active window. Each document window is divided into two. The dividing border is moveable and, consequently, each of the two window panes may be resized. The left-hand side displays a hierarchical view of the procedure and it is called the *Structure View.* The right-hand side displays the procedure graph and it is called the *Drawing View*.

The Drawing View: ViEW follows the paradigm of drawing applications to provide most of its functionality to users. So to draw tasks and links to connect them, the user just selects the corresponding tool (task and link tool respectively) and draws them on the screen.
Being able to specify the tasks and the links among tasks may constitute the framework of the procedure, but is certainly only part of the whole process. The other important aspect of workflow design is to specify what goes on inside a task. In order to enter such information the user brings up a single dialogue by double-clicking the task with the left mouse button.

The Structure View: This view displays a hierarchical view of the procedure in the form of a tree. The root of the tree is the procedure name, while the various nodes of the tree are the names of all subordinate objects: tasks, actions, applications and documents. The level of expansion may be selected by the combo box that appears in ViEW's toolbar and it is set independently for each document. Each time a new level is selected, the window displays the procedure tree up to and including the corresponding objects. Nodes in the tree may be collapsed or extended by double-clicking on the node icon (i.e. the little bitmap shown on the left of the object's name). However, notice that nodes can be expanded up to specified expansion level. The procedure node cannot be collapsed entirely, as its tasks are always visible.

The user may edit procedure objects by double-clicking on the text entry of a tree node that corresponds to an action or application. Then the corresponding (i.e. action specification or application specification) dialogue comes up displaying information on the selected object. For more information on editing objects, see the corresponding part of this manual.

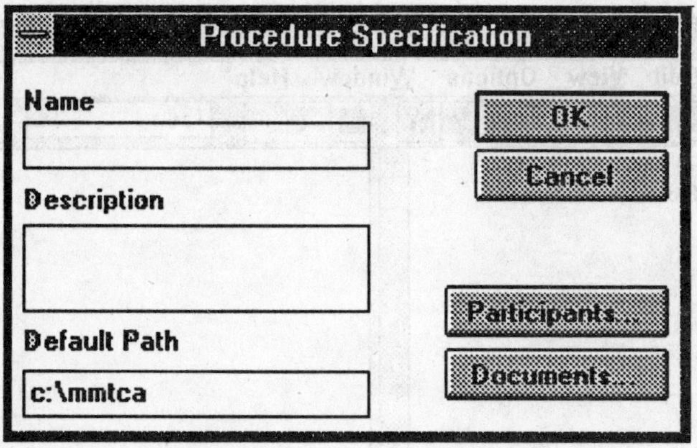

Fig. 4.8. Specifying Procedure Information

4.2.2. Creating a Procedure

A procedure consists of one, or more, *tasks* that must be executed, the *links* that specify the task execution sequence, the *users* (either individuals, or groups, in case of cooperative sessions) who will carry out each task, the *actions* that make up each task, the sets of *applications* which will be employed for each action, the list of *documents* which will be used with each application, etc.

ViEW allows users to arrange the tasks and their links graphically on the screen, carry out any necessary modifications and finally download the procedure specification to the MMTCA server.

Specifying Procedure Information: To specify procedure information the user selects the "Procedure Specification" item under the File pop-up menu. Then the dialogue shown in Fig. 4.8 appears on the screen.

The user can specify the following procedure properties:

- *Name*, the name that will appear in the Intray's procedure tray at run-time.
- *Description*, meaningful comments for the purpose of this procedure.
- *Default Path*, the path where procedure tasks are executed *on the nodes*.

The user may also get a listing of the following procedure entities:

The whole process starts with the user either starting the program, or clicking on . In both cases the user will be presented with an empty window (the process window), inside which s/he may draw the tasks and their links.

Notice that the participants and documents list are displayed in a list box attached to the right-hand side of the Procedure Information dialogue. This sub-dialogue disappears after confirming, or cancelling, the main dialogue and the information displayed in it serves only informative purposes.

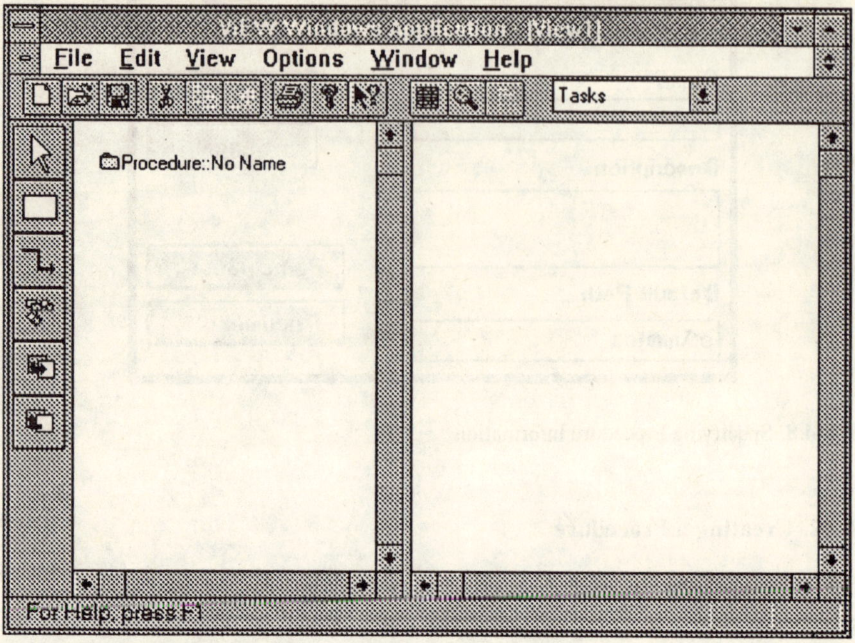

Fig. 4.9. Creating Tasks

Creating Tasks: To create a new task the user will follow these steps:

1. Click on  to be able to draw tasks.
2. When the cursor is positioned inside the process window it changes shape and looks like a pencil with a small rectangle in its tip  .
3. Click anywhere on the screen to display the task at that position.
4. Alternatively, just position the cursor (instead of clicking) and press the mouse button (but do not release it). A dotted outline of a rectangle will appear which can be moved around the screen as long as the mouse button is kept pressed.

- *Participants*, a list of all participants specified in all tasks of the procedure.
- *Documents*, a list of all documents specified in all procedure actions.

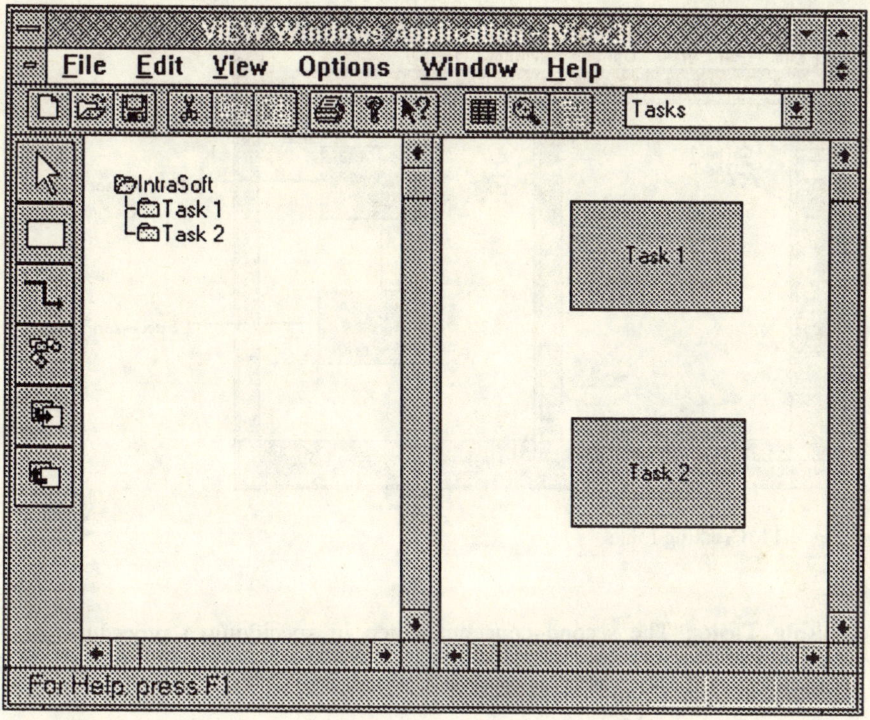

Fig. 4.10. Creating Tasks

After a task is positioned on the screen the user may of course move it to somewhere else. To do that the user will follow these steps:

1. Click on  to be able to select tasks.
2. Position the cursor over a task and click once the left button to select it. The task will appear with a dotted outline[2].
3. Press the left mouse button over the task and move the cursor around the screen. A dotted outline will follow the cursor until the user releases the mouse button. The task will then be displayed at this new position.

As usual in such cases, it is much more difficult to describe such a procedure than to actually carry it out. Using these techniques the user may create and position on the screen any number of tasks.

---

[2] Notice that if the task rectangle overlaps with other tasks, the user may have to click repeatedly over the task s/he wishes to select.

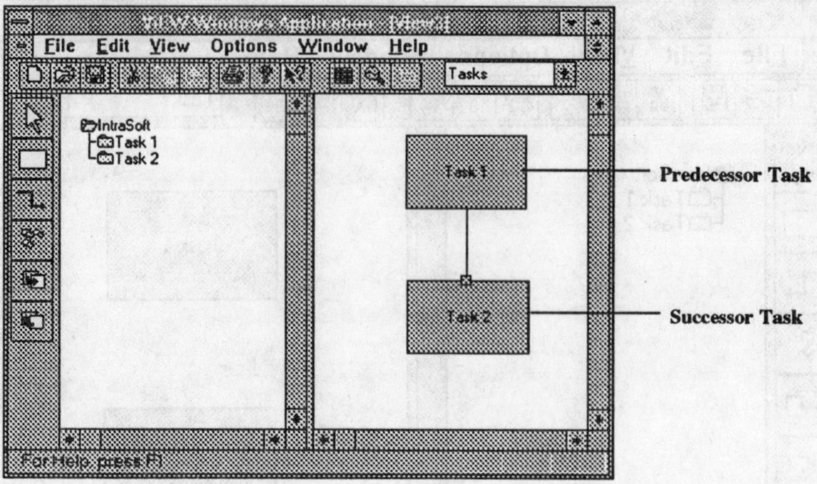

Fig. 4.11. Creating Links

Linking Tasks: The second conceptual step in specifying a procedure is to establish links among already existing tasks. ViEW supports two kinds of links: Simple Links and Conditional Links.

Simple Links: To define a simple link the user will follow these steps:

1. Click on  in order to be able to draw links.
2. When the cursor is positioned inside the procedure window, it changes shape and looks like a pencil  .
3. Position the cursor anywhere on the predecessor task and press the left mouse button.
4. Without releasing the mouse button move the cursor to point to the successor task. A dotted line will follow the cursor's movement.
5. Release the mouse button. A line will be displayed connecting the two tasks. Notice that no link is drawn when either the start, or the end, point of the link falls outside a task.

A small rectangle will be displayed at one end of the line. This is displayed at the side of the successor task to show the link's direction.

It is important to note that there is no procedure to move links around the screen, because links always follow their associated tasks. Therefore, when the user moves a task, all links originating, or terminating, to this task will be automatically re-drawn at their proper positions.

Conditional Links: To define a conditional link follow these steps:

1. Click on  in order to select the conditional link tool.
2. When the cursor is positioned inside the procedure window, it changes shape and looks like a pencil with a question mark attached at its tip .
3. Position the cursor anywhere on the screen and click the left mouse button. A diamond like shape appears in dotted outline
4. Then click on the three tasks that will be connected by the link: the *source* task, the *true destination* task and the *false destination* task. The order of tasks is important. The false destination task is optional. The link-drawing process may end by clicking on the true-destination task with the **right** mouse button. Upon finalising the drawing process the link appears in solid background along with connecting lines. The source task line is coloured red, the true task connecting line is coloured green and the false task line is coloured blue. If, for any reason, the link cannot be created, an explanatory message appears on the screen.

Notice that conditional link objects may be moved the same way that task objects are moved. All connecting lines are redrawn automatically.

After the link is created, it may be edited by double-clicking within the diamond-like object. A small dialogue appears that allows the user to specify a name and a condition for the link.

Deleting Tasks and Links: Apart from drawing and moving tasks and links, the user may need to delete tasks and links. To delete a task the user will follow these steps:

Select the task, following the process described in the section "Creating Tasks". Click on the . The selected task, along with all the links that originate, or end, in this task will be deleted. Alternatively, the user may want to delete a single link. Then the user must select the link and click again on . The selected[3] link will be deleted.

4.2.3. Editing Tasks

Task editing is performed through the task specification dialogue. As already noted this dialogue is a multi-purpose dialogue, which is brought up by positioning the cursor inside a task and double-clicking the *left* mouse button. The dialogue is multipurpose in the sense that through the same dialogue the user may enter information on all four categories available: general, cooperation, participants and actions.

---

[3] An object (task or link) is selected when it is drawn in a dotted rectangle.

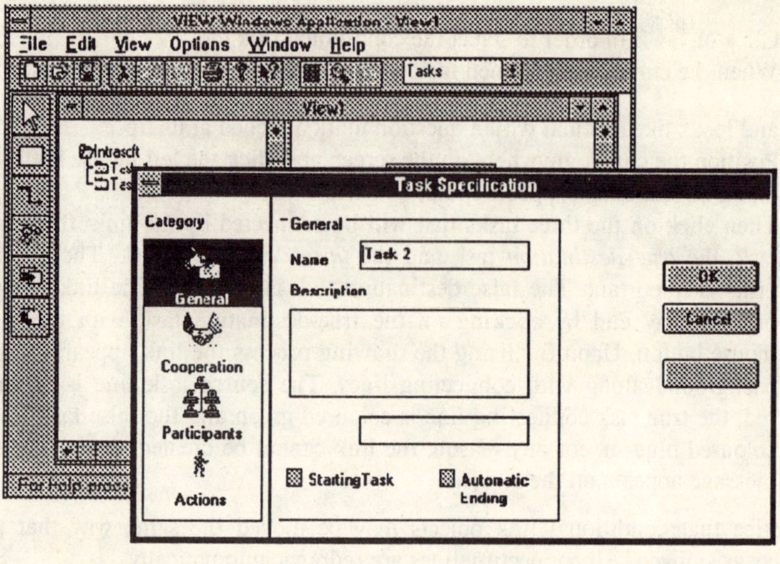

Fig. 4.12. Editing Tasks

In order to select the kind of information, the user needs just to click the corresponding icon in the list displayed in the left side of the dialogue. When an icon is selected, the dialogue's contents at the right side change to reflect the user's choice.

The following kinds of information are available and should be entered:

1. *General:* The task's name, a description, whether this task is a starting task for the procedure, whether it should end automatically, etc.
2. *Cooperation:* Whether the task is a synchronous or asynchronous task. In the former case a set of properties needs to be specified, such as: floor policy, meeting type, etc.
3. *Participants:* The users who participate in this task (a user, or a group of users).
4. *Actions:* The list of applications which will be activated in this task. Each action may activate at the same time one, or more, applications. Each application may load one or more files.

The *OK*, *Cancel* buttons at the right-hand-side of the dialogue should only be used when the user needs to close the dialogue.

Specifying General Information: The general information category is the default one, so no further selection is necessary, once the task specification dialogue is brought up.

The information which may be entered through this sub-dialogue is as follows:

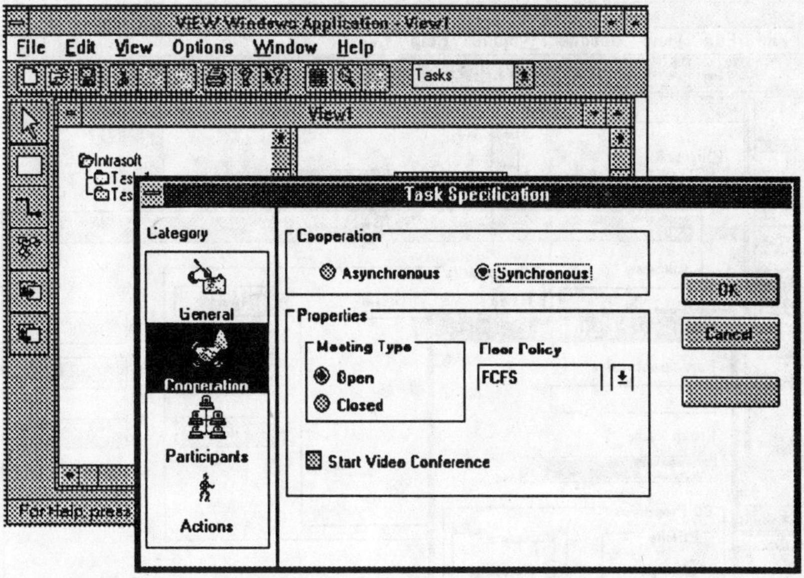

Fig. 4.13. Specifying Cooperation

- *Name:* the name that will appear in the users Intray dialogue, at run-time.
- *Description:* some meaningful comments for the purpose of this task.
- *Duration:* to be specified.
- *Initial Task:* specifies whether procedure execution starts off with this task.
- *Automatic Ending:* specifies whether MMTCA will automatically proceed with the execution of the next task, at run-time.

Specifying Cooperation: To enter cooperation information the user will double-click on a task with the right mouse button to bring up the task specification dialogue. The user will then select the cooperation category.

The information which may be entered through this dialogue is as follows:

- *Asynchronous:* specifies the task type as asynchronous.
- *Synchronous:* specifies the task type as synchronous, i.e. a cooperative session.

Notice that only one of the above buttons may be selected. If the type of the task is synchronous, then the following properties may be specified:

- *Minimum Number of Participants:* specifies the minimum number of task participants that must accept the CS invitation, before the CS chair can start the CS.

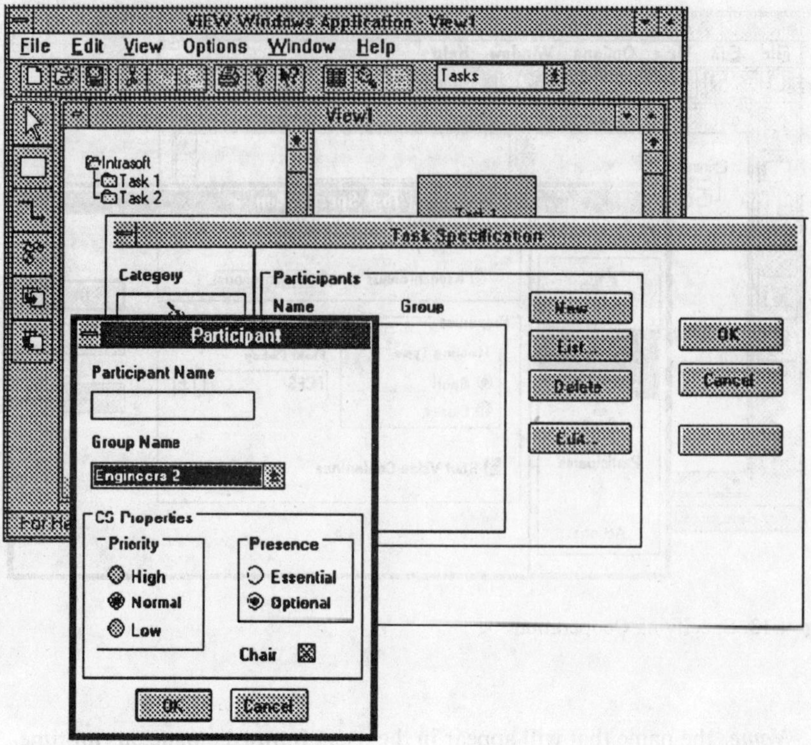

Fig. 4.14. Specifying Participants

- *Floor Policy:* specifies the policy that will be used for floor control exchange, during the CS.
- *Meeting Type:* specifies whether or not users can join an on-going CS.

Specifying Participants: To enter a task's participant information, the user will double-click on a task with the right mouse button to bring up the task specification dialogue. The user will then select the *Participants* category.

The user will enter a participant for the task by either pressing the **New** button to specify a new participant, or the **List** button, to select a participant already mentioned in previous tasks.

If the user presses New, the dialogue shown in Fig. 4.14 will be displayed, to allow the definition of a new participant for the procedure:

The user may enter a new user's name and select the group in which the user belongs. If the task type, specified in the general information sub-dialogue is *Synchronous,* then the CS Properties are enabled. Notice that the *Priority* radio buttons are enabled only if the task's Floor Policy specified in the cooperation sub-dialogue, is set to *Prioritised.*

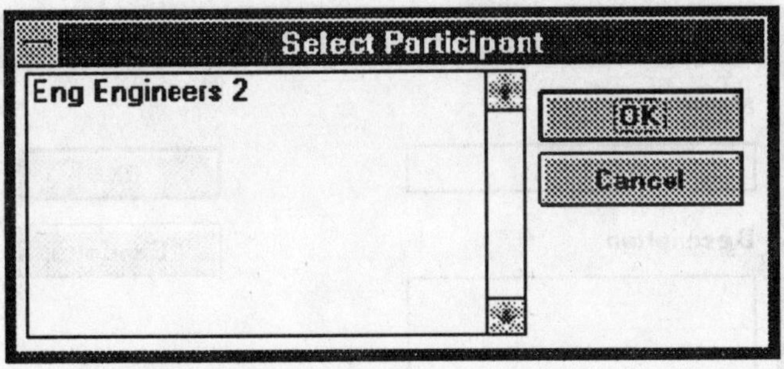

Fig. 4.15. Selecting Participants

If the user presses the List button, the dialogue shown in Fig. 4.15 will be displayed, listing all the participants defined for any procedure tasks up to this point. The user may select a user from the list.

The user may also *Delete* a task participant, or *Edit* a participant definition. When the user deletes a task participant, the participant is deleted *only* for this task. If the same participant is involved in another task, it will still appear in the procedure's participants list. If, however, the participant is not involved with another task, it will be deleted altogether from the procedure. Editing a participant definition modifies the participant definition for all tasks where the participant is involved.

4.2.4 Specifying Actions

To specify a task's actions the user will double-click on a task with the right mouse button to bring up the task specification dialogue. The user will then select the *Actions* category.

When working with actions the user can create a new action, delete an action, or edit an existing action, clicking on the *New*, *Delete*, or *Edit* button respectively. When the user clicks on the *New*, or *Edit*, button the Actions dialogue appears on the screen.

Editing Actions: This dialogue is used for action creation and action editing. The information which may be entered through this dialogue is as follows:

- *Name*, name of the action.
- *Description*, meaningful comments for the purpose of this action.

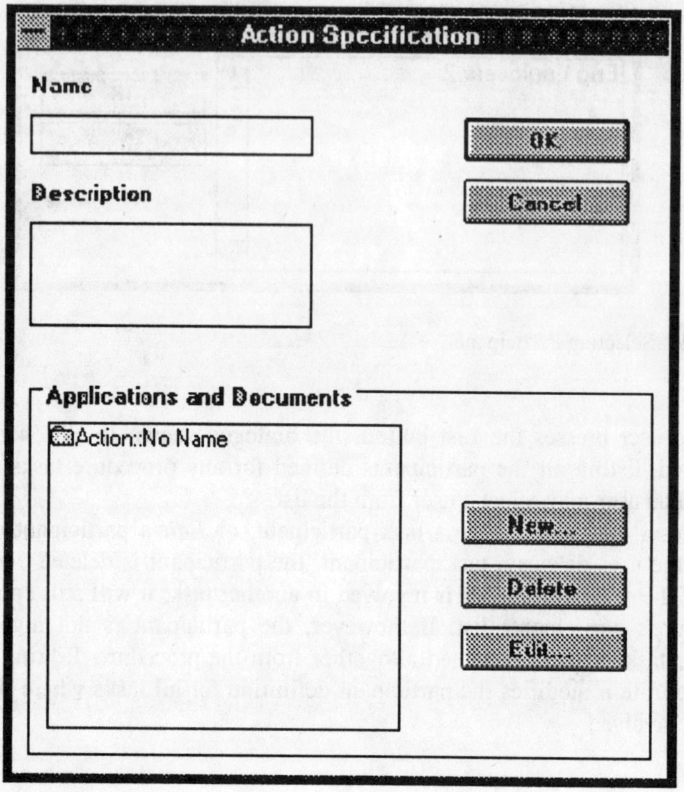

Fig. 4.16. Specifying Actions

At the bottom of the dialogue there is a list box that displays the action sub-tree. The root of the tree is the action name (set as soon as the user enters a name for the action), and the action application and document names are the tree nodes. The user may select applications and specify documents for the action, by using the *New*, *Delete*, or *Edit* buttons to create, delete, or edit applications.

Alternatively the user may edit an application by double-clicking on its name in the action sub-tree list box. In either case the application specification dialogue appears. When the user presses the *Delete* button the selected application is deleted, along with all related documents.

Selecting Applications: The dialogue shown in Fig. 4.17 is used for application selection.

The user may select an application template through the Template Name combo box that appears at the top of the dialogue. This combo box contains all application templates known to the system. If the user wishes to specify a new template, the Tools Profile Editor should be used. When the user selects a tem-

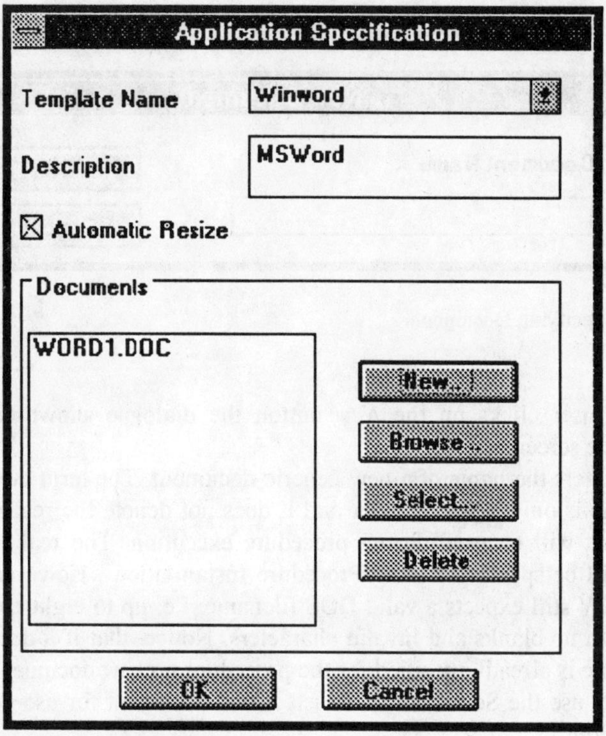

Fig. 4.17. Selecting Applications

plate, its description appears in the description field. Notice, that this field contains read-only information and the text that appears inside cannot be edited.

The list box at the bottom of the dialogue displays the names of all documents that have been specified, or selected, for this application template. Using the buttons next to the document list box the user may create a new generic document, browse on the local drives to select an existing document, select a document already specified in the procedure, or delete a document. Notice, that when the user deletes a document, the document is deleted for use with this application only. However, if the document is not used by any other application in the procedure, it is deleted entirely.

Specifying Documents: When the user specifies documents to be used with an application, the following options are available:

- Create a new generic document.
- Select a locally existing document.
- Select an already specified document (existing or generic).

Fig. 4.18. Specifying Documents

When the user clicks on the *New* button the dialogue shown in Fig. 4.18 appears on the screen.

The user enters the name of a new generic document. The term *generic* means that the name is only a place holder and it does not denote the real name of the document that will be used during procedure execution. The real name of the document will be specified during Procedure Instantiation[4]. However, for safety reasons, ViEW still expects a valid DOS filename, i.e. up to eight characters for filename, with no blanks and invalid characters. Notice, that if a document with the same name is already specified for the procedure no new document is created. The user may use the Select button to select this document for use with the current application.

When the user clicks on the *Browse* button the standard Windows open-file dialogue appears on the screen.

The user may search through the available drives and/or directories to select an existing document.

When the user clicks on the *Select* button a list box appears next to the application specification dialogue as in Fig. 4.19.

The list box contains the names of all documents used in the procedure up to this point. Generic documents are displayed with their name only, while existing files are displayed with their full path name (if the path name is too long it is truncated to display drive and filename information only). The user selects a document by clicking on its name. The document name is added to the list of documents used with this application. The list box next to the dialogue disappears. Again notice, that if the same document is already in use by the current application, it is not added again.

[4] For more information on Procedure Instantiation, see section 5.7.1.

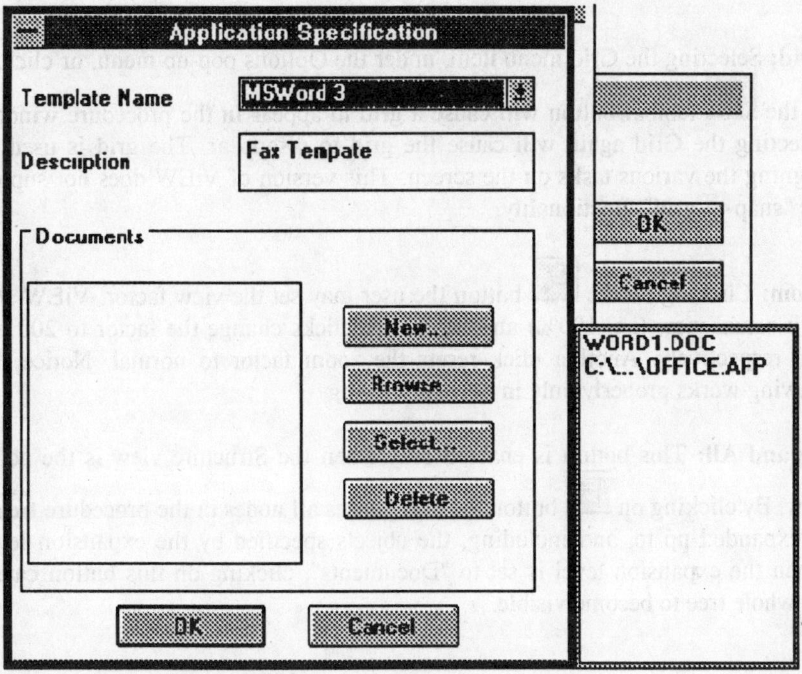

Fig. 4.19. Associating Documents with Applications

4.2.5 Uploading the Procedure

When the user is finished with the editing of the procedure and wishes to upload the procedure specification to the MMTCA server, s/he may select the "Send to Server" menu item, under the File pop-up menu. Then the process of procedure validation takes place to ensure that the user has set right kind of values for all required properties of procedure entities (i.e. tasks, actions, participants, etc.). Upon successful validation the procedure definition is converted to SQL commands for the MMTCA database server, and all required database tables are updated. An MMTCA user with the organiser privilege may then instantiate this procedure creating metadocuments out of its definition.

4.2.6 Customising ViEW

There are a number of mechanisms provided for customising the operation of the ViEW editor.

Grid: Selecting the Grid menu item, under the Options pop-up menu, or clicking on the  toolbar button will cause a grid to appear in the procedure window. Selecting the Grid again will cause the grid to disappear. The grid is used for aligning the various tasks on the screen. This version of ViEW does not support the "snap-to-grid" functionality.

Zoom: Clicking on the  button the user may set the view factor. ViEW start with actual view (i.e. 100%) and successive clicks change the factor to 200 and 300 respectively. Another click resets the zoom factor to normal. Notice that drawing works properly only in normal viewing.

Expand All: This button is enabled only when the Structure view is the active view. By clicking on  button the user causes all nodes in the procedure tree to be expanded up to, and including, the objects specified by the expansion level. When the expansion level is set to "Documents", clicking on this button causes the whole tree to become visible.

4.3 The Metadocument Browser

This tool provides an overview of Procedures defined for MMTCA and entered into the database. It also provides an overview of Instances of these procedures - these procedure instances are known as Metadocuments.

There are various facilities for manipulation of Metadocuments, both for preparation of work and for recovery after errors or system failures during work sessions.

Facilities for manipulation of Procedures are much more limited in the Metadocument Browser: they are best changed using the ViEW editor described earlier.

4.3.1 The Database Window

The Database splitter window lists all procedures in the database in the left side of the window. It is opened automatically as the Metadocument Browser starts up. It may also be opened from the *New* option from the *File* menu or the toolbar button .

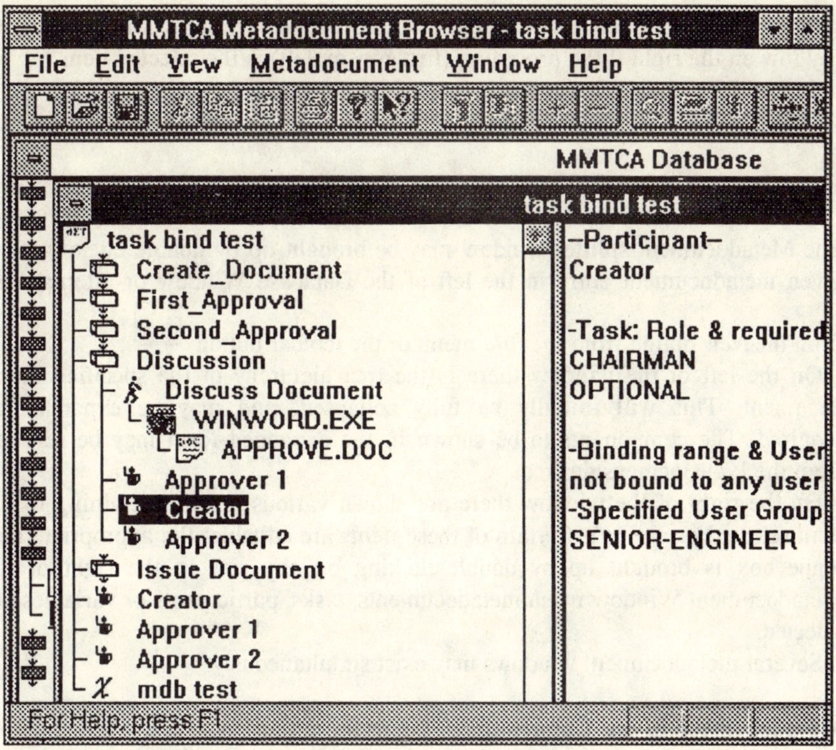

Fig. 4.23. Metadocument Browser

A double click on a procedure in the left hand window will, if possible, expand a procedure to show metadocument instances of that procedure.

An instance of the Metadocument Window will be opened by a double click on a metadocument item in the left of the database window. This may also be opened once the metadocument is selected on the left by double-clicking on the right. An instance of the Procedure Window will be opened by double clicking on the right of the database window if the selected object on the left is a procedure.

4.3.2 The Procedure Window

The Procedure splitter window may be brought up by double clicking on a given Procedure entry in the left of the Database Window or alternatively from the *New* option from the *File* menu or the toolbar button  .

On the right of the window there are shown various details pertaining to the item selected on the left. Except where otherwise stated here, these items are not editable. Procedure deletion dialogues will be popped up by double clicking on any row on the right if the procedure (first row on left) is the selected item.

Several Procedure Windows may exist simultaneously.

4.3.3 The Metadocument Window

The Metadocument splitter window may be brought up by double clicking on a given metadocument entry in the left of the Database Window or alternatively from the *New* option from the *File* menu or the toolbar button  .

On the left of the window there is the tree hierarchy of the specified metadocument. This will initially be fully collapsed, and may be expanded as required. The components to be shown in the expanded form may be selected from the *View* menu as desired.

On the right of the window there are shown various details pertaining to the item selected on the left. Certain of these items are editable; the appropriate dialogue box is brought up by double-clicking on any row in the right of the Metadocument Window when metadocuments, tasks, participants or variables are selected.

Several metadocument windows may exist simultaneously.

Metadocument Menu Commands: This menu is only available when the currently selected window is a Metadocument Window.

View Document	Look at a data file via the appropriate application
Transfer Document	Transfer data files for a task (pre start)
Set Participants	Bind a user to a participant
Toggle Links	Change the status of a link between tasks
Set Variables	Set or modify the value of a variable

4.3.4 View menu commands

The View menu offers the following commands:

Toolbar	Shows or hides the toolbar.
Status Bar	Shows or hides the status bar.
Tasks	Shows or hides the tasks in the tree
Participants	Shows or hides the participants in the tree
Documents	Shows or hides the documents in the tree
Variables	Shows or hides the variables in the tree
Links	Shows or hides the links in the tree
Actions	Shows or hides the actions and applications in the tree

Toolbar command (View menu): Use this command to display and hide the toolbar, which includes buttons for some of the most common commands in the Metadocument Browser. A check mark appears next to the menu item when the toolbar is displayed.

Status Bar command (View menu): Use this command to display and hide the status bar, which describes the action to be executed by the selected menu item or depressed toolbar button, and keyboard latch state. A check mark appears next to the menu item when the status bar is displayed.

4.3.5 Expand Tree Button

The button  to expand the tree will be highlighted if the selected item in the left of the splitter window has a sub-tree and the sub-tree is not expanded. Click on the button to expand the tree and show the sub-tree in the left splitter window. Alternatively, double click on the selected item in the left splitter window.

Note that the button is highlighted when the object potentially has a sub-tree, even though the sub-tree may contain no valid objects. This information will not be known until the attempt is made to retrieve the data from the database.

4.3.6 Collapse Tree Button

The button  to collapse the tree will be highlighted if the selected item in the left of the splitter window has a sub-tree and the sub-tree is expanded. Click on the button to collapse the tree and redisplay the collapsed tree in the left splitter window. Alternatively, double click on the selected item in the left splitter window.

4.3.7 Deleting Procedures

A procedure may be deleted only if there are no currently existing metadocuments based on the procedure in question. This restriction is necessary since the procedure description is required to make a coherent whole of the metadocument data; it is not even possible to delete a metadocument if the appropriate procedure data is not available.

Procedures may be deleted from the Procedure Window by selecting the procedure (the first item in the list) on the left of the splitter window, then double clicking on any line of the description brought up in the Right of the splitter window. A deletion dialogue will follow.

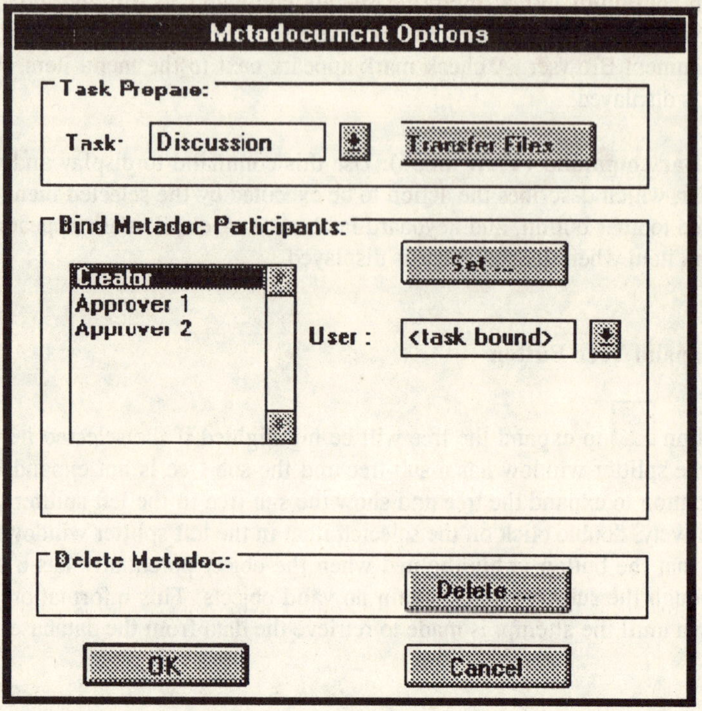

Fig. 4.24. Metadocument Options

4.3.8 Editing or Deleting Metadocuments

Double-clicking a metadocument in the right hand window brings up the dialogue box shown in Fig. 4.24.

The selected metadocument may be deleted by use of the *Delete* button. This causes permanent removal of the information pertaining to this metadocument from the database. The associated document files and any directories created are not removed at present. Currently there is no check of authorisation for this action.

The list of Tasks in the Metadocument is shown in the *Task* combo box. Pre-task file transfer may be performed by selecting the desired task from the combo box and clicking on the *Transfer Files* button. The files specified for the chosen task will be brought across to the current node. Currently there is no check of authorisation for this action.

Binding users for the scope of the whole metadocument may be performed by selecting the participant to be bound from the list box in the *Participants* area. In the combo box adjacent will be shown a list of the permitted users. If the participant is already bound for the scope of the whole metadocument then the user's name will be the single option in the combo box. If the participant is bound for the scope of one or more tasks in the metadocument, then the combo box will display <task bound>, and metadocument binding is not possible.

4.3.9 Editing Participants

Editing participant data may potentially be done in several ways. It may be important to select the correct method if you wish to achieve the desired results.

A participant may be bound to a user on a per-task basis, or alternatively bound for the whole metadocument. Once a participant is bound for the whole metadocument, little can be changed on a per-task basis.

Binding a participant for the whole metadocument may be done if the participant is currently unbound by use of the Metadocument Edit dialogue.

Binding the participant for a particular task may be done if the participant is currently unbound for the metadocument or is bound per task for a different task in this metadocument. The task specific data for the participant may be edited for per-task bound participants. The  toolbar button will be enabled in these cases, and may be used to edit participant details for the currently selected item.

Task specific participant edits may be done via the Task Edit dialogue or alternatively by the Participant Edit dialogue.

The Participant Edit dialogue (Fig. 4.25) may be brought up from the Metadocument Window when a participant is selected on the left of the window. The dialogue is brought up by double-clicking on any item on the right of the window. If the participant is directly under the metadocument in the tree hierarchy then only limited editing facilities are presented since task specific data and bindings are not appropriate. However, if the participant is under a task in the tree hierarchy, then all task specific data will be editable where possible.

If the participant is already bound in a scope that covers this task, then the user combo box will only show one option, no change is possible. For any task bound participant, it is possible to alter the *Role* and the *Requirement* for this task. The *Role* options are Chairman or Other. Chairman is selected when the check box is crossed. The *Requirement* options are Essential or Optional. Essential is selected when the check box is crossed. It is also possible to alter the *Priority* of the participant for use when the floor policy of a cooperative session is prioritised. Default priority is Normal. High and Low priority are also possible.

If the participant is not bound in a scope that covers this task, then the user may bind the participant for this task by selecting one of the choice of potential users listed in the combo box.

It is not possible to change the *Role* or *Requirement* data for metadocument bound participants from the Metadocument Browser since this information is specified for the Procedure and not for the Metadocument.

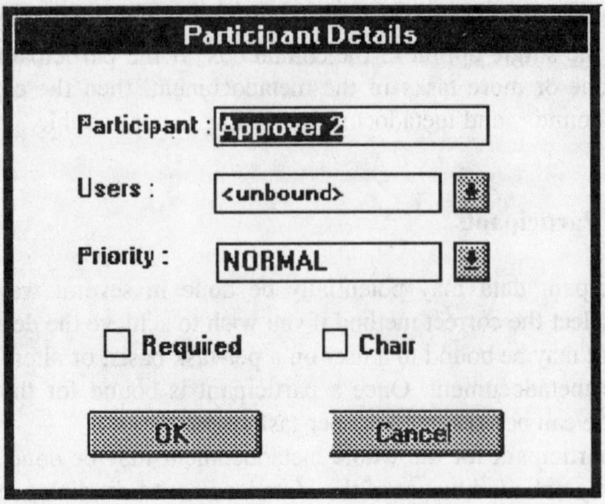

Fig. 4.25. Participant Details

4.3.10 View a Metadocument Document

This facility is available from the *Document View* button on the Toolbar or by double clicking on the appropriate document in the left of the Metadocument Window, where the document must be a subsidiary item in a task application. Once such a document is selected, the *Document View* button is enabled.

The facility will start the appropriate application with the specified document as its initial data. The parent object of the document in the tree hierarchy will be the appropriate application.

4.3.11 Editing Tasks

Double-clicking on a task in the right hand window brings up the Task Details dialogue box (Fig. 4.26).

The Task Details dialogue permits editing of details for participants who are bound to users over the scope of the task. It also permits binding of users to participants for the scope of the task if the participant is not already bound over a scope that includes this task (i.e. bound for this task or bound for the whole metadocument).

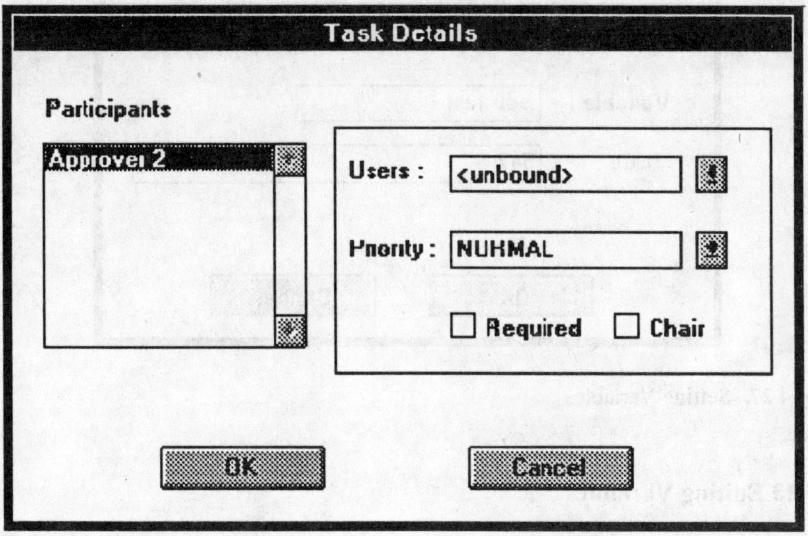

Fig. 4.26. Task Details

The list box will show the list of participants who may potentially participate in this task. If a participant is already bound to a user for this scope, then the name of that user and the relevant task specific details will be shown on the right when the participant is selected in the list box. If the participant is unbound for the task, then a list of potential users will be shown in the combo box on the right.

Task specific details may currently be modified for any participant whose binding is over the task scope rather than over the whole metadocument. These details are as for the Participant Edit dialogue in section 4.3.9.

4.3.12 Task File Transfer

If the user is a potential participant in the given task, then he/she may request that the relevant files are transferred to the current MMTCA node in advance of the start of the task, thus saving time when other users are in session.

If the files to be transferred are later changed on the file server, then the transfer of those updated files will be re-done at the start of the task.

Task file transfer may be initiated from the toolbar button  when the Metadocument splitter window is selected, and a task is selected in the left side of the window. At this time the file transfer button will be enabled, normally this button is greyed out.

Pre-task file transfer may also be initiated from the Metadocument Edit dialogue.

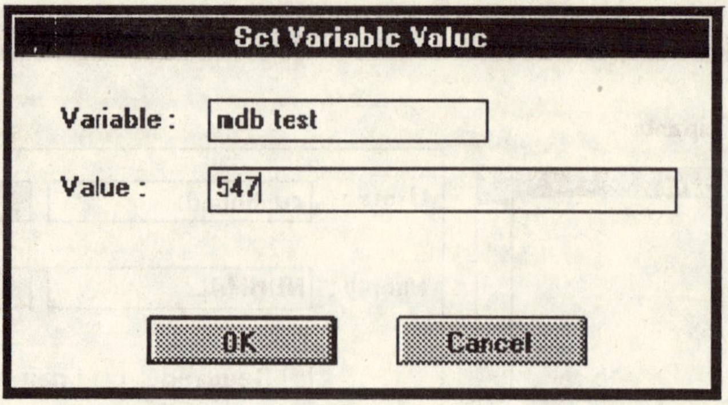

Fig. 4.27. Setting Variables

4.3.13 Editing Variables

It is important to note that various actions depend on the *existence or non-existence* of the Metadocument record for a Procedure Variable, and not only on the *value* of the variable. On the right of the Metadocument Window when the variable is selected, either its current value will be shown as part of the provided information, or a message saying that the variable does not yet exist for this metadocument.

The *Set Variable* option is available from the *Metadocument* menu when a Metadocument Window is the selected document window. It is also available from a button  on the toolbar. Neither of these options will be enabled unless the selected item on the left of the Metadocument Window is a variable.

Editing a variable may also be initiated by double-clicking on the right of the Metadocument Window when the variable to be edited is selected on the left.

If variables are not showing, it is possible to show them by toggling the *Variable* option on the *View* menu.

In all cases, there will be a Variable Edit dialogue brought up.

The name of the variable will be shown in the upper edit box (non editable), and the current value, if any, shown in the lower. Any change to the value shown will be written to the database as the *OK* button is pressed, creating a new Metadocument Variable record if necessary.

4.3.14 Metadocument Link Manipulation

Metadocument links may be set or reset for a given metadocument. This may be required to reschedule the workflow manually, either by result of user preference or for manual recovery after network or system failures, for example. Link manipulation is not to be considered a "normal" operation.

The interface to manipulate links is restricted.

The *Toggle Link* option is available from the *Metadocument* menu when a Metadocument Window is the selected document window. It is also available from a button  on the toolbar. Neither of these options will be enabled unless the selected item on the left of the Metadocument Window is a link. It is also possible to toggle the link by double-clicking on the right of the Metadocument Window when the selected item on the left is a link. An appropriate dialogue will be brought up.

If links are not showing, it is possible to show them by toggling the *Link* option on the *View* menu.

4.3.15 Update of Window Contents

An update of the contents of the displayed windows may be requested by the user from the update button  on the Toolbar or may be called automatically after an edit or deletion has changed database contents.

4.3.16 Context Help command

Use the *Context Help* command to obtain help on some portion of the MMTCA Metadocument Browser. When you choose the Toolbar's *Context Help* button, the mouse pointer will change to an arrow and question mark. Then click somewhere in the Metadocument Browser window, such as another Toolbar button. The Help topic will be shown for the item you clicked.

Context help is currently available for most parts of the Metadocument Browser. To obtain Context Help click on the *Context Help* button on the Toolbar.

4.4 Tool Profile Editor

The MMTCA Tool Profile Editor (TPE) is the application used to create and edit tool profile templates in the MMTCA database. A Tool Profile Template (TPT) is a definition in the MMTCA database which allows the user to specify a node application tool which will be used in a Cooperative Session (CS), and which configuration files it uses to customise that application. The TPT is used by the MMTCA Procedure Editor ViEW to configure applications for a CS so that the application will have the same customisations on every node in the CS by transferring the same configuration files to all the nodes.

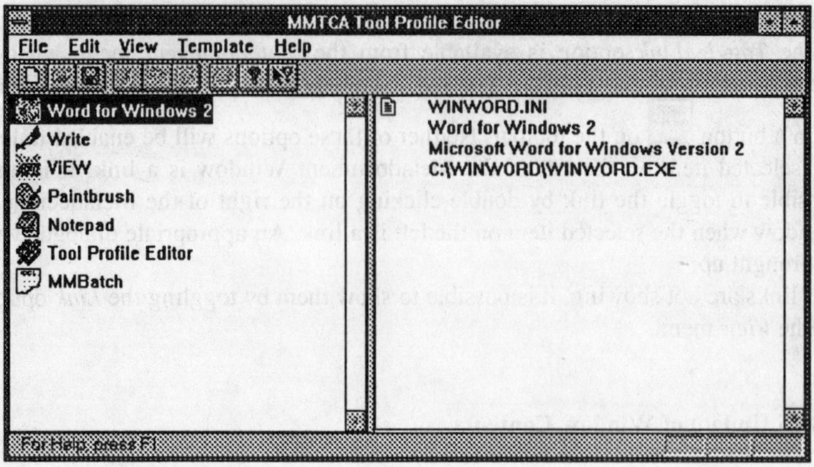

Fig. 4.28. Tool Profile Editor

The Tool Profile Editor provides a user-friendly way for tool profile templates to be created and edited for applications which will be used in the MMTCA environment, and to store the configuration files in the MMTCA server. It also provides a way for users to view the tool profiles currently in the database. The user is able to easily see if a tool profile template has its corresponding application installed on the current node.

4.4.1. Starting the Tool Profile Editor

To start the TPE, double-click the left mouse button on the Tool Profile Editor icon in the MMTCA Program Manager group. The application will start up, and automatically connect to the MMTCA server and database. The main window of the TPE will display information for the tool profile templates currently in the MMTCA database.

To exit the TPE, choose the *Exit* option from the *File* menu, or use *Close* from the system menu.

To access the on-line help for the TPE, choose the *Index* option from the *Help* menu. Use the *About* option from the *Help* menu to view the product information in the About box.

4.4.2 The Main TPE Window

When the MMTCA Tool Profile Editor is started, the main window appears. This has a menu, toolbar and status bar. The main area of the window is split horizon-

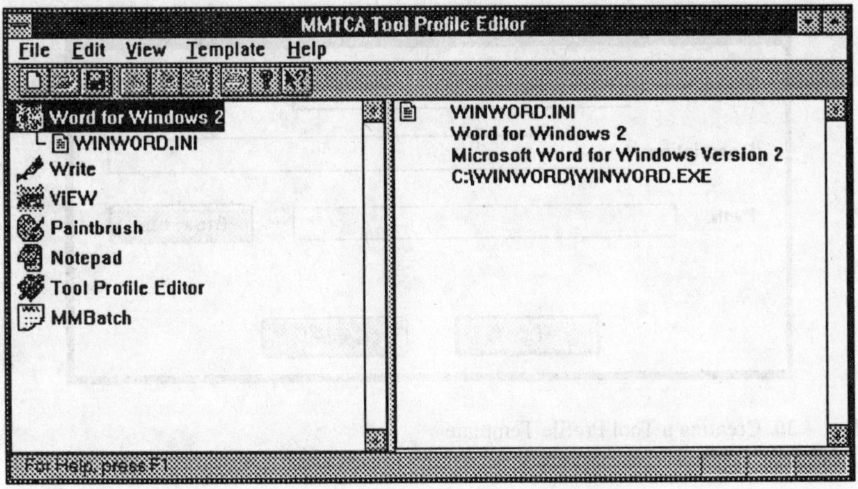

Fig. 4.29. TPE Hierarchy View

tally into two. The left side is the Hierarchy View which lists the tool profile templates and files in a hierarchy. The right side is the Data View, which contains the detailed information for the selected template or file.

The two views in the main window are divided by a splitter bar. The mouse can be used to select and drag the splitter bar to change the relative sizes of the two view windows.

4.4.3 TPE Hierarchy View Window

The Hierarchy View window is on the left side of the splitter bar in the application main window. It lists the tool profile templates and their associated files in a hierarchy. The tool profiles can be viewed at the top level of the hierarchy, and the files below them in the tree.

Double-clicking the left mouse button on a TPT will expand or collapse the tree hierarchy below it, depending on the current state (i.e. if the tree is not shown it will be expanded, and if it is shown it will be collapsed).

The hierarchy tree below a TPT will show all the files associated with that template.

For a TPT, the Hierarchy View window displays the template name and the icon of the template application. If the application cannot be found on the node machine, a generic template icon is displayed.

For a template file, the Hierarchy View window displays the template file name and a file icon.

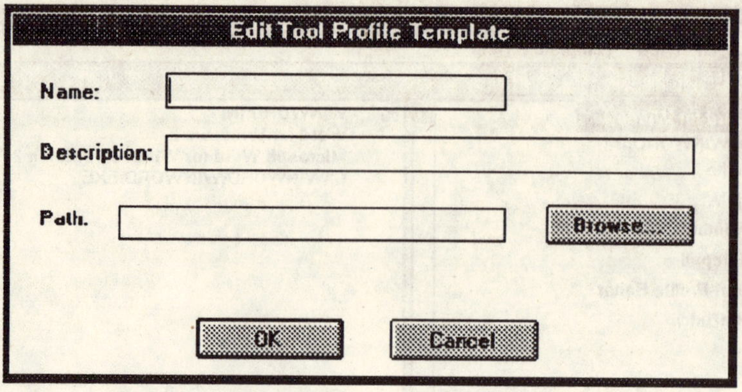

Fig. 4.30. Creating a Tool Profile Template

4.4.4 TPE Data View Window

The Data View window is on the right side of the splitter bar in the application main window. It contains the detailed information for the template or file selected in the Hierarchy View window.

For a TPT, the information displayed includes the template name, description, and the path and name of the template application. Any files associated with the template are also displayed.

For a template file, the information displayed is the file name, description, path and type.

4.4.5 Menus and Toolbars

The TPE has both a menu and toolbar. The main functions of the TPE are accessible from these.

The *Update* option on the *File* menu can be used to update the current view of the database. The MMTCA database is a multi-user system, and other users may change the contents of the database. Use the update option to retrieve the current contents of the database.

The Template menu has options for adding, editing and deleting templates and files in the MMTCA database. These options will be discussed in detail in later sections of the manual.

4.4.6 Adding a Template to the Database

To add a new TPT to the MMTCA database, select the Add item from the Template menu. This will bring up the TPT editing dialogue, with empty entries.

The TPT edit dialogue allows the user to specify the *Name*, *Description* and *Path* for a new template application. The name and description can be entered manually by the user by typing in the appropriate edit box. The name is just a descriptive name for the new template being created. The path is the full path and name of the template application, and can be entered manually using the edit box, or automatically by selecting the required application using the Browse button.

Clicking on the *Browse* button will bring up the standard Windows file dialogue. Use this to select the application for the TPT. If the *OK* button in the file dialogue is selected, the selected application's path and filename will be put into the TPT edit dialogue's *Path* edit box.

Clicking on the *OK* button in the TPT edit dialogue will bring up a confirmation dialogue asking if the user really wishes to add the new TPT to the database. If the operation is not aborted, the new TPT will be added to the MMTCA database.

Clicking on the *Cancel* button in the TPT edit dialogue will remove the dialogue and cancel the process.

4.4.7 Editing a Template

To edit a TPT already in the MMTCA database, select it in the Hierarchy View window (left side of the main window). The Data View window on the right side will display the information for the selected TPT. Now use the *Edit* option on the *Template* menu to bring up the TPT edit dialogue. Alternatively, double-click the left mouse button on the Data View window.

The TPT edit dialogue will contain the information for the selected TPT. The information can be edited by changing the values in the edit boxes, or using the Browse option to select a different template application.

Clicking on the *OK* button in the TPT edit dialogue will bring up a confirmation dialogue asking if the user really wishes to update the TPT information in the database. If the operation is not aborted, the TPT will be updated in the MMTCA database with the new values.

Clicking on the *Cancel* button in the TPT edit dialogue will remove the dialogue and cancel the process.

4.4.8 Deleting a Template

To delete a TPT from the MMTCA database, select it in the Hierarchy View window (left side of the main window). The Data View window on the right side will display the information for the selected TPT. Now use the *Delete* option on the *Template* menu. A dialogue box will appear to confirm the action. If it is not

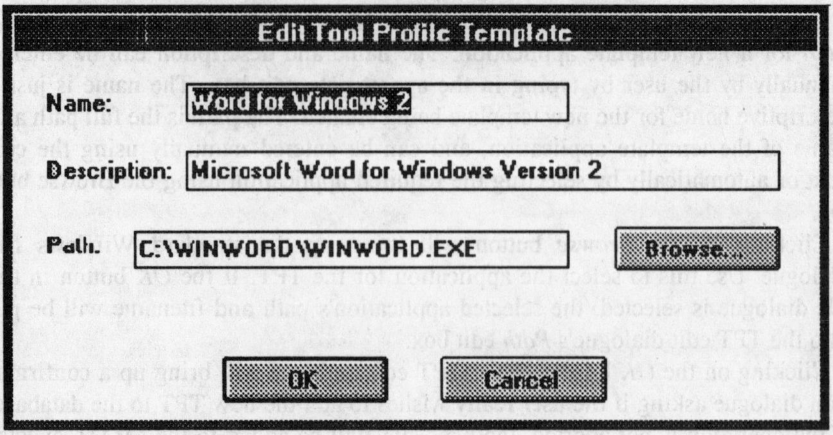

Fig. 4.31. Editing a Template

aborted, the template and any associated template file records will be removed from the MMTCA database.

It should be noted that the current version of the TPE does not remove TPT files and directories from the MMTCA server – it only removes the records from the database.

5. Carrying out the tasks

5.1 Logging in to MMTCA

A user invokes MMTCA from the Windows Program Manager, like any other Windows application - either by double-clicking its icon with the mouse, or through the run dialogue of the Program Manager. Then the user is presented with the Login Dialogue.

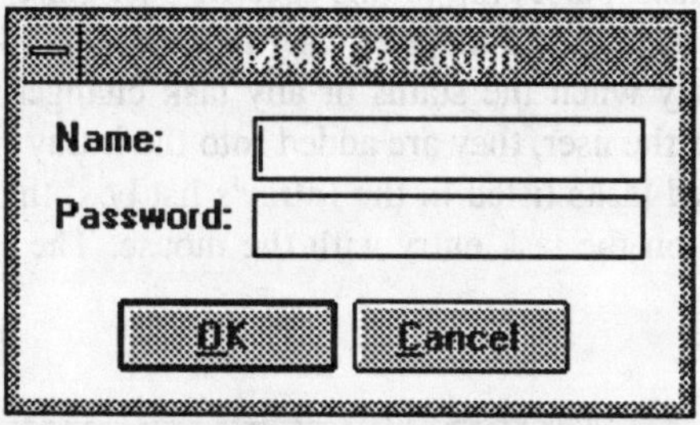

Fig. 5.1. Logging into MMTCA

The user enters his/her name and password and clicks on the *OK* button[1]. If the user clicks on the *Cancel* button MMTCA exits and the user is returned to the Windows Program Manager. If the user supplied name and password are correct, the user is presented with the MMTCA main window. If the user-supplied information is not valid an error message dialogue is presented to the user, MMTCA exits, and control returns to the Windows Program Manager.

---

[1] An operation such as clicking a dialogue button with the mouse can always be invoked through the keyboard, using standard MS Windows mechanisms.

Fig. 5.2. The Intray window

5.2 Intray

The basic monitoring functionality is provided in MMTCA through the Intray dialogue. This dialogue is invoked from the menu items *Show Intray* and *Show All*, under *Monitor*. Alternatively, it may be invoked through the toolbar by clicking on . When the Intray dialogue appears on the screen the *Show Intray* menu item changes to *Hide Intray* and the *Show All* item changes to *Hide All*. This functionality is common to all tray dialogues.

Intray lists information about all tasks that can be initiated by the particular user. If no enabled tasks belonging to this specific user exist, an informative message appears. From the Intray dialogue a user may start a task. The list of tasks is updated automatically when the status of any task changes. In addition, if new tasks are enabled for the user, they are added into the intray list automatically.

If there are enabled tasks listed in the Intray's list box, the user may select one of them by clicking on the task entry with the mouse. The selected task is highlighted.

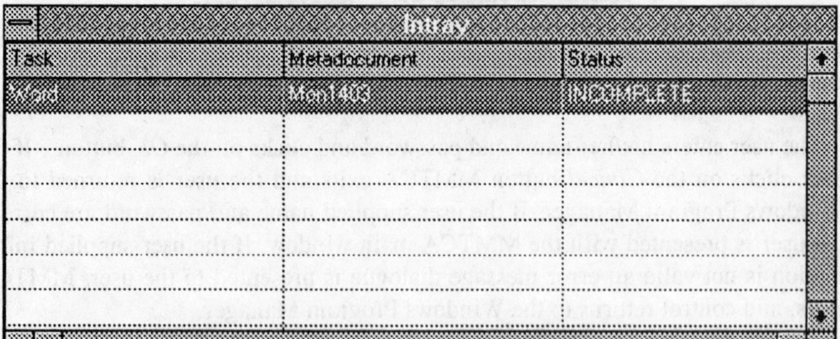

Fig. 5.3. Intray Tasks window

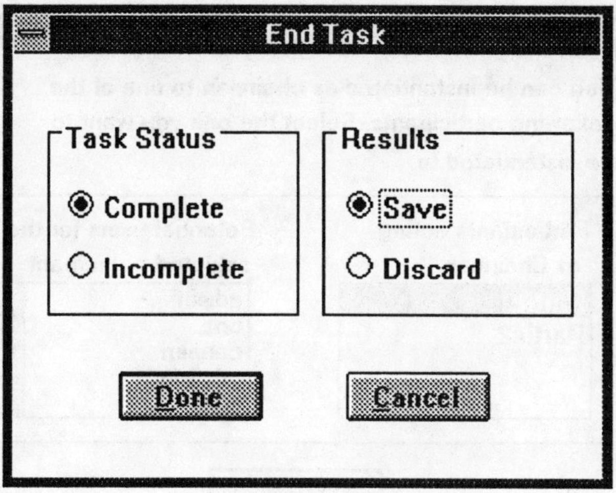

Fig. 5.4. Ending a Task

5.2.1 Running a Task

There are several alternatives to initiate a task. Common prerequisite to all is the selection of a task from the Intray dialogue's list box. Once a task is selected a user may activate the task by double-clicking the mouse on the selected task, by selecting the *Run* menu item under the *Object* pop-up menu. Alternatively, the user may click on the  toolbar button. Once the task is activated the Run menu item is disabled and the *Stop* menu item under the same pop-up menu is enabled.

The activated task may correspond to an asynchronous, or a synchronous, task. If the task is asynchronous the applications specified in the task's actions, are invoked as specified in the task script. If the task corresponds to a synchronous task, then the cooperative session process is followed.

5.2.2 Stopping a Task

A user may end an asynchronous task, by selecting the *Stop* menu item from the *Object* pop-up menu, or by clicking on the  MMTCA toolbar. A task must be active for any of these alternatives to work. If no task is running, an informative message box appears. A synchronous task is ended when the chair clicks on

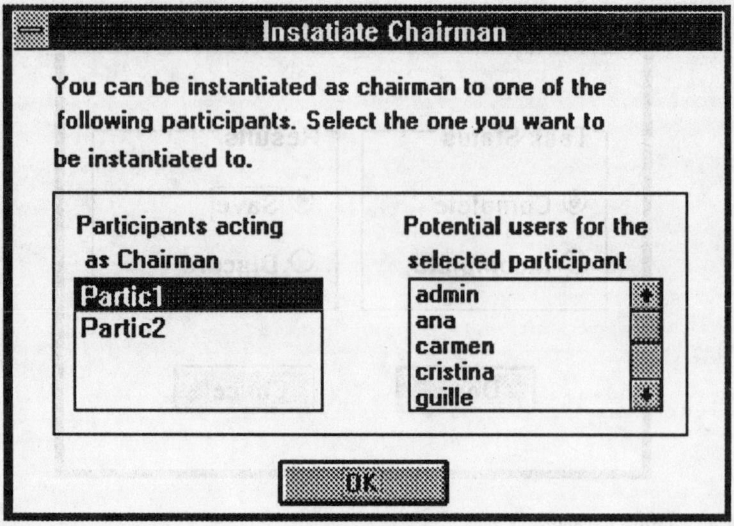

Fig. 5.5. Instantiate Chairman

the CCT Exit button. In all cases the End Task dialogue appears on the user's screen[2].

The user may select whether the task status will be complete, or incomplete, and whether the task results (i.e. produced, or modified, documents) will be saved, or discarded. When the user selects *Incomplete* as the task status, the task is actually suspended and work on this task may be resumed again. User selections are confirmed from the *Done* button. If the user clicks on the *Cancel* button the task is not ended and continues to be considered running.

Upon task completion the workflow is computed. This results in a change in the contents of the Intray dialogue. A new task entry may, or may not, appear depending on specific procedure definition. If the task status is set to incomplete again the Intray contents change to reflect the new status of the task. However, no workflow computation takes place.

5.2.3 Setting the Characteristics of the Cooperative Session

Before starting a Cooperative Session (CS), the chairman can modify the original settings of the task (bind participants, modify users' privileges, CS floor policy or meeting type).

---

[2] In the case of a synchronous task the End Task dialogue appears only on the CS chair's screen.

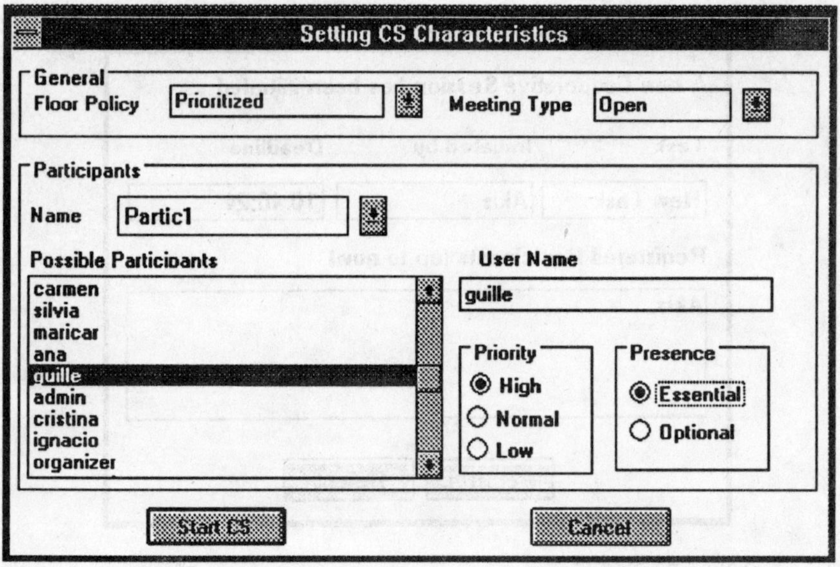

Fig. 5.6. Cooperative Session Characteristics

MMTCA supports a kind of "lazy instantiation", which means that the users are not required to be bound to a participant at procedure instantiation time. They can be bound at a later stage for the whole instance of a procedure or on a per task basis. Thus it can be the case that the chairman of a CS is not already bound to a real user when the CS is selected by a user to be started. In this case, the first action the system must accomplish is to bind the chairman of the CS.

When a user selects a CS to be executed, it is checked if that user can be bound to any of the participants whose role is Chairman. If he can not be bound to any of these participants, the user is not allowed to start the Cooperative Session.

If the user can be bound to more than one participant whose role is Chairman, he must decide which one he wants to be bound to. In this case, the dialogue box shown in Fig. 5.5 is presented to the user:

The user must have in mind that when he selects a participant to be bound to, all the other potential users for that participant (the ones in the right hand box) will be excluded from the Cooperative Session for that participant (although they could be bound to other participants for that CS).

If the user can be bound to only one participant whose role is Chairman, the previous dialogue box does not appear and the user is automatically bound to that participant.

Once the user has been bound to a participant whose role is Chairman, he is presented with the dialogue box shown in Fig. 5.6.

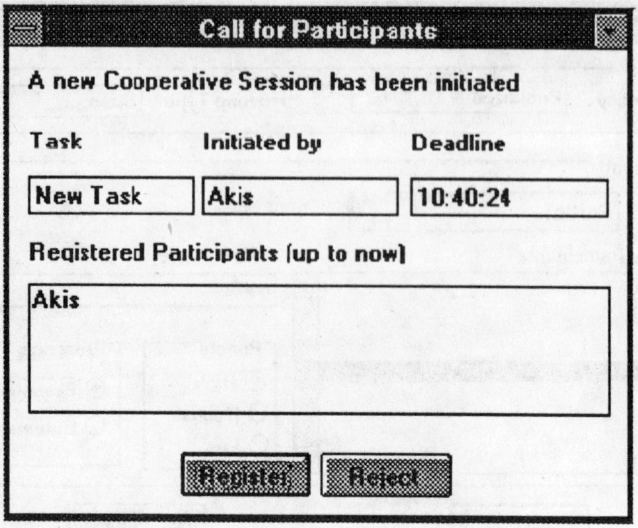

Fig. 5.7. Call for Participants

At run-time, the chairman can change some of the CS main characteristics, such as the floor policy and the meeting type.

Next, he can bind actual users to participant roles if this has not been made before. Selecting a participant from the participants' name combo box will display the possible participants for it, that means, the users that can be bound to that participant. Selecting one of the users will display the current characteristics of the user: priority (if the floor policy is prioritised) and required presence. The chairman can change these options for each bound user. If the selected user is not logged in, a warning message appears and the chairman must decide if he still wants this user to take part in the CS or not.

After binding all the participants, the *OK* button can be clicked to save these changes.

Clicking the *Cancel* button will abort all the changes already made.

5.3 Registering for a Cooperative Session

A cooperative session is initiated as a result of the activation of a synchronous task and it may be initiated only by the CS chair, who is specified in the procedure definition. When the CS chair starts the task the CS Registration Request (CSRR) dialogue appears on the screen of the chair and of all possible CS participants. However, on the chair's node the CSRR dialogue appears a little different: the *Register* and *Reject* buttons have the captions *Start* and *End*, respectively.

The CSRR dialogue displays the name of the task, the chair's name as well as the CSRR dialogue's deadline.[3] The user must respond whether, or not, s/he wishes to participate in the initiated CS by the deadline time. If s/he fails, an informative message dialogue appears on the screen and the CS request is automatically rejected. When the user clicks on any of the two CSRR buttons the selected answer is sent to the chair and the CSRR dialogue disappears from the user's screen. When a user registers for the CS, the user's name appears in the CSRRs of all other possible participants and of the chair.

After at least one user has responded affirmatively to a CSRR, the CS chair has the option to start, or cancel, the CS, by clicking on the corresponding button of his/her own CSRR dialogue. If the chair decides to cancel the CS, an informative message is sent to all users who accepted the CSRR, and they may proceed on their normal processing. If the chair decides to start the CS, the specified in the task script application is invoked on all participants' screen. Then the CS participants may use the CCT to control the CS.

5.4 Participating in a Cooperative Session

First of all, any user must be aware that cooperating with other users implies some restrictions to the functionality to be used in order to keep the synchronisation among cooperating users.

There are a few rules related to the functionality provided by the MMTCA when running Cooperative Sessions that users need to know. These are described below. As a reminder, whenever the standard functionality of Windows has been altered for the CS, a simple beep sound is played.

5.4.1 F2 Accelerator for Floor Changing Mechanism

The action associated to this key will be equivalent to the behaviour of the floor-changing button in the expanded CCT (*Request Floor, Pass Floor, Grab Floor* or *Floor Release*).

- This accelerator is only processed when a cooperative window or the Intray window is active
- The normal processing of F2 in cooperative windows is discarded.
- Local windows during a CS can use F2 normally.

For more details about floor passing, see the next section (5.5).

[3] For the MMTCA prototype the deadline has been set to 2 minutes from the moment the CSRR dialogue appears on the screen.

5.4.2 Arrow Scroll

The operation of keeping pressed an arrow box in a scroll bar is equivalent to press and immediately release that box, that is, in all the cases, independently of the time that the user keeps pressed the arrow, the cursor is moved only one position up or down in the document.

5.4.3 Switching Applications

During a CS, the *ALT+TAB* and *ALT+ESC* operations switch only to local non-cooperative applications. The information window for the *ALT+TAB* operation will not appear in the middle of the screen before activating the window, that is, the *ALT+TAB* and *ALT+ESC* operations will have exactly the same behaviour.

The Task List Window is disabled during a CS in all the nodes.

5.4.4 Iconisation

Minimisation is disallowed for cooperative windows during a CS to prevent the loss of synchronisation.

5.4.5 Screen Savers

Screen Savers are also disallowed during a CS to prevent the loss of synchronisation.

5.4.6 Maximisation

The facility of keeping free of cooperative windows the lower area of the screen allows non-floorholder users to execute local applications through the program manager icon or other icons. On the other hand, some users could prefer to maximise cooperative windows to the full screen. To handle this, a parameter is established when MMTCA is installed (LowMargin) which can be given a value between 0 and 75.

5.4.7 Double Click Time

The parameter *DoubleClickSpeed* in WIN.INI, which specifies the maximum time between two click downs, is set to the same value in all the nodes during the CS. Once the CS is finished, the previous value is re-established in each node.

5.4.8 Click Delays

MMTCA users can notice some delays in the reproduction of events between a click down and a click up. This is due to the special mechanism introduced to handle the reproduction of this chain of events.

5.5 Floor Passing in a Cooperative Session

When a CS starts, a small window called the Cooperative Control Toolbox (CCT) appears at the bottom right corner of the screen of all participants. The CS floor owner's CCT is slightly different from a normal participant's CCT. In Fig. 5.8, the basic form of the Floor Owner's (on the left), and the Normal (on the right)

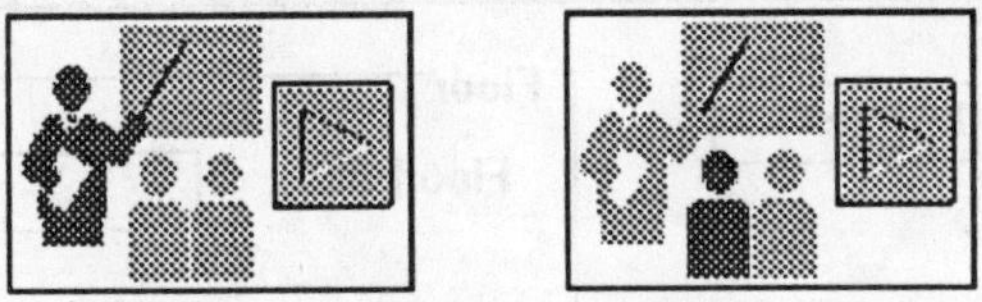

Fig. 5.8. Cooperative Control Toolboxes (Basic Form)

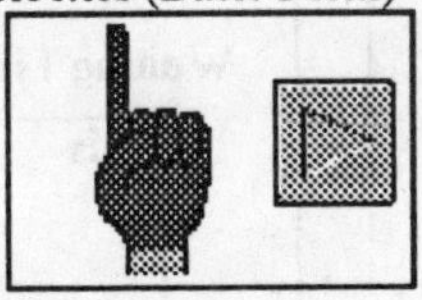

Fig. 5.9. CCT Picture after a Floor Request

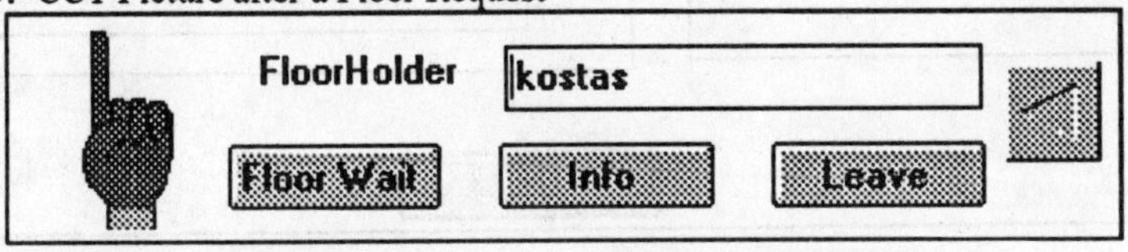

Fig. 5.10. Cooperative Control Toolbox (Extended Form)

CCT are displayed.

The only difference between the two, is a visual clue as to the role of the user with respect to floor ownership. A CS participant who does not own the floor, may request the floor by pressing the F2 function button. Then the picture of the CCT changes to provide a visual clue for the user's operation, as shown in Fig. 5.9.

The basic form of the CCT has only one button, that displays a right arrow. Clicking on this arrow, the CCT changes form and displays more information, as in Fig. 5.10.

The extended form displays a picture that corresponds to the state of the user and is the same picture that appears in the basic form, but it also provides more textual information, about the state of a floor request, and the current Floor Holder. The user may request even more information by clicking on the *Info* button. In addition, the user may leave the CS by clicking on *Leave*. Clicking on the left arrow button restores the normal form of the CCT.

When the user clicks on the *Info* button the dialogue shown in Fig. 5.11 appears.

The CS Information dialogue is a modal dialogue. In other words the user has to click the *OK* button in order to continue processing. This dialogue, displays more information about the CS, such as the CS Chair, the CS Floor Policy, The current Floor Holder, the CS Participants and a list of all participants who have

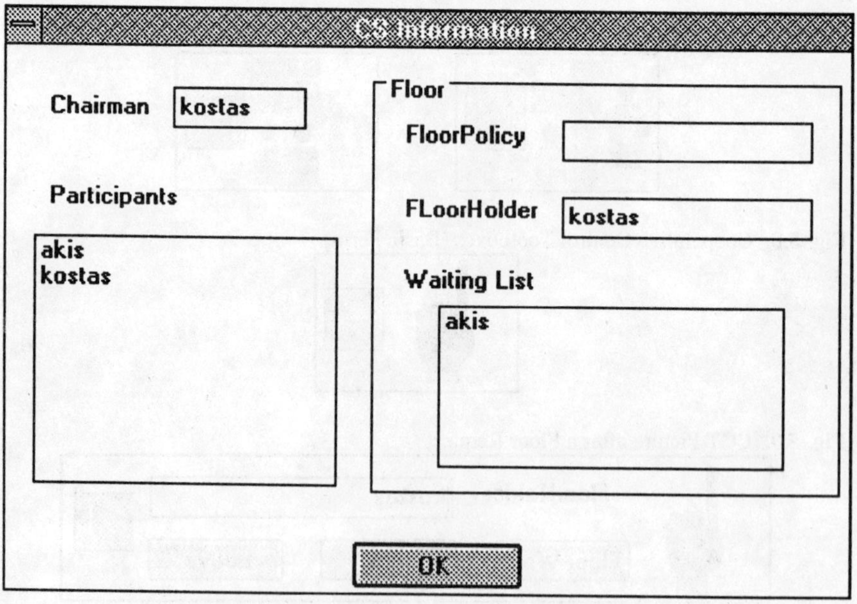

Fig. 5.11. Cooperative Session Information

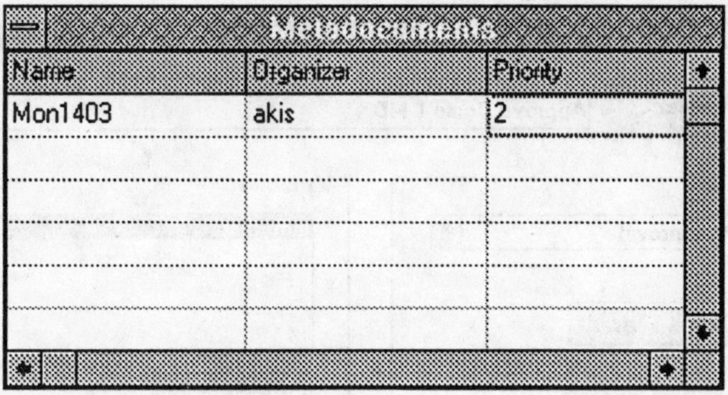

Fig. 5.12. The Metadocument Tray

requested the floor. When the user clicks on *OK* the dialogue disappears and the extended form of the CCT appears at the bottom-right corner of the screen.

5.6 Metadocument Tray

The Metadocument tray is very similar to the other four tray dialogues. It may be invoked through the main menu's *Show Metadocuments*, or *Show All*, menu items, or alternatively from the  MMTCA toolbar button. The Metadocument tray lists all active metadocuments in the system. The Metadocument tray is automatically updated each time it appears on the screen.

5.6.1 Setting Metadocument Information

The MMTCA Intray allows the user to set a number of options for an existing instance of a procedure. These include setting the values of variables in the instance, transferring documents for a task before the task is run, and setting the participants for a task in the metadocument.

5.6.2 Selecting a Metadocument

The first step in setting metadocument information is selecting a metadocument from the Metadocuments tray in MMTCA. Bring up the Metadocuments tray from menu or the toolbar. Select the metadocument for which the information is to be set, and double-click on it with the left mouse button. This will bring up the Set Metadocument Information dialogue.

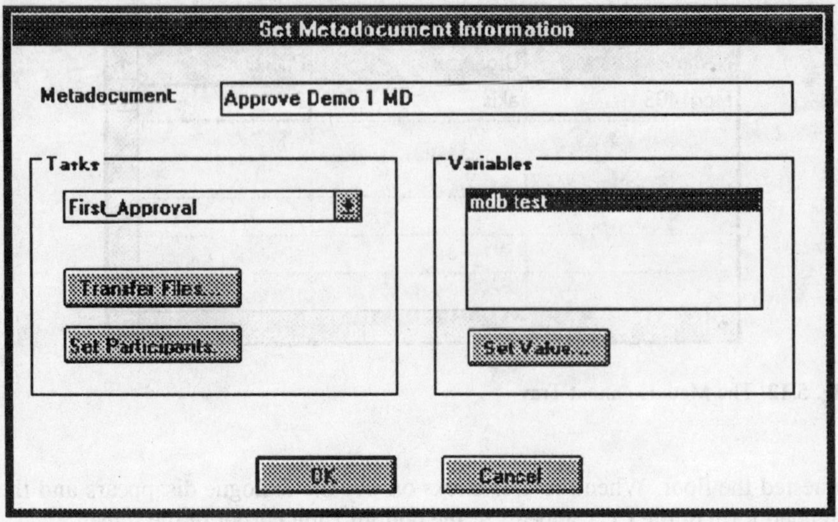

Fig. 5.13. Setting Metadocument Information

5.6.3 Metadocument Information Options

The Set Metadocument Information dialogue gives some basic information about the metadocument, and a number of options that can be set.

At the top of the dialogue the name of the Metadocument is given – this cannot be edited.

The dialogue is divided into two sections, giving options for tasks and variables.

The *Tasks* section has a combo box from which any of the tasks for the metadocument can be selected. Clicking on one of the *Tasks* options buttons will perform the options for the selected task. If no task is selected the buttons will not do anything.

The *Variables* section has a list box containing all the variables for the metadocument. The *Set Value* button will set the variable value for the selected variable. If no variable is selected the button will not do anything.

5.6.4 Transferring Task Files

To transfer document files for a task to the node from the MMTCA server, select the task in the *Tasks* combo box, then click on the *Transfer Files* button. A confirmation dialogue will appear, and responding positively to this will initiate the file transfer. The files will be transferred to the directories defined in the

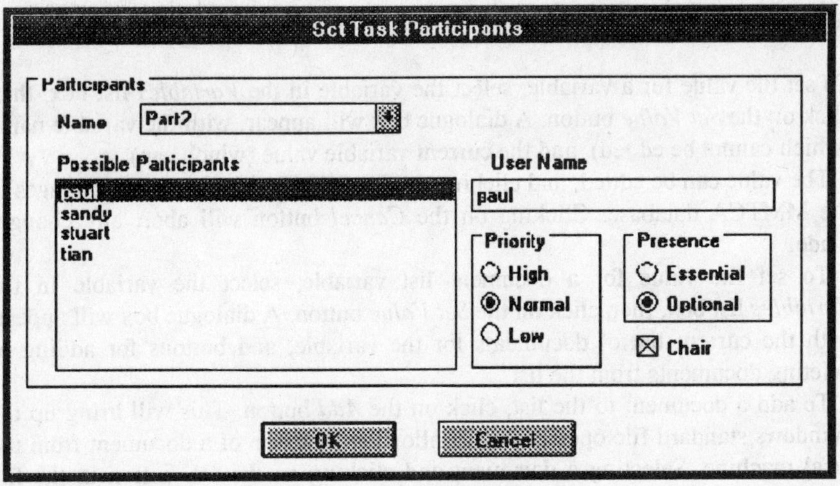

Fig. 5.14. Setting Task Participants

MMTCA database – if these do not exist, the MMTCA software will attempt to create them.

5.6.5 Setting Task Participants

To set the participants for a task, select the task in the Tasks combo box, then click on the *Set Participants* button. A dialogue box will appear, with the participant options for the selected task.

The dialogue box lists all the participants for the task in a combo box at the top. When a participant is selected in the combo box, the rest of the information in the dialogue refers to that participant. The possible users for the participant are listed in the list box on the left. When a user is selected, their name appears in the edit box on the right, and the *Priority*, *Presence*, and *Chair* options refer to the participant.

If the participant is already bound to a user, there will only be one user in the list of possible participants, shown selected, and the values for the participant will not be able to be altered. If the participant is not bound to a user, a user can be selected from the list of possible participants, and the *Priority*, *Presence* and *Chair* options can be altered.

Clicking on the *Cancel* button will remove the dialogue and any changes made to the participant bindings will be aborted.

Clicking on the *OK* button will save any changes made to the participant bindings – if users have been selected for participants, the users will be bound to those participants for the task.

5.6.6 Setting Variable Values

To set the value for a variable, select the variable in the *Variables* list box, then click on the *Set Value* button. A dialogue box will appear, with the variable name (which cannot be edited), and the current variable value (which can).

The value can be edited, and clicking on the *OK* button will save the changes to the MMTCA database. Clicking on the *Cancel* button will abort any changes made.

To set the value for a document list variable, select the variable in the *Variables* list box, then click on the *Set Value* button. A dialogue box will appear, with the current list of documents for the variable, and buttons for adding or deleting documents from the list.

To add a document to the list, click on the *Add* button. This will bring up the Windows standard file open dialogue, allowing selection of a document from the local machine. Selecting a document and clicking on the *OK* button in the file

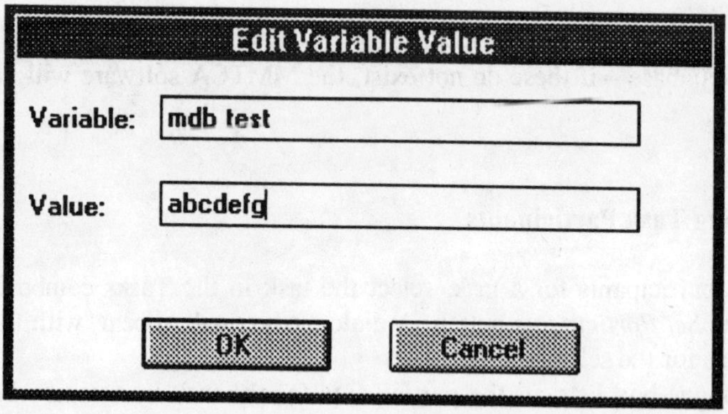

Fig. 5.15. Editing Variable Values

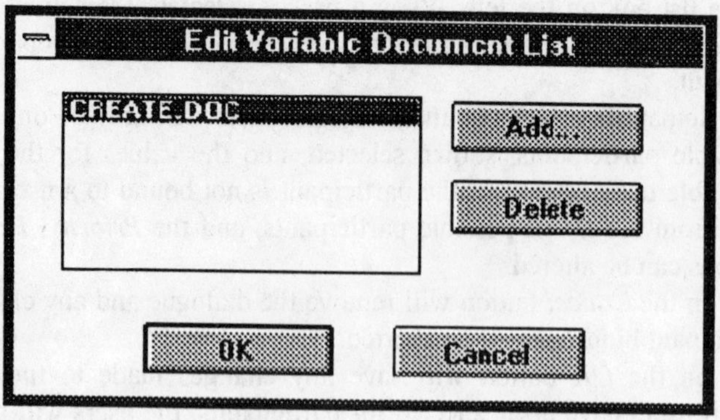

Fig. 5.16. Editing Document List Variables

open dialogue will select the document into the document list. Selecting a document in the document list and clicking on the *Delete* button will remove the document from the document list.

Clicking on the *Cancel* button will abort any changes made. Clicking on the *OK* button will save any changes made to the document list, and upload any new documents added to the list to the MMTCA server.

5.7 Procedure Tray

The Procedure tray is very similar to the other four tray dialogues. It may be invoked through the main menu's *Show Procedures*, or *Show All*, menu items, or alternatively, from the  MMTCA toolbar button. The Procedure tray lists all enabled procedures existing in the system. The Procedure tray is automatically updated each time it appears on the screen.

5.7.1. Procedure Instantiation

Procedure Instantiation is the process which allows an MMTCA procedure definition to be activated into a real executing copy of the procedure. In this process real users are bound to participants for the procedure, variable values can be set, and starting tasks for the procedure are scheduled and placed in users' intrays.

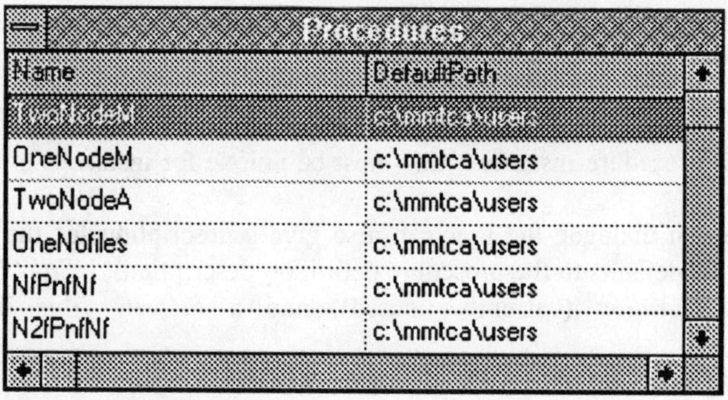

Fig. 5.17. The Procedure Tray

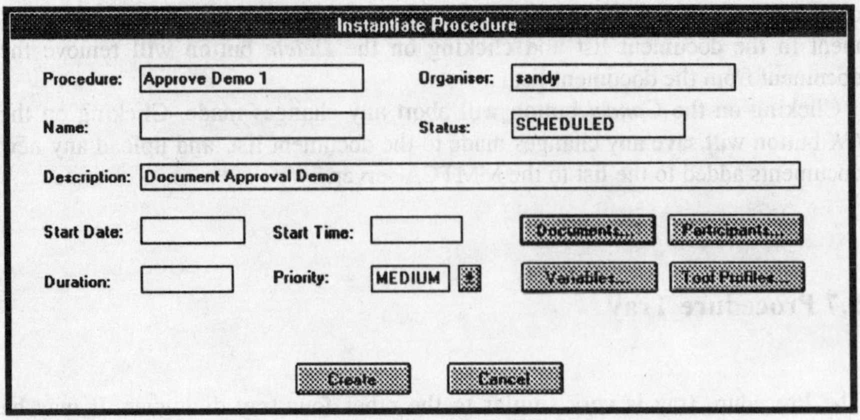

Fig. 5.18. Procedure Instantiation

5.7.2 Selecting a Procedure to Instantiate

The first step in instantiating a procedure is selecting it from the Procedures tray in MMTCA. Bring up the Procedures tray from menu or the toolbar. Select the procedure to be instantiated, and double-click on it with the left mouse button. This will bring up the Procedure Instantiation dialogue.

5.7.3 Procedure Instantiation Options

The procedure instantiation dialogue gives some basic information about the new procedure instance, and a number of options which can be set when instantiating the procedure.

At the top of the dialogue the name of the Procedure being instantiated is given, the Organiser for the new instance (the current user), and the Status of the new instance (which currently will be SCHEDULED). These options cannot be changed.

The only option in Procedure Instantiation which *must* be filled in is the Name for the new procedure instance – this must be unique for instances of the procedure.

On the main dialogue the user can also give a description for the procedure instance (this defaults to the procedure definition description), a *Start Date*, *Start Time* and *Duration* (currently unused), and a *Priority* (this defaults to MEDIUM).

There are four buttons on the dialogue, which allow the user to set further procedure instantiation options for *Participants*, *Documents*, *Variables*, and *Tool*

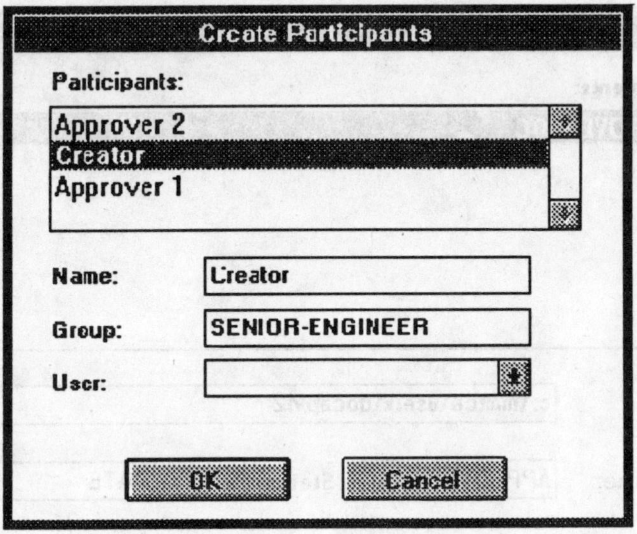

Fig. 5.19. Create Participants

Profiles. Clicking on one of these buttons will bring up the appropriate supplementary dialogue. These options are described in the following sections.

The *Cancel* button can be used at any time to exit the procedure instantiation process.

To create the new instance of the procedure, once all the options have been set, click on the *Create* button. This will create the new procedure instance in the MMTCA database, and schedule the starting tasks in the appropriate users' intrays.

5.7.4 Participants

At procedure instantiation time, the organiser can bind actual users to participant roles. These users will be bound to that participant for the whole of the procedure instance. If the participants are not bound at procedure instantiation time they can be bound to users at a later stage, for the whole instance or on a per-task basis.

To bind participants at procedure instantiation time, click on the *Participants* button on the Instantiate Procedure dialogue. This will bring up a supplementary dialogue.

The new dialogue shows a list of all the participants for the procedure. Selecting a participant in the list will display information for the current selection in the edit boxes below the list. The name will be displayed, and the user group which was selected for the participant at procedure definition time: the user can-

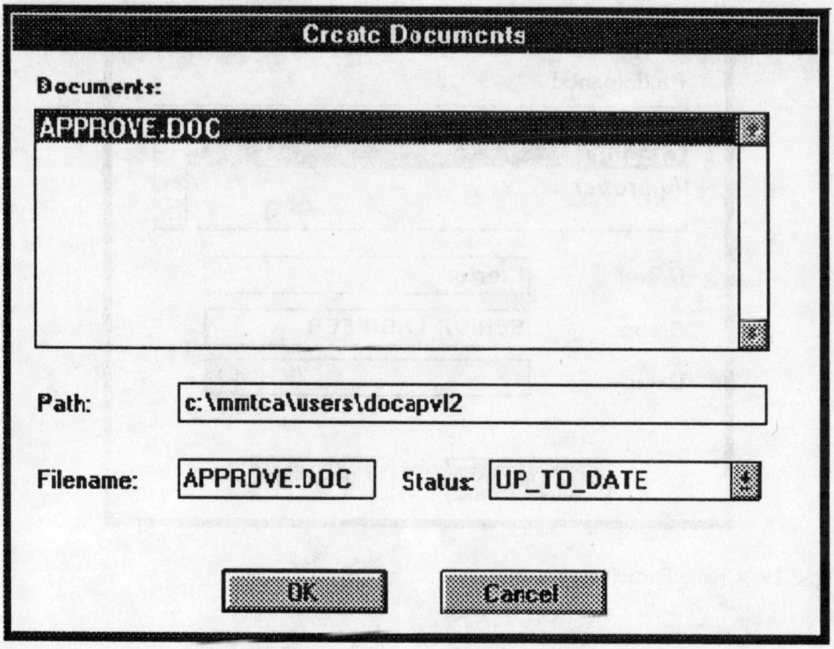

Fig. 5.14. Create Documents

not edit these options. The user combo box will contain a list of the users for the selected group, and the organiser can select one of these into the combo box to bind that user to the participant role.

Once the binding of participants to users has been completed for as many participants as the organiser desires, the *OK* button can be clicked to save these changes. Clicking the *Cancel* button will abort the participant binding selections made.

Users will not actually be bound to the participants until the procedure instance is created.

5.7.5 Documents

The Documents dialogue for procedure instantiation gives the options for setting documents at procedure instantiation time. To select document options at procedure instantiation time, click on the Documents button on the Instantiate Procedure dialogue. This will bring up a supplementary dialogue.

The dialogue lists all the documents defined for the procedure, with the edit boxes below the list box giving the information for the currently selected document. This gives the node path and filename for the document, and its status.

In the current version of MMTCA, the document options are all fixed at procedure definition time in ViEW, so the information in this dialogue cannot be changed at present.

5.7.6 Variables

The Variables dialogue for procedure instantiation gives the options for setting variables at procedure instantiation time. To select variable options at procedure instantiation time, click on the *Variables* button on the Instantiate Procedure dialogue. This will bring up a supplementary dialogue.

The dialogue lists all the variables defined for the procedure, with the edit boxes below the list box giving the information for the currently selected variable. This gives the name of the variable (which cannot be edited), and the value (which contains the default value specified in the procedure definition). The organiser can set the value for the selected variable by editing the value in the edit box.

Once the setting of variable values has been completed for as many variables as the organiser desires, the *OK* button can be clicked to save these changes. Clicking the *Cancel* button will abort the selections made.
The variable values will not actually be set until the procedure instance is created.

5.7.7. Tool Profiles

The Tool Profiles dialogue for procedure instantiation gives the options for setting tool profile files at procedure instantiation time. To select tool profile options at procedure instantiation time, click on the *Tool Profiles* button on the Instantiate Procedure dialogue. This will bring up a supplementary dialogue.

The dialogue lists all the tool profile files defined for the procedure, with the edit boxes below the list box giving the information for the currently selected file. This gives the application name for the tool profile file, the filename, neither of which can be edited. It also gives the node path for the file, which the organiser can edit.

Once the setting of tool profiles has been completed for as many tool profile files as the organiser desires, the *OK* button can be clicked to save these changes. Clicking the *Cancel* button will abort the selections made.The tool profiles will not actually be set until the procedure instance is created.

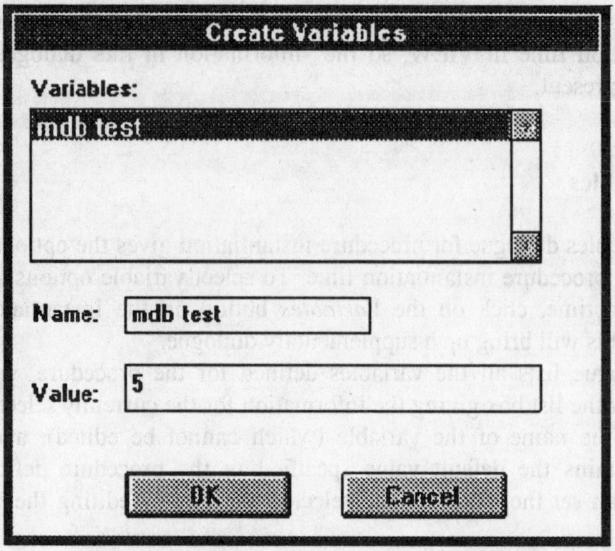

Fig. 5.15. Create Variables

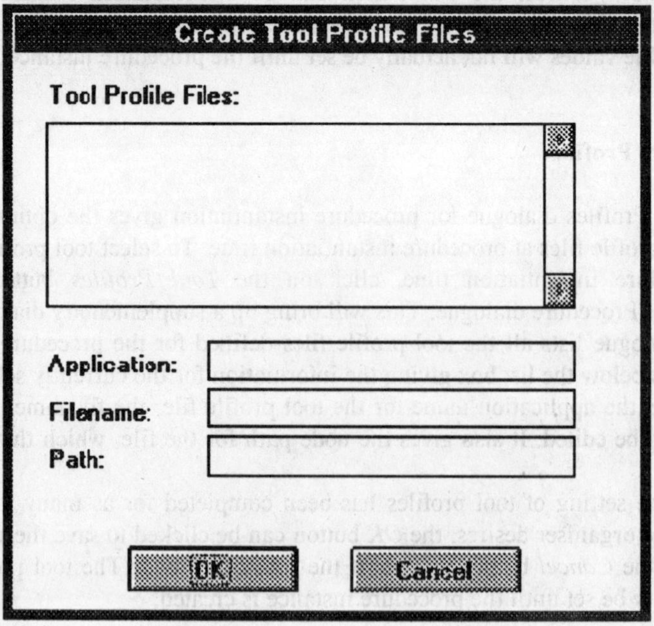

Fig. 5.16. Create Tool Profiles

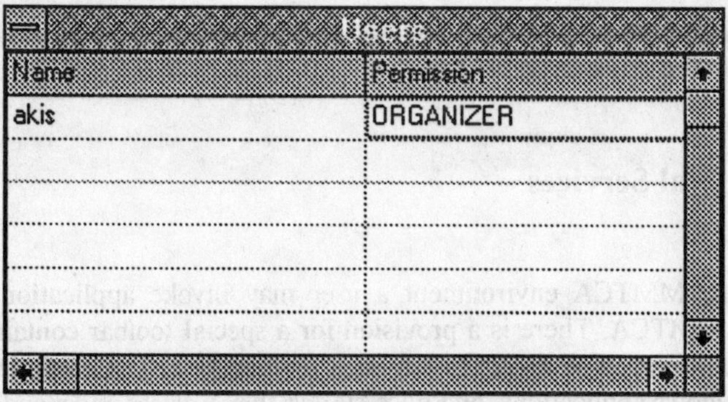

Fig. 5.17. User Tray

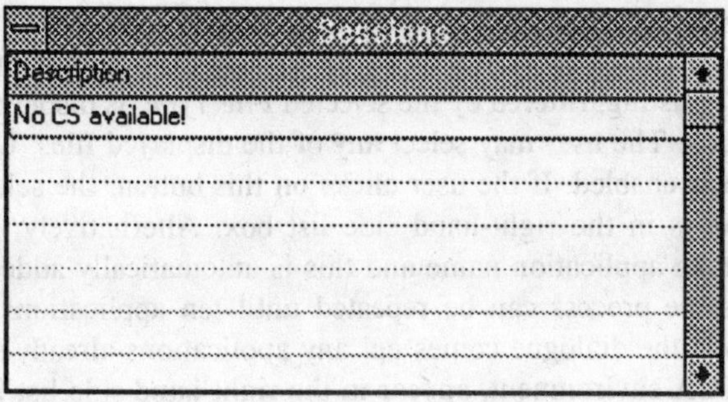

Fig. 5.18. The Session Tray

5.8 User Tray

The User tray is invoked through the main menu's *Show Users*, or *Show All*, menu items, or alternatively, from the MMTCA toolbar by clicking on . The User tray lists all currently logged in users. The User tray is updated each time it appears on the screen. In other words, if the user wishes to update the contents of the User tray, s/he must close it first and then make it appear again.

5.9 Session Tray

This is the last of the four Tray dialogues. It is similarly invoked through the main menu's *Show Sessions*, or *Show All*, menu items, or alternatively from the  MMTCA toolbar button. The Session tray lists all active cooperative sessions running in the system. The Session tray is automatically updated each time it appears on the screen.

5.10 External Services

While in the MMTCA environment a user may invoke applications that are external to MMTCA. There is a provision for a special toolbar containing icons for a user-determined set of up to ten such applications. These applications are normal Windows applications, and once started they proceed independently from MMTCA. A user may initiate this process by selecting the *Setup Applications* menu item, under *Options*. Then the dialogue shown in Fig. 5.19 appears.

The dialogue allows the user to search through the file system, in order to select applications that s/he wants to set up for use from within the Intray. The current directory listing, filtered by the selected *File Type*, is displayed in the left-hand side list box. The user may select any of the displayed files. Upon selection the *Add* button is enabled. If the user clicks on this button, the selected application name appears in the right-hand side list box. Alternatively, the user may double-click on an application name and this is automatically added in the right list box. The same process can be repeated until ten applications are selected. Notice that when the dialogue comes up, any applications already set up for use from the MMTCA environment, appear in the right-hand side list box. The user may remove applications already set up by selecting them and clicking on the *Remove* button, which is enabled as soon as a selection is made in the right-hand side list box.

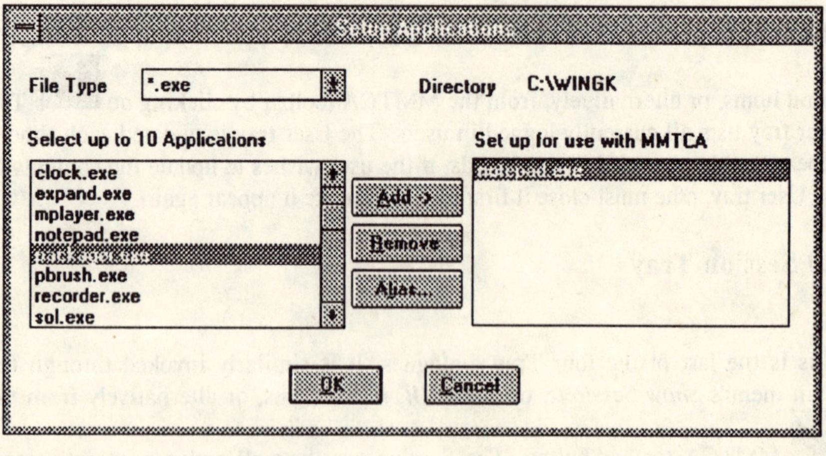

Fig. 5.19. Setting Up Applications

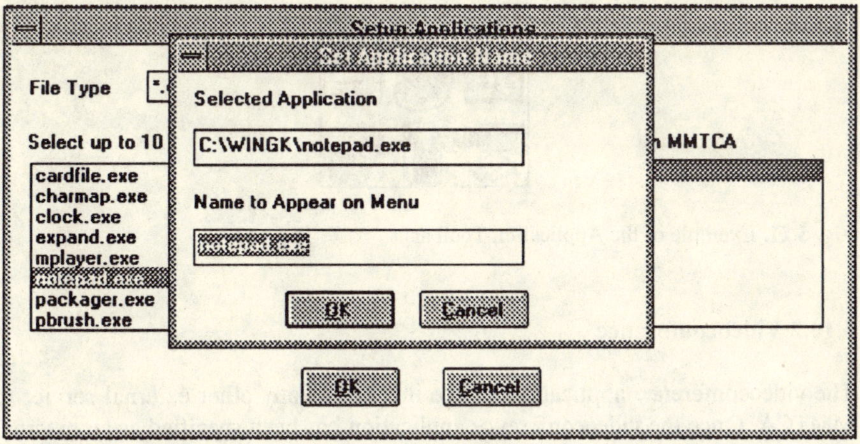

Fig. 5.20. Setting up Applications: Names

The user may change the name by which an application appears in the menu. To do this, the user must select the name of an application that has been already set up and click on the *Alias* button, or double-click on an application in the right list box. Then the dialogue shown in Fig. 5.20 appears.

The dialogue displays the full path name of the selected application and allows the user to enter the name, which will appear on the Intray's menu. If the user clicks on **OK** the dialogue disappears and the name of the application changes. The same process may be repeated many times. The applications that are set up for use from the MMTCA environment are saved each time the user logs out from MMTCA. The next time the user logs in, the same application list will be available.

Notice that MMTCA does not check the applications that the user selects. It assumes that these are valid application files, and once they start they are spawned they run independently from MMTCA.

5.10.1 Application Toolbar

The Intray user may invoke any of the selected applications from the floating application toolbar. This toolbar is created each time the user uses the *Application Setup* dialogue to select application for use from MMTCA. The toolbar displays the icon of each of the selected applications.

The user may invoke any application by double-clicking on its icon. The application toolbar may be made invisible by clicking on the *Hide AppTool* menu item under *Options*. The application toolbar may be made visible again by clicking on the *Show AppTool* menu item.

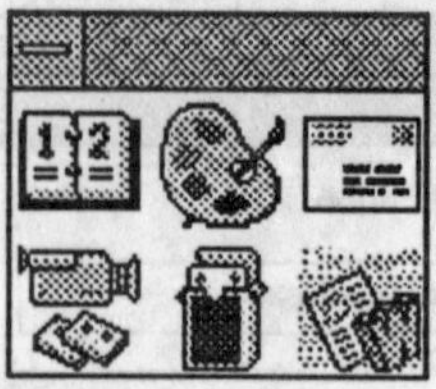

Fig. 5.21. Example of the Application Toolbar

5.10.2 Videoconference

The videoconference application can be invoked as any other external service to MMTCA. Once the videoconference application has been specified as an external application, its icon will be shown in the External Services Toolbar. The user can

Fig. 5.22. Videoconference icon

activate this service by double-clicking on the icon shown in figure 5.22 that will appear in the External Services Toolbar:

Making a connection: Once the videoconference application has been started, the window shown in Fig. 5.23 will appear showing our own camera picture. The connection menu can be used either to establish a connection with another user or to hang up an on-going connection.

Call: This is used to call a remote terminal that we want to establish a videoconference session with. The destination address can be entered using the window dialogue shown in Fig. 5.24.

Once we have introduced the name (defined in the HOSTS.TXT file) or IP address of the remote system, the remote side receives a connection notification, so that it can accept or reject the call.

Fig. 5.23. Videoconference Window: Making a Connection

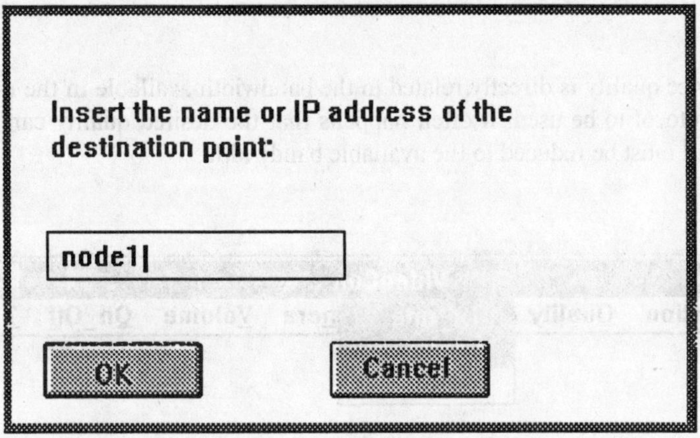

Fig. 5.24. Network address selection

The answer of the remote side is sent to the calling side. If the connection has been accepted, he can open the connection. From this moment onwards, the picture shown in the window is the one captured by the remote camera.

At any moment the window can be iconified and opened again, moved or resized and the video will still be working. If the window is closed the connection is released.

Video Service Quality: Any of the nodes can select its own video quality by changing the following parameters in the menu shown in Fig. 5.25.

- *Frames:* Number of frames per second to be transmitted. The values can be: 30, 15, 10 or 7.5 frames per second.
- *Resolution:* The picture can be shown with low or high resolution.
- *Quantizer:* The quantification to use can be chosen between coarse and sharp.

Fig. 5.25. Service Quality Selection

The service quality is directly related to the bandwidth available in the network and the protocol to be used. It often happens that the desired quality can not be reached and must be reduced to the available bandwidth.

Fig. 5.26. Transmission Speed Selection

Transmission Speed Control Menu: The menu shown in Fig. 5.26 allows the user to select the speed at which the compression/decompression board works:

- *Faster:* Set a faster working speed.
- *Slower:* Set a slower working speed.

Camera Selection Menu: Each node can have one or two cameras connected. The picture shown in the window corresponds to the camera selected in the camera selection menu (Fig. 5.27).

Volume Regulation Menu: The voice volume in the local side can be regulated from this menu (Fig. 5.28), which supports two options:

- *Higher:* This increases reception volume.
- *Lower:* This decreases reception volume.

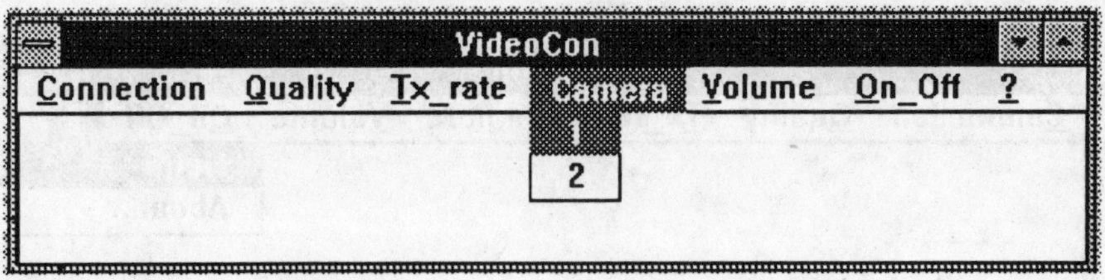

Fig. 5.27. Camera Selection

Fig. 5.28. Volume Control

Fig. 5.29. Audio Muting

Video/Audio Enable/Disable Menu: At any moment, the user can select if he wants to transmit only video, only audio or both at the same time. These features are supported through the following options from this menu (Fig 5.29):

- *Video_on/off:* Enable or disable video transmission.
- *Audio_on/off:* Enable or disable audio transmission.

Information Menu: This menu (Fig. 5.30) allows the user to ask for information about the application. It supports two options:

- *Help:* No help facility is available at the moment.
- *About...:* This shows the application version information window.

Connection Menu: Finishing a Connection: Any node can finish the connection by just hanging it up. The other side will receive a notification and each node will see its own camera picture.

Fig. 5.30. Help facility

Fig. 5.31. Finishing a connection

The Hang up menu item (Fig 5.31) is used to finish an established videoconference session with a remote terminal. The connection is hung up and all the resources are released, so that a new connection can be established.

5.11 Ready-To-Run Cooperative Session Setting

Ready-to-Run Cooperative Session setting is the process where any MMTCA user logged into the MMTCA application can start a Cooperative Session in a short way avoiding the programming phase. In this way, if any user within the MMTCA environment needs to work on some documents in a cooperative synchronous way with any of the other users logged in the system, s/he can define a Ready-to-Run CS to do so. This user will become the CS Chairman, and hence will have the rights to establish all the requirements for the session. Then a new procedure and a metadocument of that procedure are created, so that the user can be given the opportunity to run the single task within it.

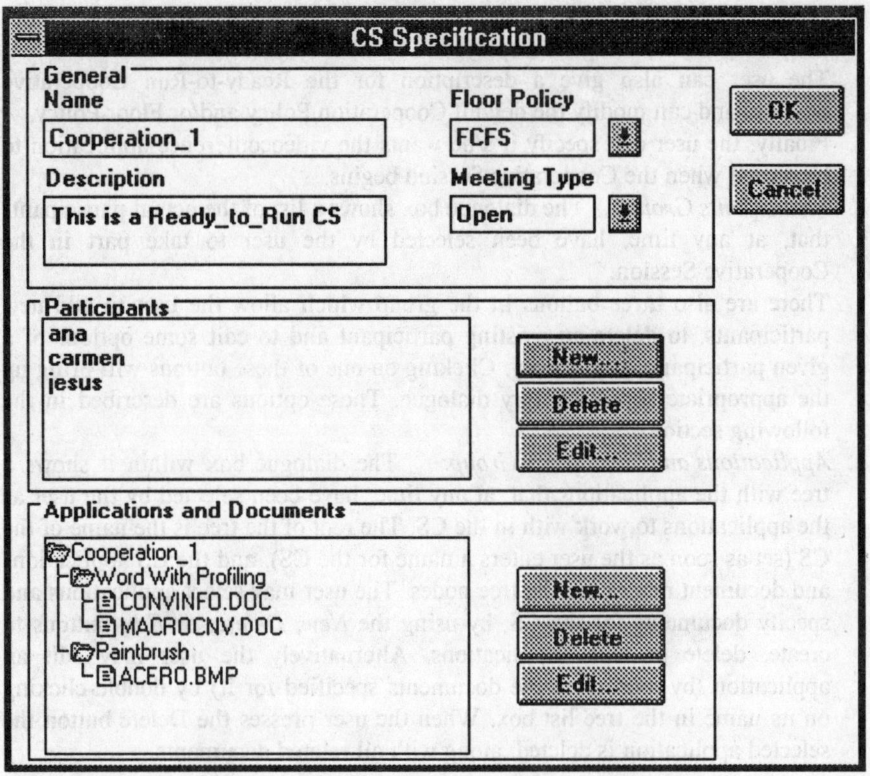

Fig. 5.32. Setting up a Ready-to-run Cooperative Session

5.11.1 Creating a Ready-to-Run CS

The first step to set up a Ready-To-Run Cooperative Session is to select the corresponding option from the main menu. This will bring up the CS Specification dialogue box.

5.11.2 Ready-To-Run CS Options

The CS Specification dialogue box (Fig. 5.32) gives some basic information that must be filled in by the user in order to set up a Ready-To-Run Cooperative Session.

The dialogue box comprises three Group boxes:

1. *General Group:* At the top of the dialogue the user is requested to provide a name for the Cooperative Session which is necessary to identify it in some of the MMTCA information trays. The name must be unique within the

Procedure database table. If the user does not provide a name or it is not unique an error message is displayed.
The user can also give a description for the Ready-to-Run Cooperative Session, and can modify the default Cooperation Policy and/or Floor Policy.
Finally, the user can specify if s/he wants the videoconference application to be started when the Cooperative Session begins.

2. *Participants Group:* The dialogue box shows a list of the actual participants that, at any time, have been selected by the user to take part in the Cooperative Session.
There are also three buttons in the group which allow the user to add new participants, to delete an existing participant and to edit some options of a given participant, respectively. Clicking on one of these buttons will bring up the appropriate supplementary dialogue. These options are described in the following sections.
3. *Applications and Documents Group:* The dialogue box within it shows a tree with the applications that, at any time, have been selected by the user as the applications to work with in the CS. The root of the tree is the name of the CS (set as soon as the user enters a name for the CS), and the CS applications and document names are the tree nodes. The user may select applications and specify documents for the CS, by using the *New*, *Delete*, or *Edit* buttons to create, delete or edit applications. Alternatively the user may edit an application (by modifying the documents specified for it) by double-clicking on its name in the tree list box. When the user presses the Delete button the selected application is deleted, along with all related documents.

The *Cancel* button can be used at any time to exit the Ready-to-Run Cooperative Session setting.

To create a new Ready-to-Run Cooperative Session, once all participants and applications have been set, click on the *OK* button. This will insert the necessary records into the MMTCA database tables, and schedule the starting task in the appropriate users' Intray.

5.11.3 Participants

The user must select at least one participant to take part in a given Ready-to-Run CS. These participants belong to the set of users that at any time are logged into the MMTCA Intray application. If the user does not select any participant an error message is displayed.

To add a new participant, click on the *New* button on the Participants Group at the CS Specification dialogue. This will bring up a supplementary dialogue (Fig. 5.33).

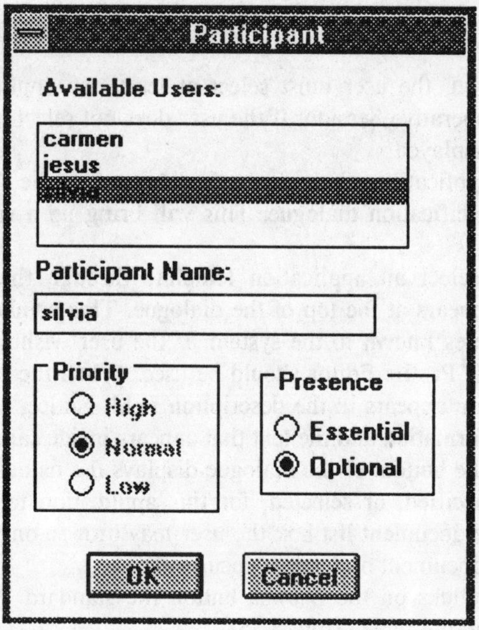

Fig. 5.33. Choosing Participants

The Available Users dialogue box shows a list of all the users that are logged into the MMTCA system and that have not yet been selected to take part in the new Ready-to-Run Cooperative Session. Selecting a participant in the list will display the name for the current selection in the edit box below the list.

The default Priority (only in case of a Prioritised floor policy) and Presence options for this participant can also be changed.

Clicking on the *Cancel* button will abort the participant selections already made.

Clicking on the *OK* button, will close the dialogue box and will add the new participant to the Participants' list at the CS Specification dialogue.

To edit a previously selected participant, select one from the Participants list on the CS Specification dialogue and click on the *Edit* button. This will also bring up the supplementary dialogue shown above.

Now, all members of the Available Users list box are disabled and the selected participant is displayed in the list box below the list. Only the default Priority (in case of a Prioritised floor policy) and Presence options for this participant can be changed.

To delete a previously existing participant, select one from the Participants' list on the CS Specification dialogue and click on the *Delete* button. The participant's name disappears from the Participants' list on the CS Specification dialogue.

5.11.4 Applications

To start cooperation, the user must select at least one application in a given Ready-to-Run Cooperative Session. If the user does not select any application an error message is displayed.

To add a new application, click on the *New* button on the Application Group Box at the CS Specification dialogue. This will bring up a supplementary dialogue (Fig. 5.34).

The user may select an application template through the Template Name combo box that appears at the top of the dialogue. This combo box contains all application templates known to the system. If the user wishes to specify a new template, the Tools Profile Editor should be used. When the user selects a template, its description appears in the description field. Notice, that this field contains read-only information and the text that appears inside cannot be edited.

The list box at the bottom of the dialogue displays the names of all documents that have been specified, or selected, for this application template. Using the buttons next to the document list box the user may browse on the local drives to select an existing document or delete a document.

When the user clicks on the *Browse* button the standard Windows open-file dialogue appears on the screen (Fig. 5.35).

The user may search through the available drives and/or directories to select an existing document.

Clicking on the *Cancel* button will abort the application specification already made.

Clicking on the *OK* button will close the dialogue box and will add the specified application, along with all related documents to the Applications and Documents tree list box at the CS Specification dialogue.

To edit a previously existing application, select one from the Applications and Documents tree list box on the CS Specification dialogue and click on the *Edit* button. Alternatively the user may edit an application by double-clicking on its name in the Applications and Documents tree list box. In either case the application specification dialogue appears and the user can modify the list of documents specified for that application.

To delete a previously existing application, select one from the Applications and Documents tree list box on the CS Specification dialogue and click on the *Delete* button. The selected application, along with all related documents, is deleted from the tree list box.

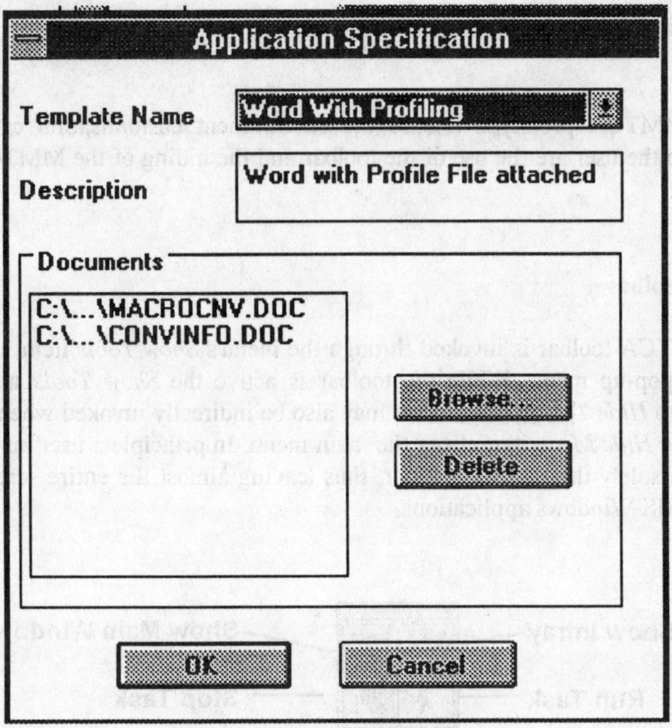

Fig. 5.34. Selecting Applications

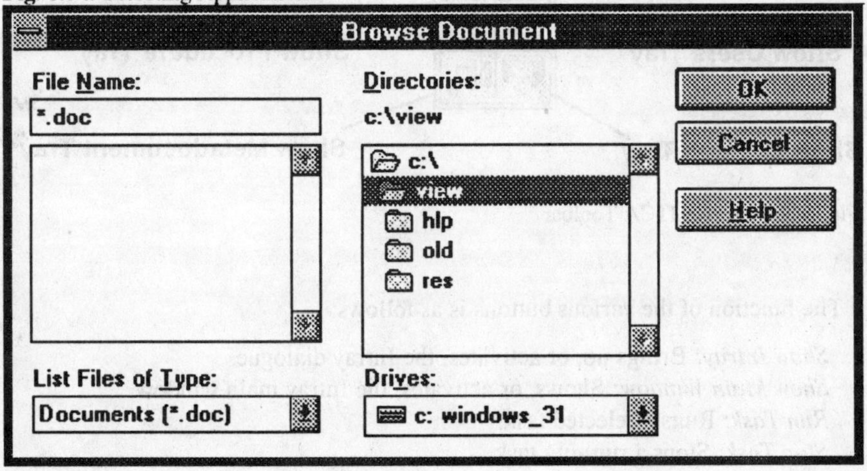

Fig. 5.35. Browse Documents

5.12 Customising the Environment

In the MMTCA prototype release the environment customisation capabilities offered to the user are the use of the toolbar and the hiding of the MMTCA main window.

5.12.1 Toolbar

The MMTCA toolbar is invoked through the menu's *Show Tools* item, under the *Options* pop-up menu. While the toolbar is active the *Show Tools* menu item changes to *Hide Tools*. The toolbar may also be indirectly invoked when the user selects the *Hide Menu* item, from the main menu. In principle a user may operate MMTCA solely through the toolbar, thus leaving almost the entire screen space to other MS Windows applications.

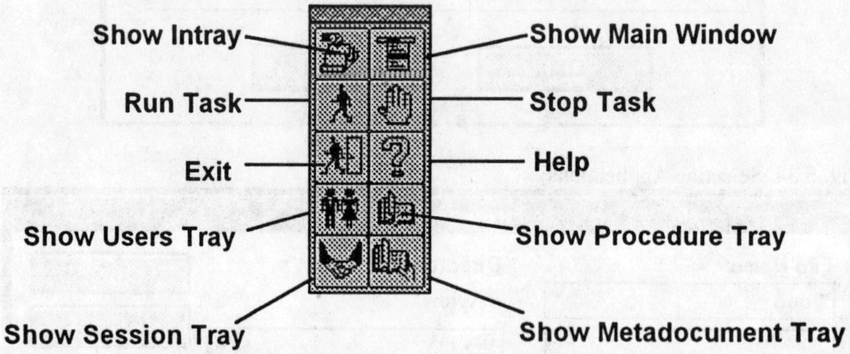

Fig. 5.36. The MMTCA Toolbar

The function of the various buttons is as follows:

- *Show Intray:* Brings up, or activates, the Intray dialogue.
- *Show Main Window:* Shows, or activates, the Intray main window.
- *Run Task:* Runs a selected task.
- *Stop Task:* Stops a running task.
- *Exit:* Exits the Intray application.
- *Help:* Invokes the Intray's help facility.
- *Show Users Tray:* Shows, or activates, the Users tray.
- *Show Procedure Tray:* Shows, or activates, the Procedure tray.
- *Show Session Tray:* Shows, or activates, the Session tray.
- *Show Metadocument Tray:* Shows, or activates, the Metadocument tray.

5.12.2 Hide Main Window

The *Hide Menu* menu item under *Options*, causes the MMTCA main window to disappear. If the toolbar is not visible, it automatically appears in the position it had the last time it was visible. If the toolbar is visible it becomes the active MMTCA window. The main window becomes visible again by clicking on the *Show Main Window* toolbar button. This way, the user always has some means of accessing the MMTCA application.

5.12.3 Getting Help

On-line help to MMTCA users is provided through the *Help* menu item.

5.12.4 Tray Dialogue Customisation

All tray dialogues, except the Intray dialogue, may be customised to display various combinations of information fields. The customisation process is the same for

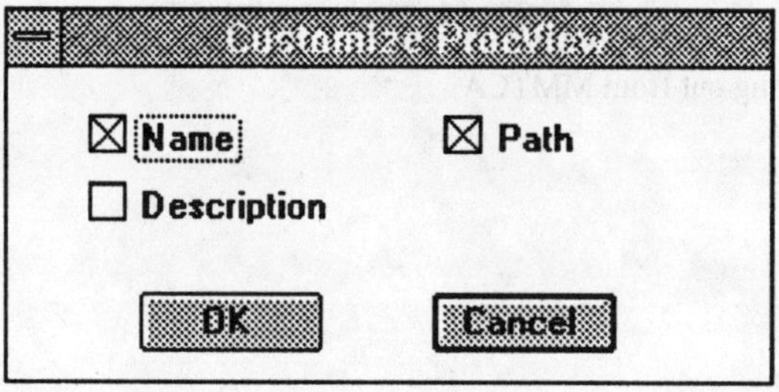

Fig. 5.37. Customising the Procedure View

all trays. The user selects the *Customize View* field under the dialogue's system menu[4]. Then the customisation dialogue shown in Fig. 5.37 appears.

The user checks any of the fields s/he wishes to display on the tray dialogue. Notice, that the fields that appear are different for each tray and depend on the particular tray. When the user clicks on **OK** the tray dialogue displays all requested fields. The user can use the tray dialogue's scrollbars to bring invisible fields in view.

---

[4] The system menu is the pop up menu that appears when the user clicks the top-left square in a Window's caption bar.

5.13 Logout Process

The user exits MMTCA from the main window menu[5]. The *Logout* menu item is invoked under the *File* pop-up menu, or by clicking on . Then the confirmation dialogue shown in Fig. 5.38 is displayed.

If the user clicks on the *No* button, control returns to MMTCA, while if the *Yes* button is clicked, MMTCA exits and control returns to the Windows Program Manager. Logout is not allowed while a task is running (see section End Task Process).

Fig. 5.38. Logging out from MMTCA

---

[5] The MMTCA Toolbar provides an alternative way of invoking basic MMTCA functionality. See the Toolbar in the Customize Environment subsection.

6. Case study: Banking

The MMTCA consortium included a bank (Banco del Comercio, Madrid), which was interested in using computer-supported cooperative work technology in order to enhance its delivery of banking services.

Present-day banking products are very complex and they appear on the market very rapidly. This means that the commercial departments in a branch of a bank have very little time to acquire a deep knowledge of new products.

In addition, the sale of a banking product is complex, and requires the cooperative work of people working in different departments. Many banks have development programmes in hand to ensure better integration and coordination of the computer-base infrastructure, but in the meantime the lack of up-to-date skills and time-consuming steps can cause a waste of time for customers, and a loss of profit to the bank.

Banco del Comercio's main aim is to provide its branch network with an integrated information platform that allows branches quick remote access to complete and up-to-date information on banking products for marketing purposes and the execution of all the necessary steps in a coordinated way without any unnecessary waste of time. In this respect, the main objectives for the bank are

- *Product Marketing Support*: using multimedia facilities, and
- *Cooperative Work Integration*: allowing users to share and to interchange documents.

Within MMTCA a prototype demonstrator was developed to demonstrate that MMTCA could contribute to achieving both of these objectives.

The Banco del Comercio Information System is centralised in structure, with no distributed intelligence among remote sites. It consists of a Central Data Processing Centre and a network of 250 branches.

The data processing centre is an IBM environment with CICS/DLI as its teleprocessing platform. The network uses several different types of communication lines (IBERPAC X.25, switched and leased lines). It also has several connections to external services, usually through leased lines of up to 64 Kbps.

The typical branch office has a cluster controller and a cash machine both using SDLC protocol and connected to the X.25 network through a PAD. The cluster controller is attached to the central host and the cash machine is connected to an external one using the same X.25 line. At present, branches do not have a LAN.

The central services are a special site in the information system with several financial branches inside it and several point-to-point connections to the IBM host for 320 emulation. It also has no LAN structure.

6.1 The Pilot Hardware Architecture

The bank is currently planning a major upgrade to its facilities and equipment. As a first step, a pilot configuration is being developed. Fig. 6.1 shows the pilot environment which consists of five locations. All the client stations are interconnected through Ethernet to the server station.

IBM HOST: The mainframe of Banco del Comercio, where all databases (Accounts, Clients, etc.) are stored. In order to provide 3270 sessions to client stations it is possible to make connections in local or remote mode.

SERVER: Currently located in the data processing centre, this provides common services to client stations through an Ethernet (TCP/IP) connection. It consists of a 486 PC running SCO Unix.

Data Processing Centre. CLIENT: From this station, technical support staff from the data processing centre can assist the branch office staff in order to solve technical problems with the new platform and application environments. It runs Windows and includes all the software components to develop, debug and test the application. It is in local connection using Ethernet with the server.

Headquarters CLIENT: From this station, banking experts can assist the branch office staff in order to solve banking product questions that could arise when selling the products to customers. It also runs Windows and includes only run-time modules to execute the application. It is connected to the bank network using either a point-to-point link or X25 link.

Branch Office CLIENT: In this station, branch staff can execute the full application in order to sell products and can also contact the other clients to ask for technical and banking advice. It runs Windows and as with the Headquarters client, includes only run-time modules. It is connected to the bank network using the X25 link

Each station has the peripherals and services indicated in Fig. 6.1.

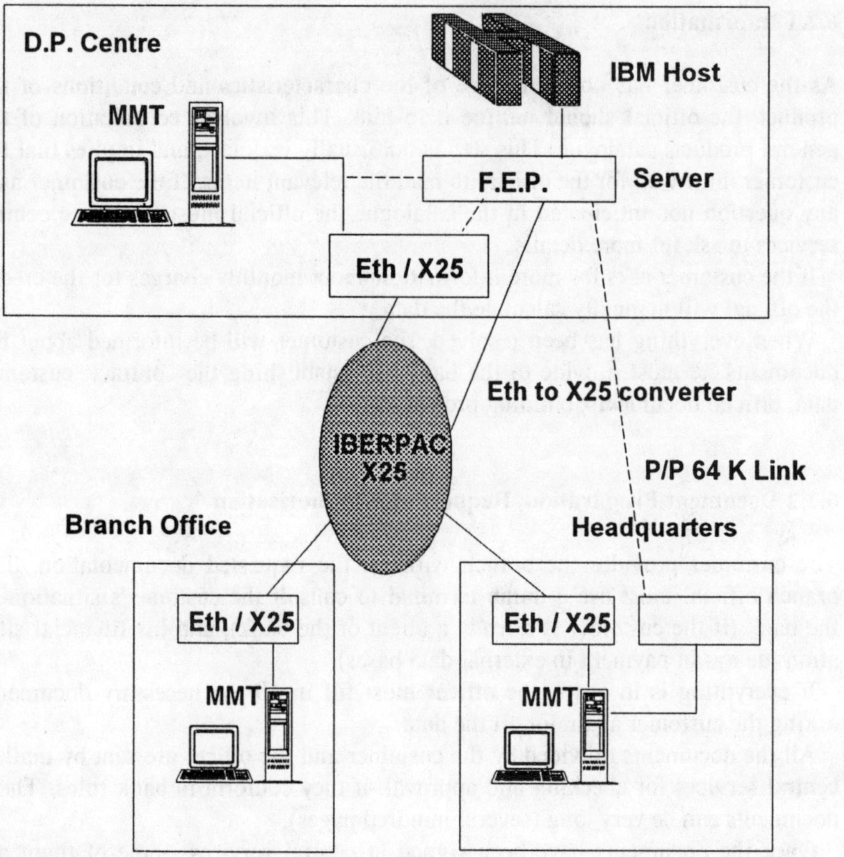

Fig. 6.1. The Bank Pilot Application Setup

6.2 Existing System for Mortgage Credit

The demonstrator application was for a contract for mortgage credit. This application is only one of a set of general Banking Product Sales that the bank would like to have in the future. It is envisaged as a standard procedure that employees of the bank would follow.

To take into account all the possible processes involved in the application, the starting situation would be a customer with no relationship with the bank coming into a branch to ask for a mortgage credit. It is assumed that the bank official has only a limited knowledge of the product.

To simplify the description of the different processes, the procedure is split up into three phases. The next few sections describe the existing procedure (without CSCW).

6.2.1 Information

As the customer has no knowledge of the characteristics and conditions of the product, the official should outline it to him. This involves consultation of the general products catalogue. This step is not usually very fast, and implies that the customer must wait for the official to read the relevant items. If the customer asks any question not anticipated in the catalogue the official must telephone central services to ask for more details.

If the customer asks for more information about monthly charges for the credit, the official will manually calculate the data.

When everything has been resolved, the customer will be informed about the documents he must provide to the bank for establishing the contract: customer data, official documents, building project, etc.

6.2.2 Document Preparation, Request and Authorisation

The customer provides the branch with all the requested documentation. The branch official must use a dumb terminal to consult the customer's situation in the bank (if the customer is already a client of the bank), and his financial situation (delays in payment in external data bases).

If everything is in order, the officer must fill in all the necessary documents asking the customer again for all the data.

All the documents provided by the customer and the officer are sent by mail to central services for checking and approval, if they conform to bank rules. These documents can be very long (several hundred pages).

Once the documents have been signed at central services, some of them are returned to the branch with the approval or refusal.

6.2.3 Contract Signature

The officer then must fill in (on a typewriter) the contract and other necessary documents for the signature. Also, he must access the host machine to open the account and to update the central data bases.

The customer must sign the documents. The official must finally send the required copies of the documents by mail to central services.

After this long and time consuming exchange of documents the mortgage credit process is complete.

6.3 Prototype Application

Using MMTCA, with the pilot hardware configuration described in section 6.1, the manual procedure described above is transformed as follows. Note that there is no intention here to develop a futuristic scenario. These represent serious developments being put in hand by the bank.

6.3.1 Information

As the customer has no knowledge of the characteristics and conditions of the product, the official must give him a general introduction. The official makes a video presentation of the product through a multimedia PC (MMT) executing one local application to access the product data (Fig. 6.2). This application is based on standard presentation software.

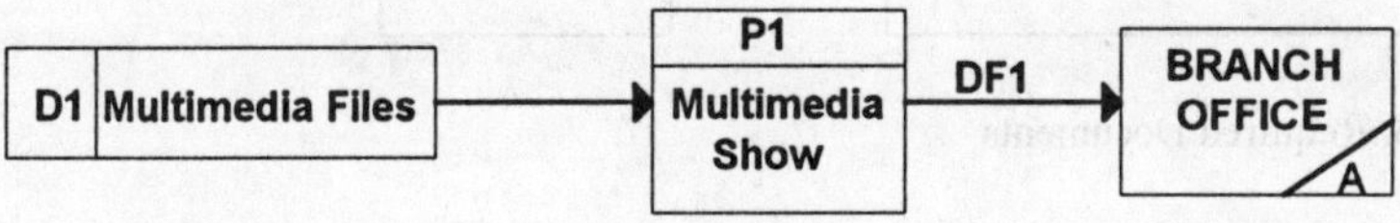

Fig. 6.2. Multimedia Show

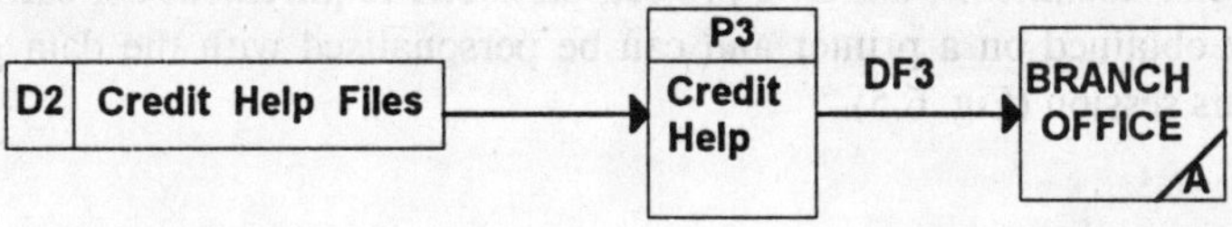

Fig. 6.3. Credit Help

If the customer asks any question not exactly included in the on-line presentation, the official can connect, through the MMT, with help files (Fig. 6.3).

If the customer asks for more details about, for example, the monthly charges for credit, the official, using the MMT facilities, can execute a simulation of the customer's own case and immediately obtain the results on a printer and give it to the customer. Once again, the MMT can access standard banking simulation software (Fig. 6.4).

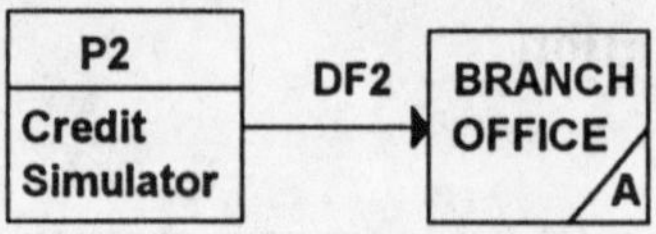

Fig. 6.4. Credit Simulation

When everything has been resolved, the customer will be informed about all the documents he must provide to the Bank for establishing the contract (customer

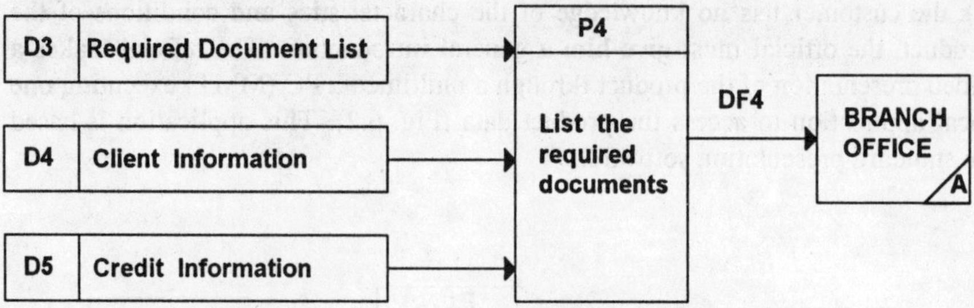

Fig. 6.5. Required Documents

data, official documents, building project, etc). The requirement list can be automatically obtained on a printer and can be personalised with the data gathered during this session (Fig. 6.5).

6.3.2 Document Preparation, Request and Authorisation

The customer provides the branch with all the required documents.

The branch official must consult (through the MMT, using 3270 emulation facilities) the situation of the customer in the Bank (if the customer is already a client of the Bank) by connecting to the Central DP Services, and his financial situation (i.e. delays in payments in existing external data bases) by connecting to external systems. These consultations can be made through a dumb terminal emulation or generated through an intelligent interface that inserts the necessary data in the transactions.

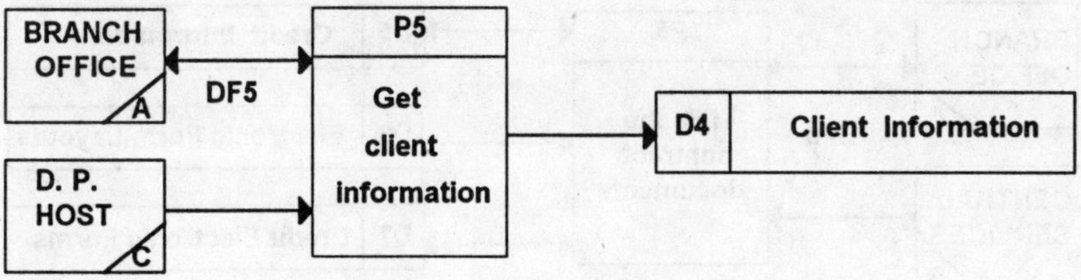

Fig. 6.6. Client Information

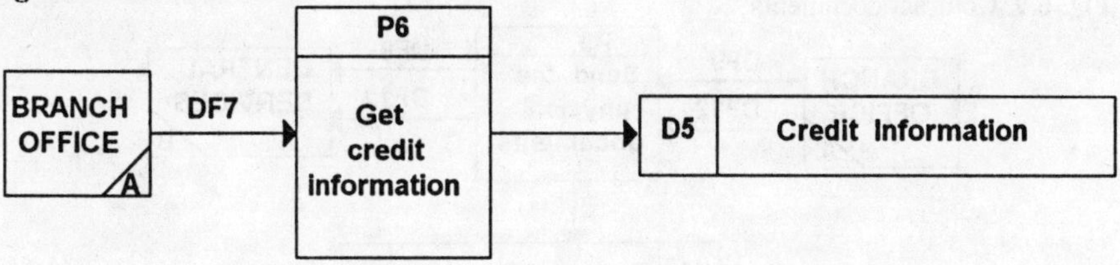

Fig. 6.7. Credit information

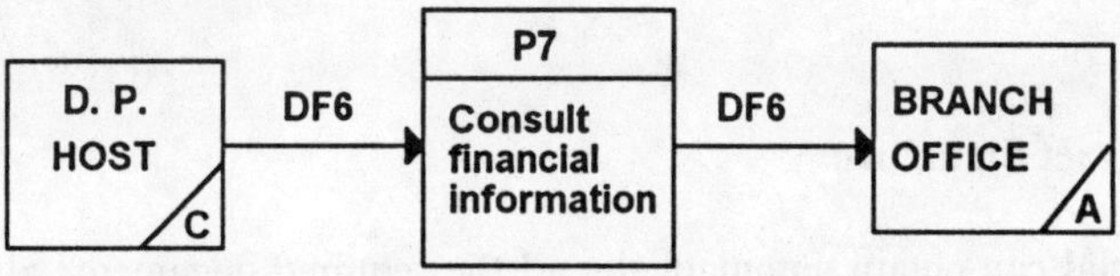

Fig. 6.8. Financial information

If everything is in order, the official must fill in all the necessary documents using the data already provided by the customer. In this case, the data which were provided before are already available in the MMT and do not need to be asked for again.

The documents can be locally or remotely stored in electronic form (image documents where necessary).

All the documents provided by both the customer and the official can be sent by fax or as a file using the scanner, but, in both cases, through the same connection and using the MMT interfaces. These documents can be very long (several hundred pages).

On signing the documents at Central Services, part of them must be sent back to the branch with approval or rejection. All the document changes can be made through the MMT.

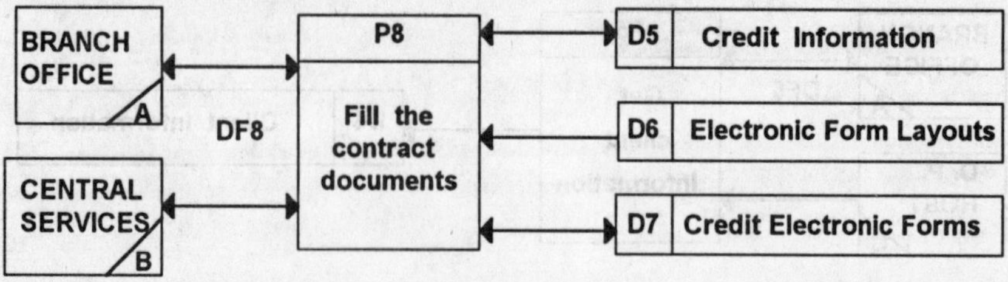

Fig. 6.9. Contract documents

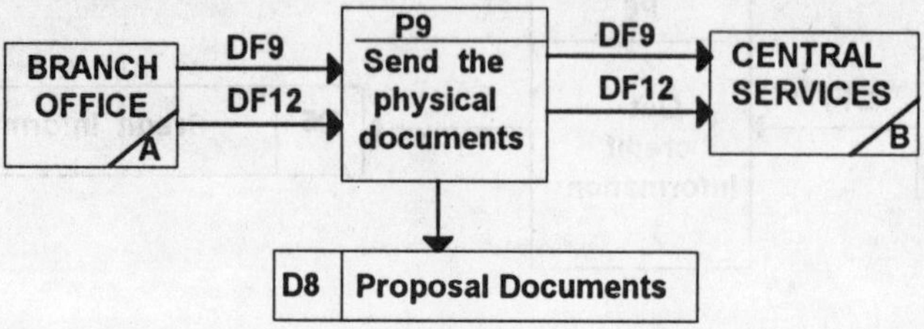

Fig. 6.10. Sending the documents

6.3.3 Contract Signature

The official can obtain automatically all the required documents already filled in with the right data. Also, he must access the central host to open the account and to update the central data bases. As was said above, this connection can be made
using a dumb terminal emulation or by generating automatically all the required transactions.

After the customer has signed them, he must finally send the required copies of the documents to the central services through the MMT.

All the local applications and data must, of course, be remotely updated and this process must be controlled by the MMT.

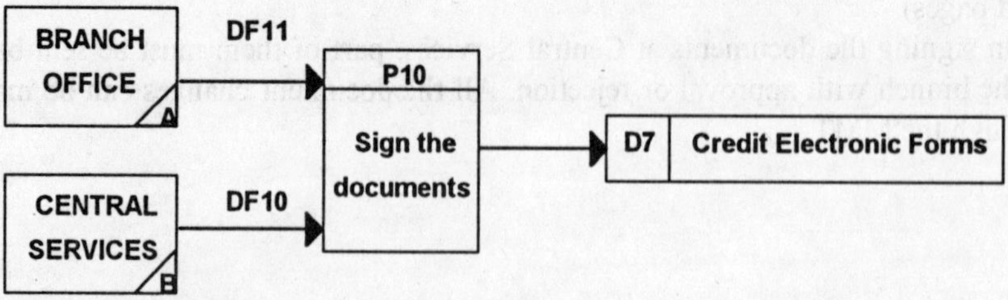

Fig. 6.11. Contract Signature

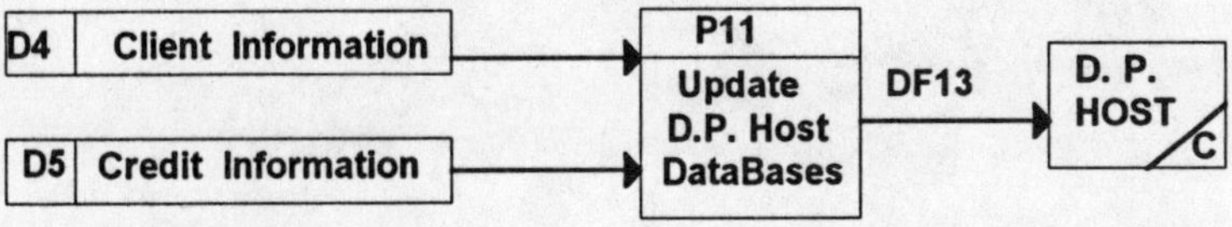

Fig. 6.12. Update Databases

From this case study it can be seen that the workflow and document control aspects of MMTCA are the most important for the bank. Future developments at the bank envisage assistance with decisions within workflow, using the support provided within MMTCA. Examples of the decision facilities are a feature of the case study described in the next chapter.

7. Case study: Shipping

In the MMTCA project, it was considered important to include an application area where remoteness and the need for cooperative technical work. Such an application area is afforded by the shipping sector. Workflow is less important than the need to exchange multimedia documents such as pictures of damage, technical drawings with modifications highlighted, etc.

The Institut für Seeverkehrswirtschaft und Logistik (ISL) was already involved in such a project (MOEBIUS), and welcomed the opportunity to include appropriate software for cooperation, as offered by MMTCA.

7.1 The Shipping Application Environment

The MMTCA user for the shipping application was the Institute of Shipping Economics and Logistics (ISL) in Bremen, Germany. ISL is a non-profit making independent foundation. Its research work includes theoretical and empirical aspects in the field of shipping, shipbuilding, ports and other areas related to the maritime sector. With the logistics branch of the institute technical aspects of maritime traffic and information flows are also covered.

The shipping application was realised in connection with the European Union's RACE project R2040 MOEBIUS ("Mobile Experimental Broadband Interconnections Using Satellites", 1992-1995), where ISL is also a consortium member. The objective of this project is, in very short words, to realise satellite-based, mobile, multimedia communication between a mobile unit (car with satellite antenna and multimedia terminal equipment) and a head office (also equipped with multimedia terminal equipment).

Mounting all the equipment on the mobile side in a car makes land-mobile applications possible in addition to maritime applications, where the car is located in an open top container.

On one hand, ISL was a user in MMTCA; on the other hand, it is a developer in MOEBIUS. In that project, one of the users is the Bremer Vulkan (BV), a very large enterprise engaged in ship and Diesel engine newbuilding and repair as well as in information and telecommunication technology. This is the Application User, for which ISL developed applications with MMTCA.

Two branches of the BV were involved:

- the service department of the Diesel engine factory, and
- the service department of one of the yards.

The objective of Bremer Vulkan is to improve its relations with the customers with the help of advanced telecommunications. To this end, a telecommunication office (TCO, see below) was created, which will be used to offer video and computer supported services for engine maintenance and repair.

7.2 Technology Background

The basic technology of the MOEBIUS system for mobile multi-media communication is to multiplex three different kinds of information flows (video, audio and computer data) into one single digital signal. This is done by a special device, a Codec (coder/decoder), which consists of two computer extension boards.

This digital signal is transmitted between the mobile unit and the TCO via satellite and ISDN, where the connection between the satellite system and the ISDN at the satellite land earth station in Eik (Norway) was one of the main achievements of MOEBIUS:

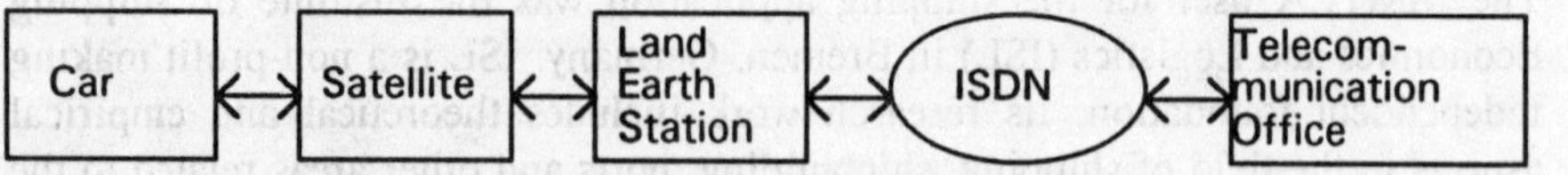

Fig. 7.1. Digital signal transmission between car and TCO

For the satellite transmission a special service of INMARSAT ("International Maritime Satellite Organisation") is used: DHSD ("Duplex High Speed Data") which offers one digital 64 kbit/sec channel. This seems to be not very much compared with several hundreds of Mbit/sec in terrestrial networks. But remember, the objective of the project was *Mobile* Communication, and in this field 64 kbit/sec is already a considerable bandwidth. Whereas analogue voice and fax as well as low speed (up to 9.6 kbit/sec) data communication between ship and shore is usual practice already several years ago DHSD is a new service. It was launched in 1993 and allows high quality audio and high speed data communication in addition to the most important aspect for MMTCA: integrated multimedia communication containing voice, video and computer data.

For the MMTCA tests, two different bandwidth-combinations were used:

- 16 kbit/sec audio + 40 kbit/sec video + 8 kbit/sec computer data for low volume data communication needs (cooperative work between ship and shore, i.e. writing, drawing, scrolling, mouse movements, ...)
- 16 kbit/sec audio + 8 kbit/sec video + 40 kbit/sec computer data for large volume data communication needs (file transfer).

The car is fitted, among other multimedia and satellite equipment, with two 50 MHz 486 computers in 19 inch racks: One under MS-Windows for codec operation and one under SCO-Unix for cooperative sketching applications under XWindow. These two computers are connected via Ethernet and the second one can also be operated under DOS and MS-Windows to be used as an MMTCA node. Because of restricted space inside the car there is only one keyboard and one screen for both computers - with a switch for alternative use.

In the TCO there are access points for the BV LAN as well as for ISDN (S_0 with two B-channels, 64 kbit/sec each). The TCO is fitted, among other multimedia and ISDN equipment, with the following computers:

- one 50 MHz 486 under MS-Windows for codec operation and
- one 50 MHz 486 under SCO-Unix for cooperative sketching applications under XWindow. This one is used as the MMTCA server with the data base Ingres at the same time.
- Another 50 MHz 486 under MS-Windows to be used as MMTCA node.

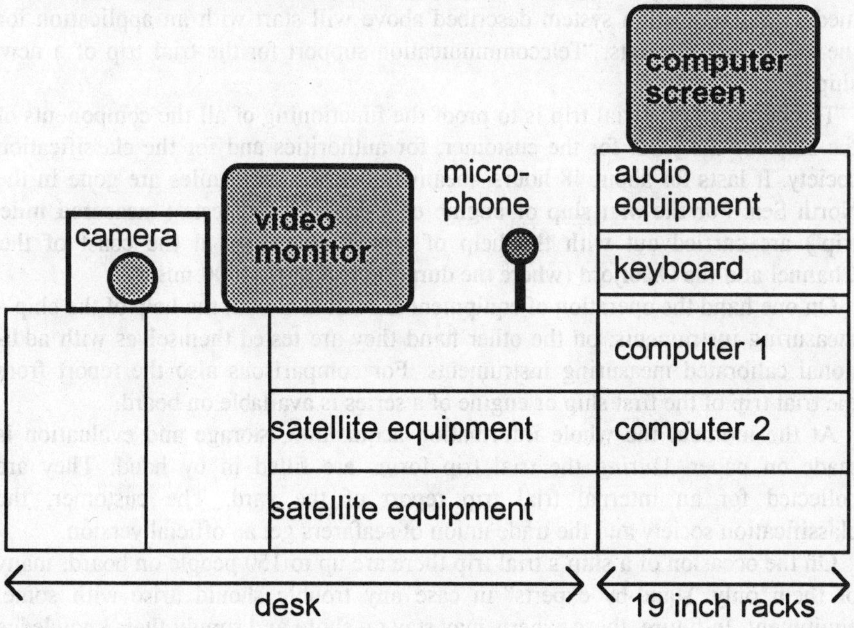

Fig. 7.2 Car equipment

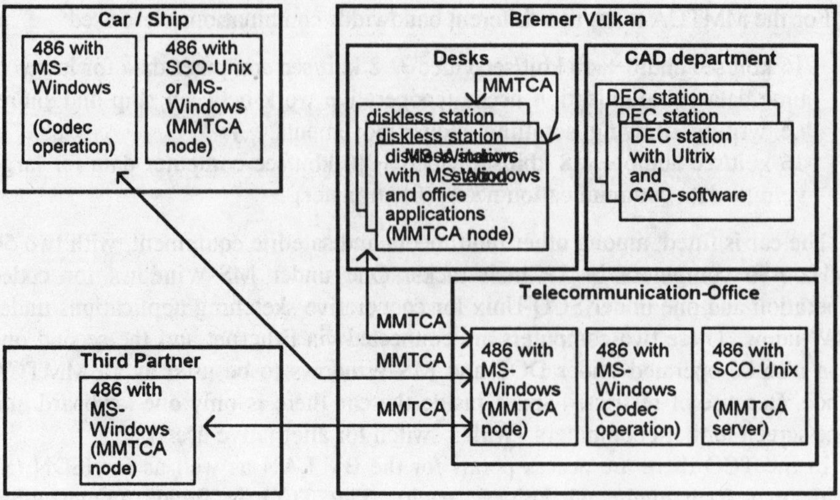

Fig. 7.3. The use of MMTCA for cooperative work in the shipping application

7.3 Application Background

The usage of computer supported cooperative work within the mobile, multimedia communication system described above will start with an application for the yards own interests: "Telecommunication support for the trial trip of a new ship".

The objective of a trial trip is to proof the functioning of all the components of the ship for the yard, for the customer, for authorities and for the classification society. It lasts for about 48 hours, meanwhile 400 to 500 miles are gone in the North Sea. For the first ship or engine of a series speed tests ("measured mile trip") are carried out with the help of special markings at the coast of the Channel and the Oslofjord (where the duration is 4 days, 1000 miles).

On one hand the operation of equipment is evaluated with the help of the ship's measuring instruments; on the other hand they are tested themselves with additional calibrated measuring instruments. For comparisons also the report from the trial trip of the first ship or engine of a series is available on board.

At the moment the whole information acquisition, storage and evaluation is made on paper. During the trial trip forms are filled in by hand. They are collected for an internal trial trip report of the yard. The customer, the classification society and the trade union of seafarers get an official version.

On the occasion of a ship's trial trip there are up to 150 people on board, many of them only "stand-by experts" in case any trouble should arise with some equipment. In future, these experts may stay on shore and supply their knowledge from there via integrated video, voice and data communication.

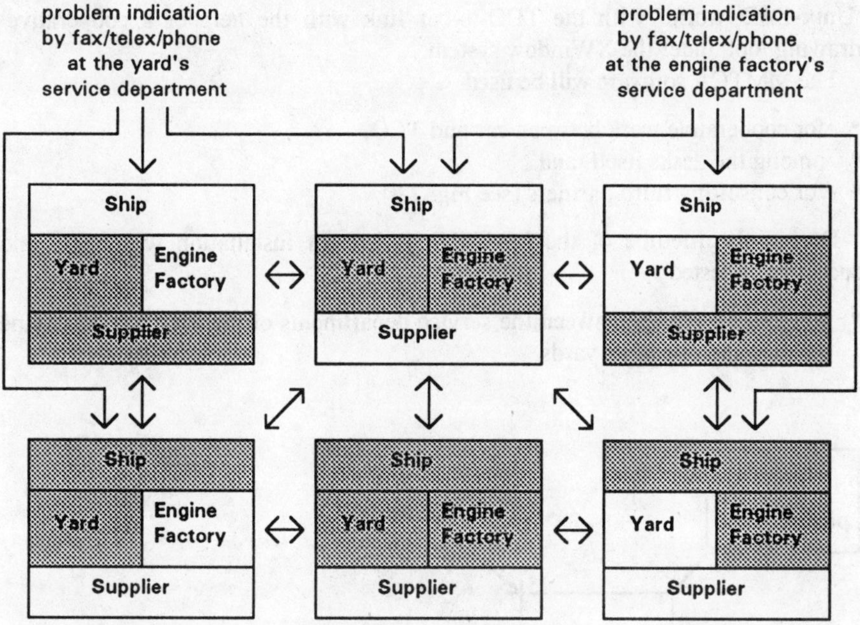

Fig. 7.4. The shipping application scenario

The effective usage of MMTCA for cooperative work between ship and shore via satellite with its restricted data transmission rate is possible, because both partners have most of the necessary information available on their computers (drawings, photos, text, tables). Therefore, the transmission of large amounts of data will be the exceptional case. This may happen, if, for example, photos of a damage on the ship are needed for the cooperative problem discussion. In that case, the cooperative session must be prepared by a file transfer.

During the lifetime of the MMTCA project tests for cooperative writing and drawing with MS-Notepad and MS-Paintbrush were made via satellite between car and TCO. Because of the low amounts of data to be transmitted during cooperative work, performance, even with only 8 kbit/sec for data, was very good.

Interest in using MMTCA at the BV started with the need for shared screen software to be used between car and TCO. But then, stimulated by MMTCA, the idea grew of extending this kind of work also to the communication between different departments and/or companies of the BV as well as with its customers and suppliers.

The BV TCO is connected to the enterprise-wide LAN with about 400 discless stations, 25 LAN-Manager servers and 100 DEC-VAX stations. According to this hardware, there are two "computing worlds" at the BV: the "Unix-CAD world" and the "MS-Windows desktop world". MOEBIUS itself will connect the

"Unix-CAD world" with the TCO-to-car link with the help of a cooperative drawing tool under the XWindow system.

The MMTCA software will be used

- for cooperative work between car and TCO,
- among the desks itself, and
- for consulting third partners (see Fig. 7.3).

During the lifetime of the MMTCA project an installation was made and successfully tested

- via Ethernet LAN between the service departments of the BV's Diesel engine factory and one of its yards

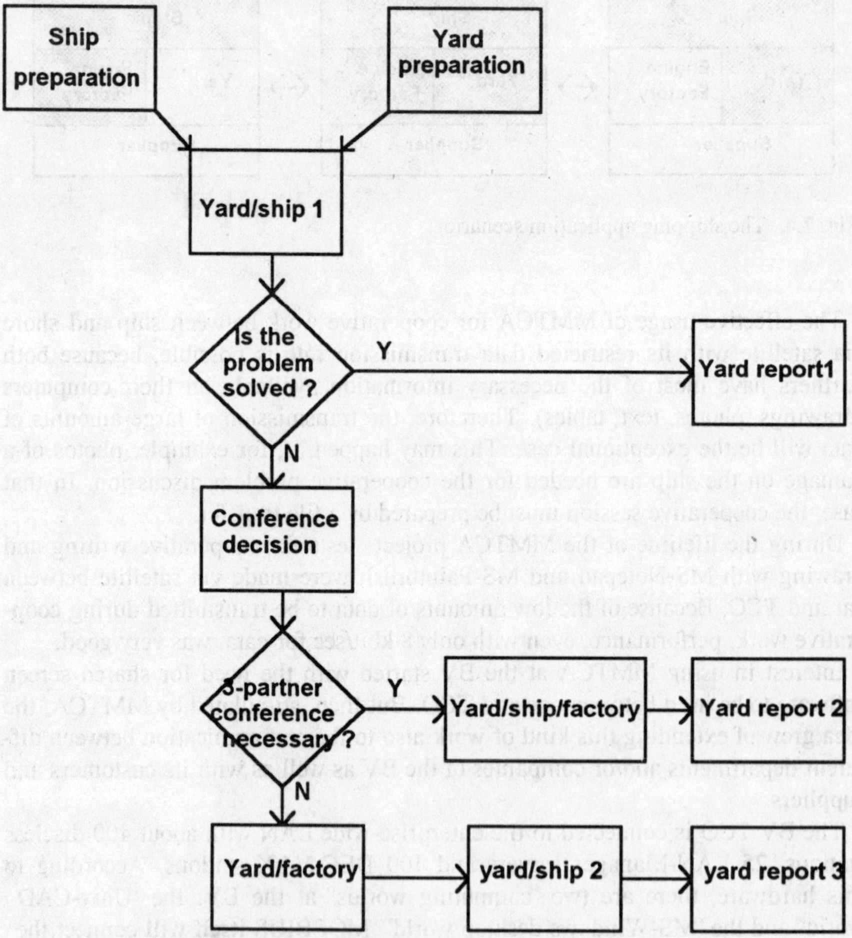

Fig. 7.5. The shipping application workflow

- via ISDN between the TCO and ISL.

7.4 Scenario and Workflow

In the scenario, the problem indication will arrive by telephone, fax or telex either at the yard's or at the diesel engine factory's service department. Both of them can

- contact the ship immediately to try a problem solution
- contact each other first, or
- contact a supplier first.

Also a three-party conference between ship, yard and factory is possible.

The MMTCA workflow for the shipping application is shown in Fig. 7.5. According to the scenario the problem indication has arrived at the yard's service department. Now, both the ship as well as the yard's service department have to prepare the cooperative session. At the ship, a photo of the damage is taken, stored on the local harddisk and uploaded to the server ("ship preparation"). On the other hand, at the yard some repair instructions are written by the service manager ("yard preparation"). For this he can use the MMTCA metadocument browser to have a look at the results of former cooperative sessions.

When ship and yard have completed their preparations, the cooperative session between them can start ("yard/ship 1"). It will open different tools for shared editing of text, drawings and photos simultaneously.

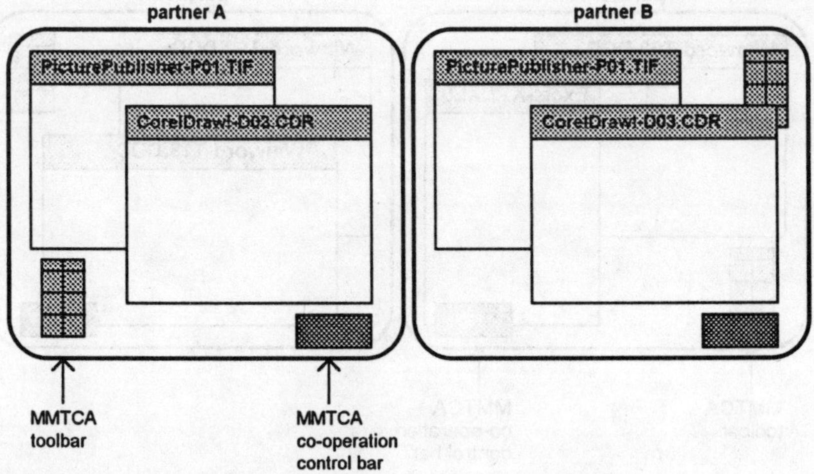

Fig. 7.6. Screen layout for simultaneous cooperative work with different document types

After the cooperative session between ship and yard has ended, the problem is either solved or not. In the first case, the yard's service manager has to write a report ("yard report 1"). In the latter case, it must be decided ("conference decision"), whether a three-party conference between yard, ship and factory has to take place ("yard/ship/factory") or whether the participants want to have two two-party conferences between yard and factory ("yard/factory") and between yard and ship ("yard/ship 2"), respectively. In both cases the workflow will end again with writing a corresponding report at the yard ("yard report 2" and "yard report 3"). This report may contain all the documents created and discussed within the workflow.

7.5 The User Interface

Two typical screen layouts for the shipping application are shown in Fig. 7.6 and 7.7, respectively.

Fig. 7.6 shows a screen layout for simultaneous cooperative work with different document types in several shared windows, which is very important for the solution of technical problems. Usually, the service engineer on shore and the chief on board have to work with photos of a damage on the ship, drawings taken from engine manuals and text (spare parts list, repair instructions, ...) at the same time. Also cut-and-paste between the shared windows works fine and proved to be very helpful during the MMTCA tests.

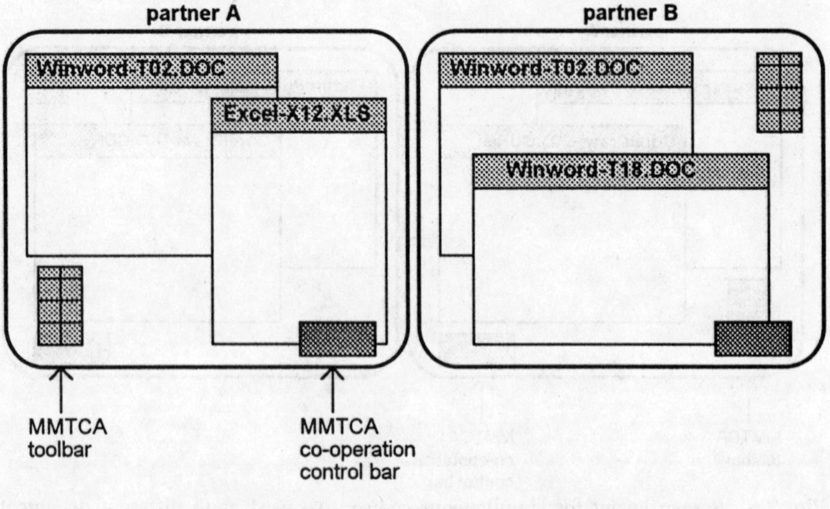

Fig. 7.7. Screen layout for simultaneous work in shared and private windows

Fig. 7.7 shows a screen layout for simultaneous work in shared and private windows. This can be used very effectively in connection with the MMTCA metadocument browser. Consider, for example, the following case: The service engineer, just discussing a problem with the ship, remembers, that he has solved already a similar problem with another ship some time ago. Then he can retrieve this information from the MMTCA database with the help of the metadocument browser, have a look at the documents from the former problem solution and use them for the current case.

8. Case study: Computer Integrated Manufacturing

This chapter describes the CIM Application Design in the MMTCA demonstrators. In the first section a summary of the application scenario is provided, and analyzed in a set of distinct procedures. In the second section the application scenario is mapped on the PTA model of MMTCA Toolbox. In this case study, the main focus of attention becomes the notion of open meetings and flexible working arrangements.

The chapter discusses actual and potential working practices in a CIM company, and so contains many proprietary names and registered trade marks, which are the property of their owners.

8.1 Elements of the CIM Application Scenario

The CIM application aims at the integration of the existing product design procedures within Intracom in a single integrated collaborative environment. As the design environment in Intracom consists of heterogeneous platforms, only part of this integration will be addressed by the MMTCA project, as the solution provided by the MMTCA Toolbox concerns only tools running on an MS-Windows environment.

Product design within Intracom can be decomposed in several distinct procedures concerning different departments along with the interaction among them.

A product design procedure is initiated by the Marketing Department usually in response to the request of an external customer. This initiation is associated to the definition of the *Product Design Requirements Specification*.

The initiation of product design project is followed by the creation of a *product design project team*. This team is usually centred in the Engineering Department and comprises a senior designer as project leader, a mechanical parts design team, an electronics parts design team, an associated quality engineer, an associated production engineer, an associated materials engineer and an associated purchasing officer.

The first task of the design process is the *Industrial Design of the product* which consists in a conceptual and aesthetic overall initial design, based on the user requirements, and becomes part of the technical specifications for the rest of the project. As a result of this procedure the final form of the product is defined and the available spaces for the product components are determined. On the basis of this information a decomposition of the project in *Electronics parts design* (PCBs – Printed Circuit Boards) and *mechanical parts design* is effected.

PCB design is undertaken by the electronics design team belonging to the R&D Department whether mechanical parts design is undertaken by the Engineering Department. Electronics parts design is effected by using the Mentor Tools electronics CAD package, whether mechanical parts design is effected by using SDRC's I-DEAS and AUTODESK's AutoCAD CAD packages.

The *Interaction between electronics parts design team and mechanical parts design team* is effected by exporting PCBs' data from Mentor Graphics Board Station (PCB's CAD tool) to SDRC I-DEAS system. Calculation of mechanical characteristics (solid models) of PCB by using I-DEAS Mentor Graphics Board Station EDA Interface. Integration of PCBs' mechanical CAD drawings with mechanical parts drawings after translating them in IGES format and exporting them from the I-DEAS system to the AutoCAD system. The objective of this interaction is the identification of possible adaptation problems leading to redesign of mechanical and/or electronics parts with possible selection of alternative materials (components).

In the following paragraphs further steps in the product design procedure are described in more details. These steps are aimed to be integrated in a collaborative design environment, to be installed in INTRACOM, based on the MMTCA Toolbox. These steps fall within the scope of the MMTCA project as they are basically based on tools running in the MS-Windows environment. (AutoCAD for Windows, MS-Word, Corel Draw etc...).

8.2 Mechanical Parts Design

According to the decomposition of the product to be designed in distinct parts, the project leader proceeds in the work allocation to the mechanical parts design team.

After the initial work allocation, the design team members may work individually on their parts. During their individual work, design team members may request the interaction with other design team members for exchange of ideas or expert consultation. More experienced members of the design team or the project

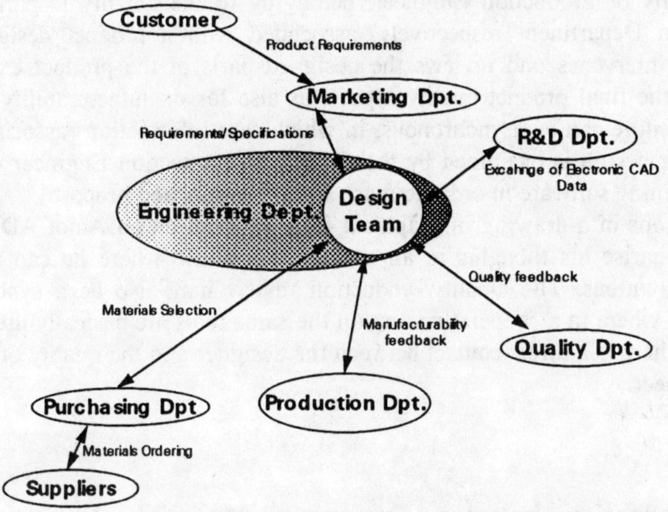

Fig. 8.1. Agents involved in the Product Design procedure

leader may be asked to intervene to modify a drawing or the project leader may ask to control a designer's work.

The project leader may request a common Design review of the parts under design at different stages of the design process. During these reviews all members of the design team assist and comment on each other's work.

The cooperation cases described above normally are synchronous, but the possibility for an asynchronous cooperation mode should also be provided. Such an asynchronous cooperation mode can be based on the use of redlining graphics overlaid on the drawings and the use of associated comments in text and/or voice form.

The views of the final CAD drawings of the product are included in specific forms of the Production folder of the product.

8.3 Quality/Production Review

A Quality or Production Engineer, belonging to the Quality Department or Production Department respectively, associated with a product design team, regularly intervenes and reviews the designed parts of the product examining them for the final product quality aspects as also for manufacturability aspects. This procedure can be asynchronous, in which case information associated to a part under design is examined by the Quality or Production Engineer who can use a redlining software in order to mark specific points and propose modifications of a drawing in graphical form overlaid on an AutoCAD file. He may summarise his thoughts in an associated text file where he can also add voice annotations. The Quality/Production review may also be a synchronous procedure where in a cooperative session the same tools are basically used but in this case there is a direct contact between the designer and the quality or production engineer.

8.4 Interaction between Designers, Materials Engineer and Purchasing Officer

Usually a product under design, apart from electronic PCB's which are designed by the electronics design team, also contains numerous mechanical components which are provided by subcontractors or exist in the market. Information on these materials concerning their characteristics, cost, providers, stock in the warehouse, is maintained in a particular database. The selection of the appropriate components to be included in the product is the responsibility of the materials engineer based on the product specifications, cost, availability and adaptability with the overall product under design. The selection of a particular material and the possible effects in the product design are the object of the interaction between the materials engineer and the design team. The materials engineer belongs to the Engineering Department. The final selection of a material may require the feedback of a purchasing officer who will comment on the cost and availability of a material to be selected. The purchasing officer belongs to the Purchasing Department.

This interaction can also be synchronous or asynchronous, requires the access to the materials database and to the CAD drawings and its results may be summarised in a text file associated with voice comments. The conclusion of the work of the materials engineer is the creation of the E-BOM (Engineering-Bill of Materials) and M-BOM (Manufacturing-Bill of Materials) of the product to be included in the appropriate section of the Production folder of the product.

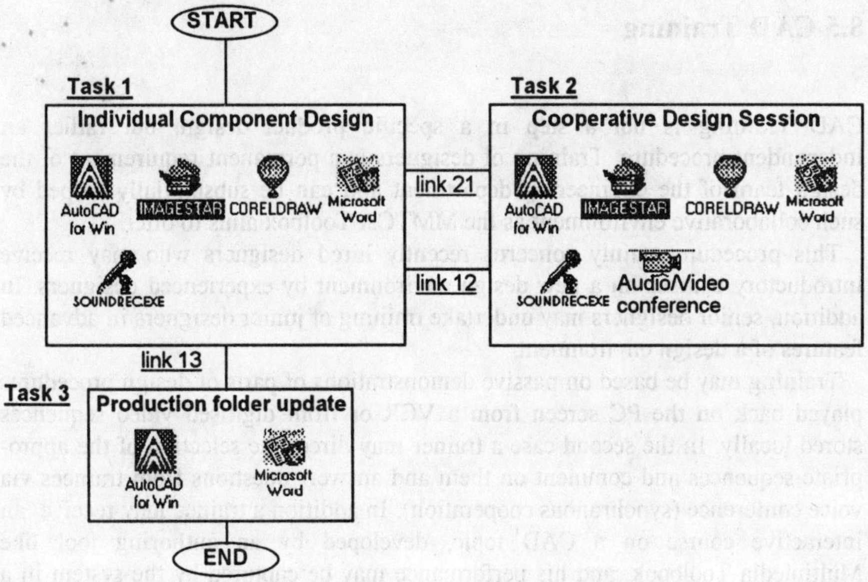

Fig. 8.2. Mechanical Parts Design

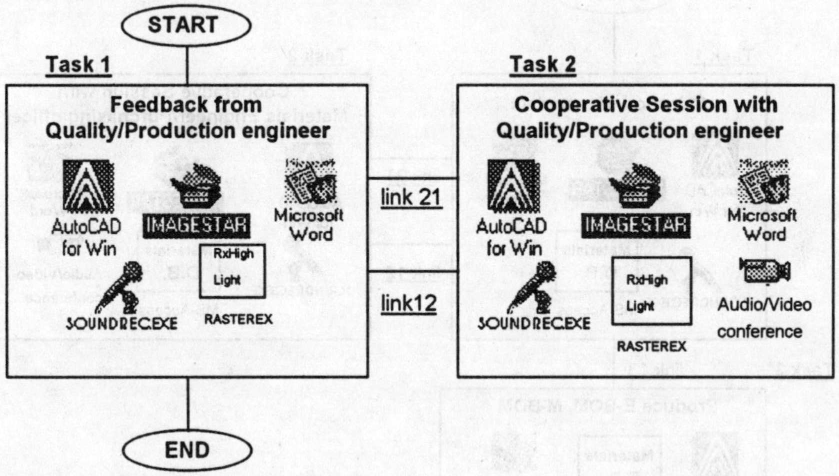

Fig. 8.3. Production/Quality review procedure

8.5 CAD Training

CAD Training is not a step in a specific product design, but rather an independent procedure. Training of designers is a permanent requirement of the design team of the engineering department and can be substantially helped by such collaborative environment as the MMTCA Toolbox aims to offer.

This procedure mainly concerns recently hired designers who may receive introductory courses on a new design environment by experienced designers. In addition, senior designers may undertake training of junior designers in advanced features of a design environment.

Training may be based on passive demonstrations of parts of design procedures played back on the PC screen from a VCR or from digitised video sequences stored locally. In the second case a trainer may direct the selection of the appropriate sequences and comment on them and answer questions from trainees via voice conference (synchronous cooperation). In addition a trainee may receive an interactive course on a CAD topic, developed by an authoring tool like Multimedia Toolbook, and his performance may be captured by the system in a

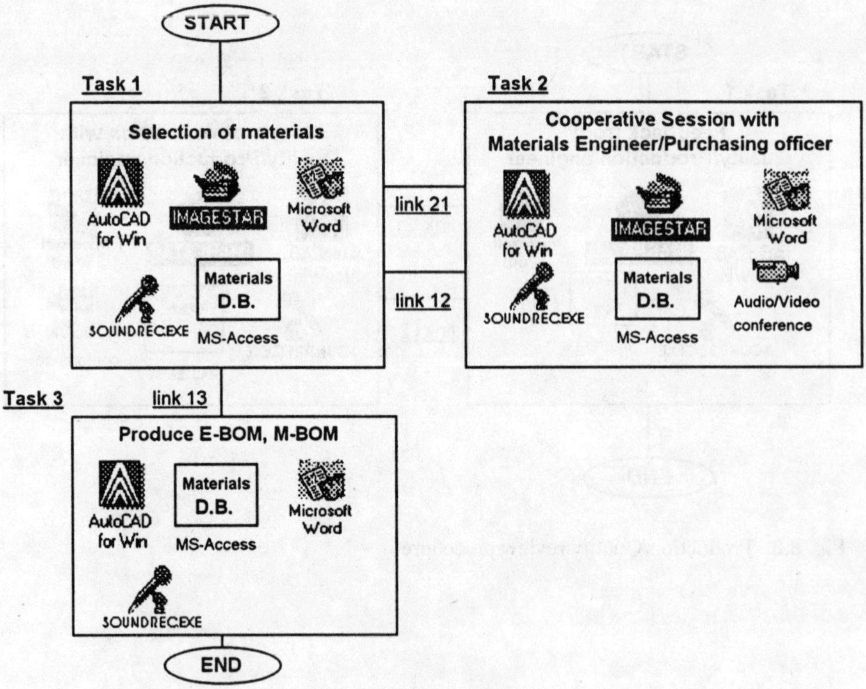

Fig. 8.4. Materials/Purchasing Interaction procedure

file and communicated to the trainer. The trainer can make comments and suggestions based on the trainee's performance (asynchronous cooperation).

In addition a trainee may interact directly with a design environment (CAD tool) and the trainer may follow up his work and intervene or comment if needed, or inversely a trainer may give demonstrations on the use of a specific CAD tool for different design topics (synchronous cooperation).

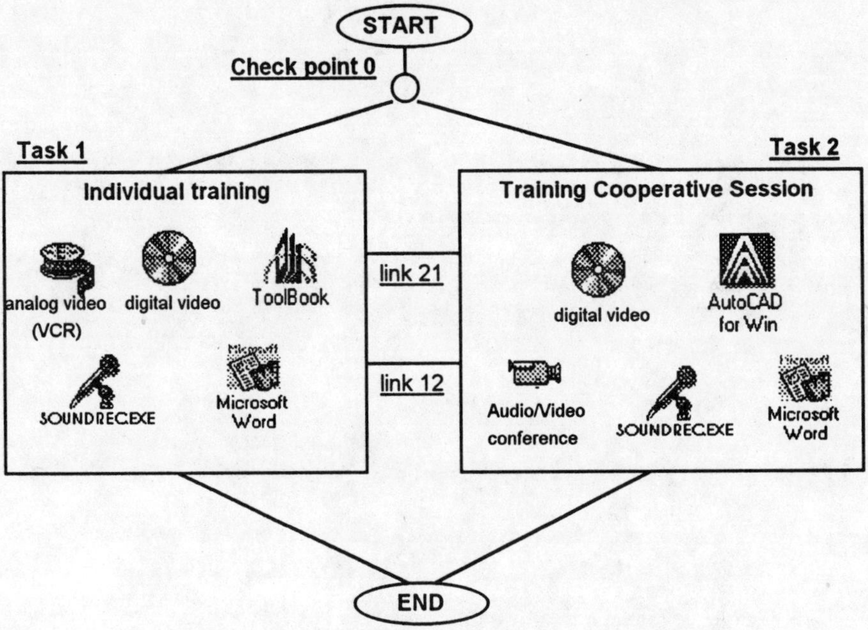

Fig. 8.5. CAD Training procedure

Part 3: A Technical Introduction

The purpose of the following chapters is

- to explain the procedures for installing MMTCA and integrating new applications with it
- to explain the nature and contents of the MMTCA database
- to give sufficient explanation of the internal functioning of MMTCA to enable access to its advanced features.

Chapter 9 gives an overview of the MMTCA architecture, dealing with the kernel, the network manager, and the architecture of the procedure design system (organising work to be done), and the run-time system (carrying out the tasks).

Chapter 10 deals with setting up the MMTCA system, installing and configuring the software.

Chapter 11 presents the MMTCA database, which is an essential part of MMTCA's operation. It is occasionally useful to know the details of the tables that MMTCA uses in the database to control its operation. Intervention in these tables can be used by system administrators when cleaning up or archiving software, or moving procedures from one MMTCA system to another.

Chapter 12 gives the application program interface of MMTCA. These functions are all in dynamic link libraries used by MMTCA, and can therefore be used from many Windows applications.

9. MMTCA Architecture

Précis: MMTCA models user cooperation on a hierarchical procedure→task→ action structure. Fundamental to this approach is an ability to clearly analyse and break down the steps and processes a group may go through to produce a specific target object(s) or effect(s).

There are two aspects of MMTCA: its program time tools and its run-time system. By explaining each in turn, an understanding of how MMTCA achieves its ambitious aims should be developed.

9.1 MMTCA Kernel

In MMTCA, the message passing between nodes is managed by a Network Manager module. To ensure scalability, all messages pass through the server, so that clients communicate only with the server. On each node the MMTCA kernel is set up as shown in Fig. 9.1.

9.2 The Network Manager

The Network Manager is aimed to provide communication:

- between a Node and the Server.
- between several Nodes, using the Server as intermediary.

At the level of the Network Manager Kernel logical unit, this communication is understood in terms of the export of any kind of services or functions from modules in one side (Node or Server) to the other side (Server or Node). The implementation of service export and remote invocation is based on the exchange of requests and answers between server and node Network Manager modules.

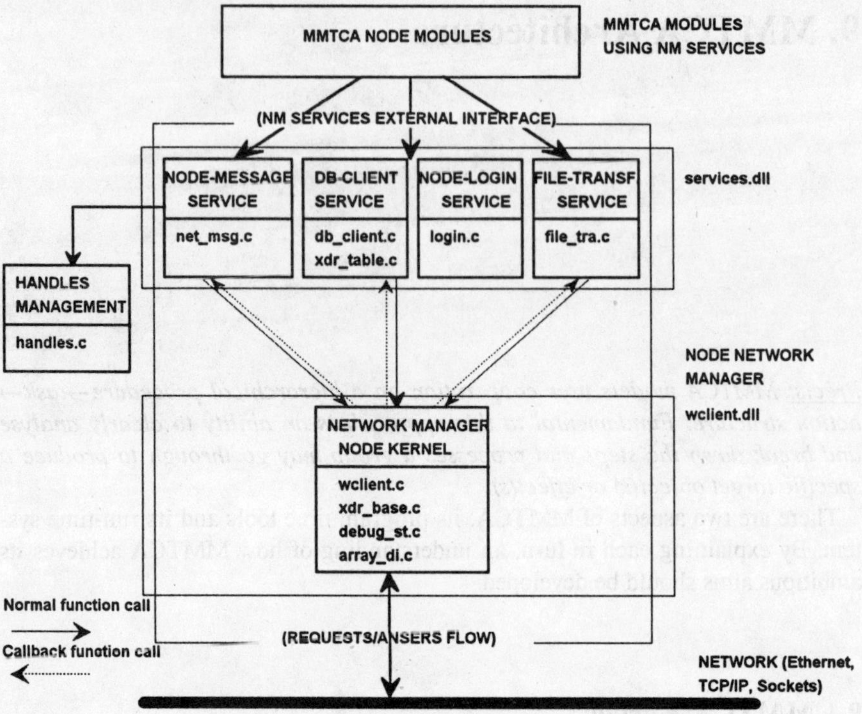

Fig. 9.1. Node side architecture

At the level of the Network Manager Services logical unit, some general Function services have been implemented on top of that service exportation mechanism, addressed to the rest of the modules in MMTCA. These services are:

- *Message Communication/Dispatching* between modules at the Nodes through the Server.
- *Database Access* from the module Nodes to the Server database.
- *Login Control* in MMTCA Nodes, centralised in the Server.

Fig. 9.2 shows the Network Manager server side architecture.
In this diagram, the following modules are shown:

- *Network Manager Server Kernel module*, which implements the Server part of the mechanism of exporting services to the Node and uses remote services from the Node. It provides the Node-Server connection facility and controls the request and answer flow to and from the Nodes.

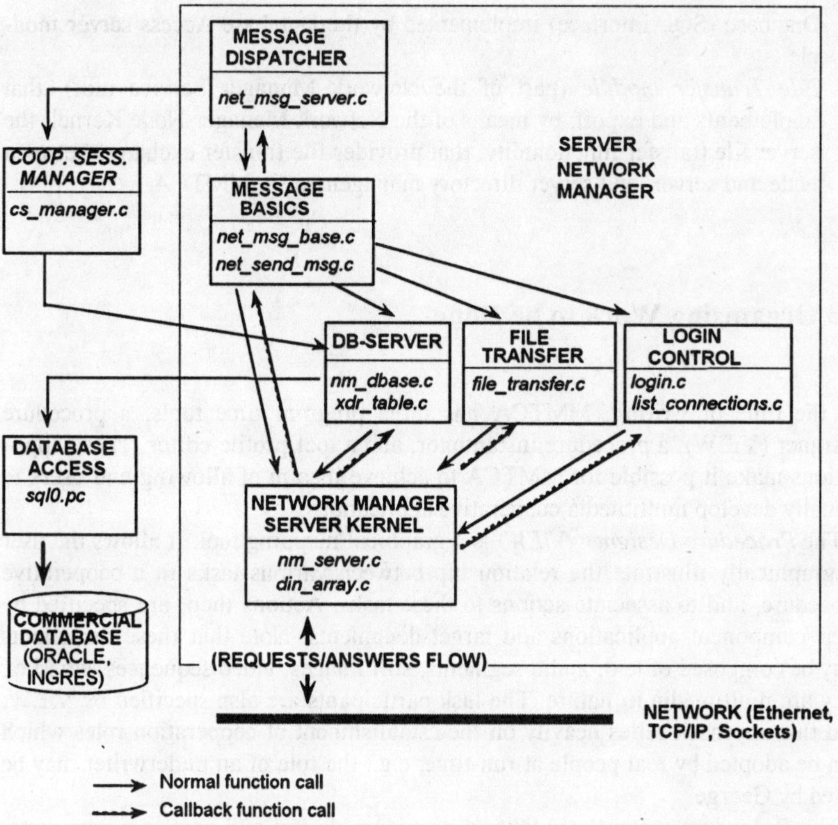

Fig. 9.2. Server side architecture

- *Message Basics module*, which implements, on top of the Network Manager Server Kernel and using the Database Server's database access facilities and Login Control module, the basic mechanisms for sending and receiving messages to and from the nodes.
- *Message Dispatcher module*, which implements, on top of the Message Basics, the Server part of the Message Service: message reception from a node and dispatching to other nodes, depending on the kind of message. It accesses the Cooperative Session Manager, to invoke functions associated to the reception of specific Cooperative Session messages.
- *Login Control module*, which implements and exports, by means of the Network Manager Node Kernel, the server login control functionality, that provides security control in MMTCA.
- *DB-Server module* (part of the Network Manager Service unit), that exports, by means of the Network Manager Server Kernel, the access to the server

Database (SQL interface) implemented by the Database Access server module.

- *File Transfer module* (part of the Network Manager Service unit), that implements and export, by means of the Network Manager Node Kernel, the server file transfer functionality, that provides file transfer exchange between node and server, and server directory management in MMTCA.

9.3 Organising Work to be Done

At the time of writing, MMTCA has three program time tools: a procedure designer (ViEW); a procedure instantiator; and a tool profile editor. These applications make it possible for MMTCA to achieve its aim of allowing end users to actually develop multimedia cooperative applications.

The *Procedure Designer (ViEW)* is a graphical mapping tool. It allows the user to graphically illustrate the relationship between various tasks in a cooperative procedure, and to associate actions to these tasks. Actions then, are specified by their component applications and target documents. Note that these documents may be composed of text, audio segments, still images, video sequences, etc., i.e., they are multimedia in nature. The task participants are also specified by ViEW, and this approach relies heavily on the establishment of cooperation roles which can be adopted by real people at run-time, e.g., the role of an underwriter may be filled by George.

The *Procedure Instantiator* takes a procedure design and creates a new metadocument. This metadocument can be looked upon as a running instance of a procedure.

The *Tool Profile Editor (TPE)* is used to manipulate tool profile templates (TPT's). A TPT is a user specification of a node application tool (e.g., Microsoft Word) which will be used in a cooperative session, together with a definition of which configuration files are used to customise that application (e.g., winword.ini). The TPT's are used by ViEW to configure applications for a cooperative session, such that the same configuration files are used on every node participating in a cooperative session. This approach has successfully managed to overcome synchronisation difficulties caused by the inconsistent starting states of applications used for cooperative sessions.

9.4 Carrying out the Tasks

MMTCA uses only one system pointer. During asynchronous cooperation, this pointer is under complete control of the local user. However, during a cooperative session there is only a single controlling user (the floor holder): when this user is actively typing, or moving his mouse (i.e., generating input to his local application replica), all other passive user input (on remote nodes) is prevented. When the floor holder is inactive - even momentarily - passive users are free to work in their own private windows, but will be pre-empted when the active user 'takes up the chalk' again. This mechanism is made possible by the use of special filters available to Windows 3.1 system programmers. Using these, user input can be diverted to the network (and hence to other nodes), or disabled and taken from the network (i.e., from another node), as illustrated in Fig. 9.3. Note that node to node communication only takes place via a central server.

All PCs participating in a conference run the same MS Windows applications at the same time. MMTCA keeps all applications synchronised by feeding them with the same events so that they generate identical displays. One of the most interesting aspects of MMTCA lies in the fact that no changes are required to the Windows operating system or to the applications running on it, but yet applications can be operated in a strict WYSIWIS manner. This approach (shared-input architecture) generates significantly less traffic than sharing the display (shared-output architecture), which in any case requires changes to the operating system or hardware; and about 95% of WYSIWIS performance is achieved.

Some of these limitations on WYSIWIS performance in MMTCA were mentioned earlier in section 5.4. The main problem relates to the treatment of events between a click down and a click up (click and drag, double click, scrolling, selecting options in menus, etc.) The chain of these events is handled in all cases by a special mechanism, called the click and drag mechanism. In many applications that support painting, interrupts are disabled during drawing operations, and so the events need to be queued up and sent as a group to the network manager. This is done for all sequences that begin with left mouse button down, and special processing is performed for detecting and reproducing double-click events. This mechanism works well in most cases, but gives undesired results in some circumstances, because (apart from double-click) events are reproduced without considering the time at which they were generated.

Expanded menus, where the whole operation of selecting a submenu item is carried out without releasing the mouse button, represent a WYSIWIS performance fault in MMTCA. Another problem occurs with automatic scrolling, which is supported by some applications when the mouse is dragged into the border area of the window. Such automatic scrolling is governed by different messages in different application, making it impossible for MMTCA to provide a general solution, and the rate of scrolling depends on the internal clock in each machine.

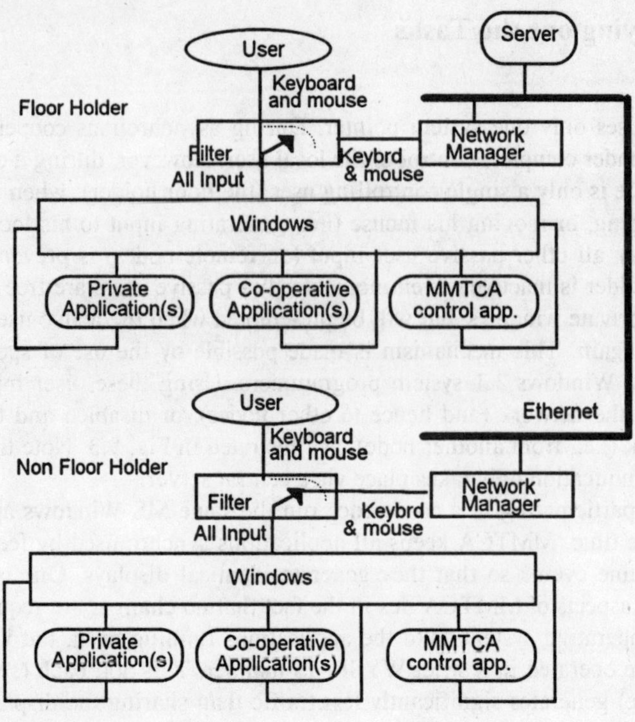

Fig. 9.3. MMTCA architecture

In future development of MMTCA it is intended to achieve further improvements to WYSIWIS performance by taking account of the timing of events when it is strictly necessary for a particular application, and adjusting for the internal clock rates and control panel settings of the participating machines.

10. MMTCA Installation

10.1. Node Installation

This section details the setup of the MMTCA node software, using the MMTCA Setup application MMTCASET to configure the software for your system. MMTCASET should be installed and run from the same directory as the other node software applications.

MMTCASET is designed to let the user easily configure the main options for their MMTCA node software applications. It allows the user to specify the name and port number for the MMTCA server they wish to connect to, the database type the server is using, and some details of cooperative sessions and videoconference.

Start MMTCASET by double-clicking the left mouse button on the MMTCA Setup icon in the MMTCA group in Program Manager, or choose run from the File menu in Program Manager and select MMTCASET.EXE from the MMTCA\RUN directory.

When the MMTCASET application starts it will display a dialogue on the screen:

The first section in the dialogue allows the user to set the options for the MMTCA server they wish to connect to.

Name specifies the name of the server – type in the name of the server to be used. If the node software has been configured previously, the *Name* edit box will hold the name of the server which is currently used – edit this if a different server is to be used.

The *Port Number* is the number of the port at which the server is listening for connections - the default number for an MMTCA server is 1603. If the MMTCA server chosen is using a different port, edit the value to reflect this.

The second section of the dialogue allows the user to configure the option for the type of database which the MMTCA server is using. The default option is to use an Oracle database. If the MMTCA server to be connected to is using another

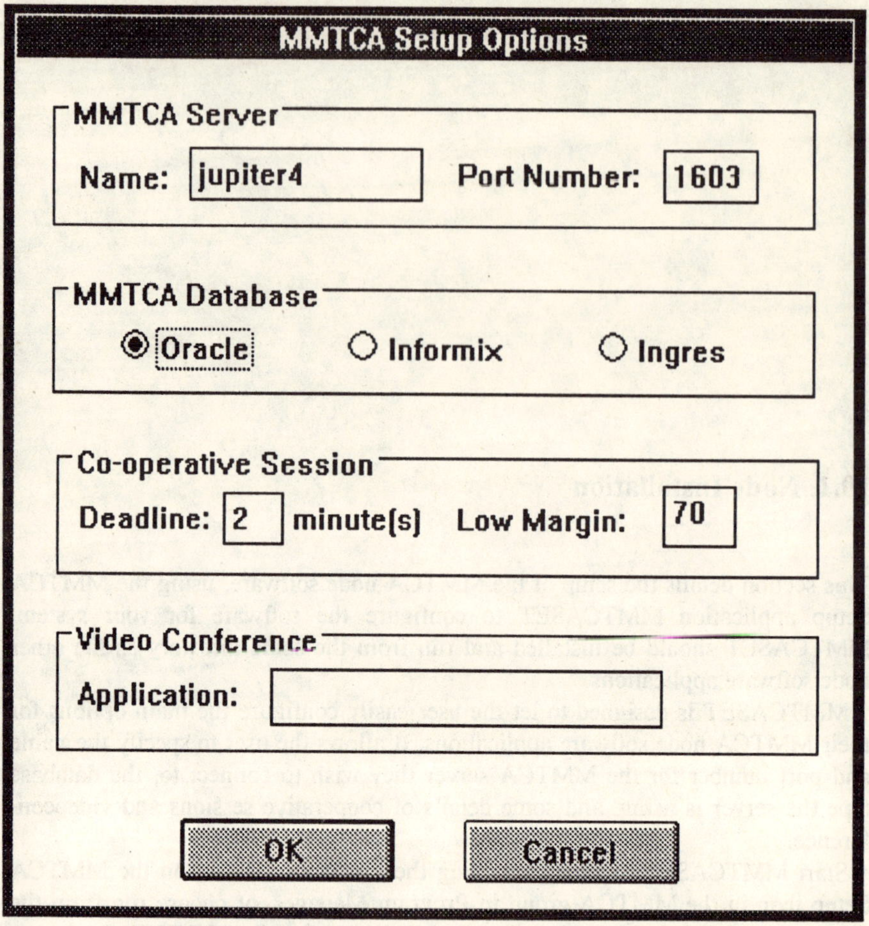

Fig. 10.1. MMTCA Installation

of the supported databases (Informix or Ingres), select the appropriate radio button on the dialogue.

The third section of the dialogue allows the user to configure parameters for use in a Cooperative Session (CS). The *Deadline* allows the user to set the deadline in minutes that will be used when inviting other users to participate in a CS. The default deadline is 2 minutes. The *Low Margin* option allows the user to specify the space that will be reserved at the bottom of the screen during a CS, so that even maximising applications will leave this space free. If it is required to have maximised applications filling the whole of the screen, set this value to 0. If private application icons should always be visible when a CS is in progress, set the *Low Margin* to 70.

The last section of the dialogue allows the user to configure the videoconference application that will be used when including a videoconference in a CS using ViEW or the Ready-to-Run CS facility in the Intray. The application specified should be the name of the application template for the videoconference application.

Once the desired options have been selected, click the *OK* button to save the changes, or the *Cancel* button to abort the changes.

10.2 Server Installation

The MMTCA server may run on several hardware platforms and DBMSs. To facilitate this, the installation of the server has to be made from the source files, to customise the compilation and linking for the specific server chosen.

This section gives details of how to install the MMTCA server. It covers the following steps:

- *Sources/directories load*
- *Customisation* for the specific platform and DBMS chosen
- *Building* of the server executable
- *Preparation* of the running environment
- *Running* the MMTCA server

10.2.1 Sources/directories load

The MMTCA server sources are shipped in their original directory structure. They just have to be extracted from the distribution files by using the appropriate UNIX tools: 'uudecode', 'uncompress', 'tar', etc., to get the sources and makefiles organised in this structure.

The directory structure is:

```
<server_root_directory>/
  debug
  gen_obj
  timer
  nm_server
  mmtca_server
  lib
```

Because of ownership and access rights on UNIX files, it is recommended to use the same UNIX user when loading the server directories and when operating the server. In case of access conflicts with the read files, the UNIX commands 'chown' and 'chmod' can be used by the superuser to change the file ownership and access rights.

10.2.2 Choice of server and DBMS

In this step, the makefiles in the subdirectories are prepared according to the chosen server platform and DBMS. This is made by invoking the corresponding 'make install_xxxx' command.

For the moment, the MMTCA server is available for four combinations of platform (OS) and DBMS. Depending to the one you have you should use one of the following commands:

- to install MMTCA Server for HP-UX/Oracle platforms
  `make install_hp_orac`
- to install MMTCA Server for SUN-OS/Informix platforms
  `make install_sun_infx`
- to install MMTCA Server for SCO/Ingres platforms
  `make install_sco_ingr`
- to install MMTCA Server for SCO/Informix platforms
  `make install_sco_infx`

10.2.3 Building the Server Executable

In this step, the makefiles in each subdirectory are automatically invoked to compile and link the sources, obtaining the libraries and server executable file.

To build the MMTCA Server for the installed platform you should invoke the following command:

make mmtca_server

10.2.4 Preparation of the Running Environment

Before executing the MMTCA server in the server, two new services (for using sockets) must be added to the file */etc/services* at any point of the file, by the superuser. The file has to look like this:

```
#
#   MMTCA services   ######
#
mmtca           1603/tcp    nm_server
mmtcaudp        1604/udp    nm_serverudp
```

where

`mmtca` (`mmtcaudp`) is the service name
1603 (1604) is the port number (default values)
`tcp` (`udp`) is the socket protocol type
`nm_server` (`nm_serverudp`) is an alias

The port number of the `'mmtca'` service has to be the one specified when installing the nodes using MMTCASET tool. The port number of the 'mmtcaudp' service is assumed to be the next one. Be sure that there are no other services in the file using the same port numbers.

10.2.5 Running the MMTCA Server

The server executable is generated in the subdirectory

<server_root_directory>/mmtca_server

under the name 'nm_server'. You should go to this subdirectory to execute it from there.

The MMTCA server is executed by invoking the following command:

nm_server [-s*service-name* -db*database-string* -tr|-trdb|-trmsg]

where,

service-name is the name of the alternative service used. By default this is 'mmtca' (see previous section)

database-string is the string to be passed in the connection to the database containing DB name (password, ...). By default the one for Oracle is 'mmtca/mmtca'.

the flag '-trdb' enables a trace of the SQL sentences issued and executed against the server DB during the execution. The flag '-trmsg' enables a trace of the MMTCA messages dispatched by the server. The flag -tr' enables all the traces.

Optionally, two environment variables MMTCA_SERVICE and/or MMTCA_DATABASE can be defined to avoid specifying the service name and/or the database string in the command line every time the server is executed. Depending on the UNIX version and the shell used, the environment variables are defined in a different way: refer to your OS manuals.

10.3 Videoconference

VIDEOCON is a videoconference system that allows users who are connected to the same local area network, to establish voice and video communication between them. To do so, the participants must be provided with a personal computer and several devices as camera, microphone and loudspeaker, plus the VIDEOCON software application. The TCP/IP protocol support is necessary for this software to run.

The general system architecture is shown in Fig. 10.2.

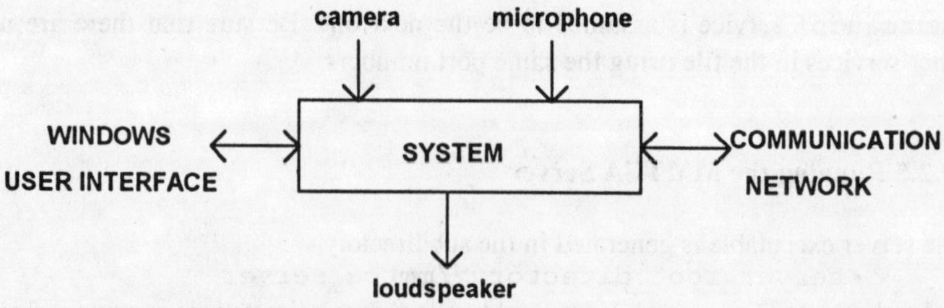

Fig. 10.2. Videoconference architecture

The system communicates with the user through the interfaces provided by the MS-Windows. With it, the user can select the different options available in the system, show the video images, etc.

The camera provides the video input to the system. In the same way, the microphone provides the audio input.

The video output system is the same PC monitor, using the mentioned windowing environment. On the other hand, the audio output is made through a loudspeaker connected to the system.

There is another alternative for the system audio input/output, as the telephone o any other audio input/output line.

Finally, the network provides the communication media between remote systems. In this way, the network is in charge of distributing the video and audio information that the user wants to transmit to the remote system, and recovering the information sent from the remote sites to the local one.

10.3.1 Hardware Platform

The minimum equipment required to run a videoconference is the following:

- Personal Computer with a 386-25 MHz processor, ISA bus, VGA monitor. The minimum RAM memory allowed is 4 MB. A better system improves the quality of the service.
- Communications network supporting the TCP/IP protocol.
- Bitfield H.261 compression board plus an optional daughter board for movement estimation.
- Bitfield G.711A audio board.
- For audio input/output, the user can select between a telephone or a microphone + loudspeaker system.
  The telephone can be connected through an RJ11 connector.
  The microphone or any other audio input line must be connected to the board using a RCA connector (the closest one to the adapter cable). This connector must have and input impedance of 47 kohm (not balanced) and a nominal

sensivity of 70 mV for the microphone or 700 mV for any other audio input line.
The loudspeaker or any other audio output line can be use the RCA connector sited furthest of the adapter cable. This connector has a low output impedance, that is of >4 ohm (not balanced) for the loudspeaker or 700 mV nominal output level for any other audio output line.

- For video input the user can choose between a camera or any other device supporting an Y/C video signal or one/two composed video device
- For video output the user can use any monitor supporting composed video or Y/C video. However, to integrate al the system in a PC environment, a video overlay board is required to show real video in an VGA monitor (i.e. Screen Machine board).

10.3.2 Installation of the Bitfield Compression/Decompression Board

Install the board in one of the computer slots following its installation manual.

There is an adapter cable to connect all the different devices to the board. The cable has a 15 pin D connector in the board side and several jack connectors in the other side.

Choose any of the four available I/O addresses so that there is not conflict with other installed hardware.

10.3.3 Camera Installation

Camera number 1 must be connected to the black female jack of the adapter cable. An optional second camera can be connected to the yellow female jack.

If a camera with S-Video output is used, the red female jack must be used for the crominance and the black/yellow female jacks for the luminance.

10.3.4 Audio Devices Installation

For audio input/output, a telephone or a microphone + loudspeaker system can be chosen.

The telephone can be connected directly to the board using the RJ11 connector provided in it.

The microphone or any other audio input line must be connected to the board using a RCA connector (the closest one to the adapter cable). This connector must have and input impedance of 47 kohm (not balanced) and a nominal sensitivity of 70 mV for the microphone or 700 mV for any other audio input line.

The loudspeaker or any other audio output line can be use the RCA connector sited furthest of the adapter cable. This connector has a low output impedance, that is of >4 ohm (not balanced) for the loudspeaker or 700 mV nominal output level for any other audio output line.

10.3.5 Connection to the Digitiser Board

This board must be installed following its installation manual. The compression/decompression board must be connected to the digitiser board using the black male connector. If the board supports Super-VHS, the black male connector must be used for the luminance and the red male one for the chrominance.

10.3.6 Software Installation

All the following installation requirements will be supported in the procedure for the installation of the MMTCA software.

Pre-Requisites: To run the VIDEOCON application, it is necessary to load the ETHDRV kernel that implements the TCP/IP protocol. To get the maximum throughput of the system, it is advised to change the following parameters in the PCTCP configuration file:

window = 5840
large-packets = 15
small-packets = 7

(The third parameter must be set to 10 for running the videoconference service from within MMTCA)

It is also necessary to have loaded the MCI driver of the digitiser board.

On the other hand, the following change must be introduced in the Windows SYSTEM.INI file:

NetHeapSize = 64 (in the [386Enh] section)

Board Initialisation: Before running the VIDEOCON application, it is necessary to initialise the compression/ decompression board. The following line must be executed:

startup [-c cfg*] [-b* base*] [-p* path*]*

cfg: configuration (default 1). The available configurations are as follows:

1	→	PAL, no audio
2	→	PAL, audio
101	→	NTSC, no audio
102	→	NTSC, audio

base: board base address in hexadecimal format (default 320h) path: directory where the configuration files are stored. If nothing is stated, the files are located in the current directory.

Normally, default parameters are used and the initialisation instruction is reduced to :

startup

VIDEOCON Application: To run the VIDEOCON application, the following files must be in the same directory:

BFLLI.DLL
CMDLL.DLL
PCTCPAPI.DLL
WNET386.DLL
VIDEOCON.EXE

To start the videoconference application the VIDEOCON.EXE program must be executed within Windows.

11. The MMTCA Database

The MMTCA Database module represents the storage of all the workflow schema generated at the node. It consists of a set of tables defined to store all the relevant information about:

- Procedure Definition:
  - the procedures defined,
  - the tasks defined within a procedure,
  - the participants, i.e. users which participate in a task,
  - the actions defined within a task,
  - the links defined between tasks,
  - the set of applications that must be activated to perform an action,
  - the list of documents to be processed by an application.
  - the list of profile files related to an application on definition.
- Run-Time i.e. Procedure Instantiation, Metadocument or Execution:
  - the metadocuments, i.e. procedure instances,
  - the Intray tasks
  - the document instance handled, i.e. actual documents processed,
  - the link instances between tasks,
  - the participant instances and real participants, i.e. actual users involved,
  - the cooperative sessions
  - the profile files instances related to an application on execution.
- For Administration purposes:
  - the nodes potentially involved,
  - the users groups or profiles,
  - the users potentially involved,
  - the current login,
  - the login history,
  - the profile templates and files related to an application.

11.1 MMTCA Database Overview

The MMTCA Database structure is shown is Fig. 11.1, using the Entity-Relationship formalism.

The squared corner rectangles represent Entities, i.e. supported in a dB table and the lines between them are Relations, supported by attributes in a DB table. The relations are only nominated when they are not evident composition or PD-MD relations. Ellipses also indicate Relations, but with the difference that they are supported in the DB by a table.

11.2 Procedure definition (PD) tables description

11.2.1 PD_PROCEDURE

This table will contain all the procedures defined in the MMTCA environment.

`PROC_ID` Identifier of the procedure. The system will assign a unique identifier for each procedure defined within the MMTCA environment.

`NAME` Descriptive name of the procedure.

`DESCRIPTION` Description of the purpose of the procedure.

`TYPE` Type of the procedure (enumerated value supported by the auxiliary table `PD_ENUM_PROC_TYPE`). Possible values for this field are:

- `'NORMAL'`: Standard MMTCA procedure.
- `'CS_PROCEDURE'`: Ready-to-run Cooperative Session procedure.

`DEFAULT_PATH` The default path of the metadocuments.

Table 11.1. PD_PROCEDURE

Column	Format	Constraint
PROC_ID	Numeric	Primary Key
NAME	Alphanumeric	NOT NULL
DESCRIPTION	Alphanumeric	OPTIONAL
TYPE	Enumerated	PD_ENUM_PROC_TYPE
DEFAULT_PATH	Alphanumeric	NOT NULL

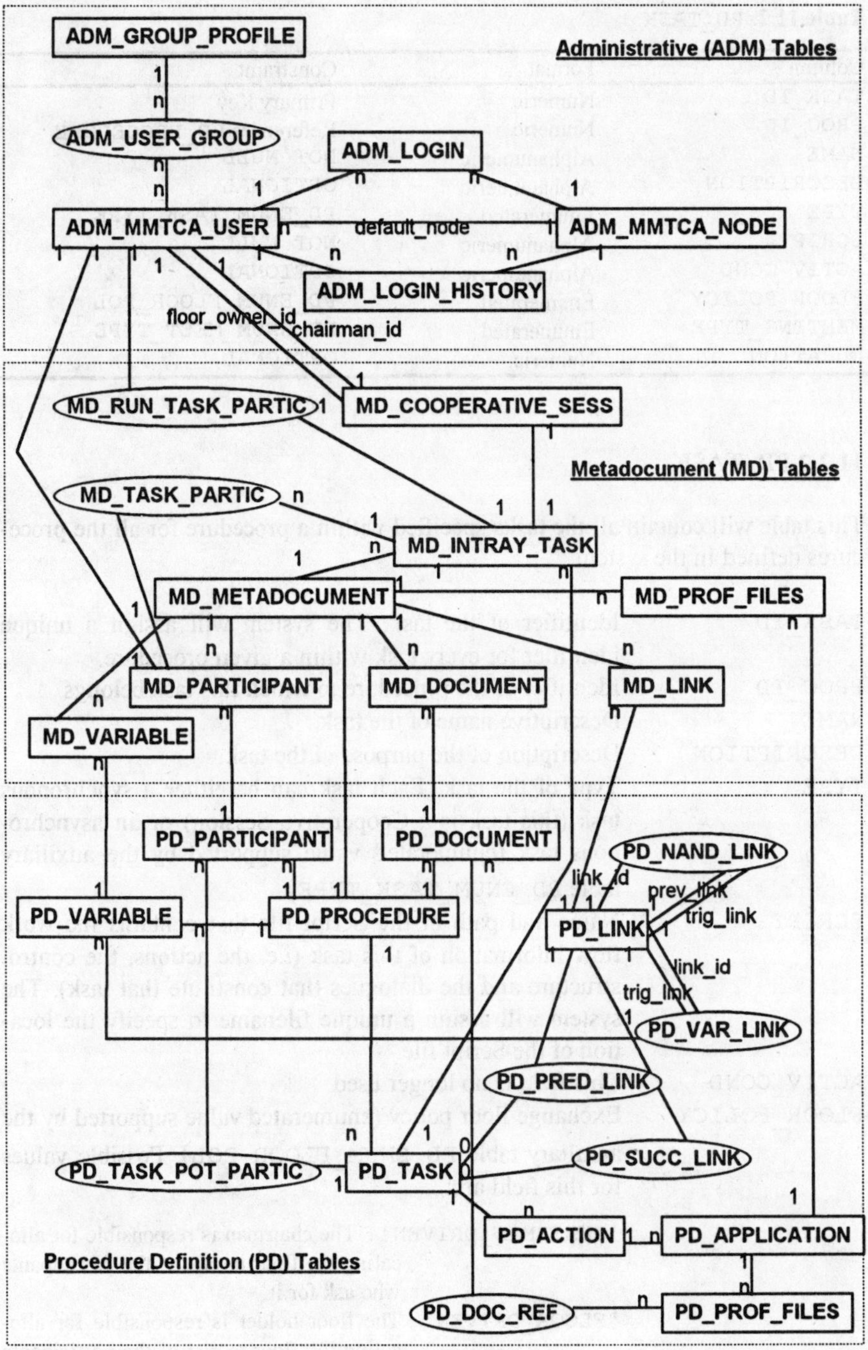

Fig. 11.1 Entity-Relationship Database Diagram

Table 11.2. PD_TASK

Column	Format	Constraint
TASK_ID	Numeric	Primary Key
PROC_ID	Numeric	References PD_PROCEDURE
NAME	Alphanumeric	NOT NULL
DESCRIPTION	Alphanumeric	OPTIONAL
TYPE	Enumerated	PD_ENUM_TASK_TYPE
SCRIPT	Alphanumeric	NOT NULL
ACTIV_COND	Alphanumeric	OPTIONAL
FLOOR_POLICY	Enumerated	PD_ENUM_FLOOR_POL
MEETING_TYPE	Enumerated	PD_ENUM_MEET_TYPE
DURATION	Numeric	OPTIONAL

11.2.2 PD_TASK

This table will contain all the tasks specified within a procedure for all the procedures defined in the system.

TASK_ID — Identifier of the task. The system will assign a unique identifier for every task within a given procedure.

PROC_ID — Identifier of the procedure to which this task belongs.

NAME — Descriptive name of the task.

DESCRIPTION — Description of the purpose of the task.

TYPE — Type of the task. Each task can be either a synchronous task (this task is a Cooperative Session) or an asynchronous task (enumerated value supported by the auxiliary table PD_ENUM_TASK_TYPE).

SCRIPT — Name and path of the Script file that contains the work flow information of this task (i.e. the actions, the control structure and the dialogues that constitute that task). The system will assign a unique filename to specify the location of the Script file.

ACTIV_COND — This field is no longer used.

FLOOR_POLICY — Exchange floor policy (enumerated value supported by the auxiliary table PD_ENUM_FLOOR_POL). Possible values for this field are:

- 'CHAIRMAN_DRIVEN': The chairman is responsible for allocating the floor to one of the participants who ask for it.
- 'FLOOR_DRIVEN': The floor holder is responsible for allocating the floor to one of the participants who ask for it.

'FCFS':	Floor allocation follows First Come First Served once the floor holder releases it.
'PRIORITIZED':	The floor is allocated to the requester participant with higher priority once the floor holder releases it.
'NONE':	No applicable floor policy (asynchronous task).

MEETING_TYPE Meeting type in a cooperative session (enumerated value supported by the auxiliary table PD_ENUM_MEET_TYPE). Possible values for this field are:

'OPEN':	Open meeting, where joining to it when already on-going is allowed.
'CLOSED':	Closed meeting, where joining it when already on-going is not allowed.

DURATION Estimated duration of the task.

Table 11.3. PD_ACTION

Column	Format	Constraint
ACTION_ID	Numeric	Primary Key
TASK_ID	Numeric	References PD_TASK
NAME	Alphanumeric	NOT NULL
DESCRIPTION	Alphanumeric	OPTIONAL

11.2.3 PD_ACTION

This table will contain all the actions specified within a task for all the tasks in the system.

ACTION_ID	Identifier of the action. The system will assign a unique identifier for every action within a task.
TASK_ID	Identifier of the task the action belongs to.
NAME	Descriptive name of the action.
DESCRIPTION	Description of the purpose of the action.

Table 11.4. PD_APPLICATION

Column	Format	Constraint
APPL_ID	Numeric	Primary Key
ACTION_ID	Numeric	References PD_ACTION
NAME	Alphanumeric	NOT NULL
FULL_NAME	Alphanumeric	NOT NULL
LEFT	Numeric	
TOP	Numeric	
WIDTH	Numeric	
HEIGHT	Numeric	

11.2.4 PD_APPLICATION

This table will contain all the applications that need to be activated to perform an action for all the actions in the system.

APPL_ID — Identifier of the application to be activated within an action. The system will assign a unique identifier for every application within an action.

ACTION_ID — Identifier of the action the application belongs to.

NAME — Logical name that identifies the application in the procedure definition.

FULL_NAME — Default physical name of the application.

LEFT — Default initial X coordinate of the left-up corner position of the application window.

TOP — Default initial Y coordinate of the left-up corner position of the application window.

WIDTH — Default initial width of the application window.

HEIGHT — Default initial height of the application window.

11.2.5 PD_DOCUMENT

This table describes all the documents used or produced in the execution of the procedure. Input and output documents are considered.

DOC_ID — Identifier of the document. The system will assign a unique identifier for every document.

PROC_ID — Identifier of the procedure to which the document refers.

Table 11.5. PD_DOCUMENT

Column	Format	Constraint
DOC_ID	Numeric	Primary Key
PROC_ID	Numeric	References PD_PROCEDURE
NAME	Alphanumeric	NOT NULL
DESCRIPTION	Alphanumeric	OPTIONAL
VAR_ID	Numeric	
PATH_TYPE	Enumerated	PD_ENUM_PATH_TYPE
PATH	Alphanumeric	NOT NULL
FNAME_TYPE	Enumerated	PD_ENUM_FNAME_TYPE
FILE_NAME	Alphanumeric	OPTIONAL

NAME — Logical name that identifies the document in the procedure definition.

DESCRIPTION — Description of the purpose and contents of the document.

VAR_ID — In the case of a document list, this contains the identifier of the variable that support the names of the documents.

PATH_TYPE — Indication of the way to obtain the document filename path (enumerated value supported by the auxiliary table PD_ENUM_PATH_TYPE). Possible values for this field are:

- 'DEF_TIME_PATH': The path of the document is specified at procedure definition time.
- 'INHERIT_PATH': The path of the document is the default path associated to the metadocument.
- 'RUN_TIME_PATH': The path of the document will be specified either at instantiation or at run time.

PATH — When specified, it is the physical path of the document.

FNAME_TYPE — Indication of the way to obtain the document filename (enumerated value supported by the auxiliary table PD_ENUM_FNAME_TYPE). Possible values for this field are:

- 'DEF_TIME_FILENAME': The filename of the document is specified at procedure definition time.
- 'RUN_TIME_FILENAME': The filename of the document will be specified either at instantiation or at run time.

FILE_NAME — When specified, it is the physical filename of the document.

Table 11.6. PD_DOC_REF

Column	Format	Constraint
APPL_ID	Numeric	References PD_APPLICATION
DOC_ID	Numeric	References PD_DOCUMENT
EDIT_ACTION	Enumerated	PD_ENUM_EDIT_ACT

11.2.6 PD_DOC_REF

This table describes the relation between the documents handled by the procedure and the applications that operate with it.

APPL_ID — Identifier of the application to be activated with the document.

DOC_ID — Identifier of the document handled by the application.

EDIT_ACTION — Indication of the action supposed to be carried out in the document in the task with the application (enumerated value supported by the auxiliary table PD_ENUM_EDIT_ACT), used in the pre/post file process actions. Possible values for this field are:

- 'CREATED': The document is created in this task.
- 'CONSULTED': The document is consulted in this task but not modified.
- 'UPDATED': The document is modified in this task.
- 'DELETED': The document is deleted in this task.

11.2.7 PD_VARIABLE

This table describes all the variables used in the execution of the procedure.

VAR_ID — Identifier of the variable. The system will assign a unique identifier for every variable.

PROC_ID — Identifier of the procedure to which the variable is attached.

NAME — Name of the variable (for documentation purposes).

DESCRIPTION — Variable role description.

TYPE — Type of the variable (enumerated value supported by the auxiliary table PD_ENUM_VAR_TYPE). Possible values for this field are:

Table 11.7. PD_VARIABLE

Column	Format	Constraint
VAR_ID	Numeric	Primary Key
PROC_ID	Numeric	References PD_PROCEDURE
NAME	Alphanumeric	NOT NULL
DESCRIPTION	Alphanumeric	
TYPE	Enumerated	PD_ENUM_VAR_TYPE
DEF_VALUE	Alphanumeric	OPTIONAL

'NORMAL': Standard MMTCA variable.
'DOC_LIST': Variable supporting a document list.

DEF_VALUE When specified, a default value specified on the procedure definition time.

11.2.8 LINK support tables

The set of tables described in this section provides the means of expressing the topological and logical (predecessor, successor, conditions, etc.) relationships between tasks in the procedure work-flow.

PD_LINK: This table describes the link entities.

LINK_ID Identifier of the link The system will automatically assign a unique identifier for every link.
PROC_ID Identifier of the procedure to which the link belongs to.

PD_PRED_LINK: This table describes the link predecessor task relation.

LINK_ID Identifier of the link.
TASK_PRED Identifier of the predecessor task of the link.

PD_SUCC_LINK: This table describes the link successor task relation.

LINK_ID Identifier of the link.
TASK_SUCC Identifier of the successor task of the link.

PD_NAND_LINK: This table is used to express the link enabling conditions. It provides the basis for the activation of tasks depending on their predecessor links, by describing a NAND link relation. A NAND is described by one or more records in the PD_NAND_LINK table with the same TRIG_LINK and LINK_ID. When the TRIG_LINK is enabled the output link (LINK_ID) will be enabled, depending on the existence of the NAND input links (PREV_LINK) in

Table 11.8. PD_LINK

Column	Format	Constraint
LINK_ID	Numeric	Primary Key
PROC_ID	Numeric	References PD_PROCEDURE

Table 11.9. PD_PRED_LINK

Column	Format	Constraint
LINK_ID	Numeric	References PD_LINK
TASK_PRED	Numeric	References PD_TASK

Table 11.10. PD_SUCC_LINK

Column	Format	Constraint
LINK_ID	Numeric	References PD_LINK
TASK_SUCC	Numeric	References PD_TASK

records with this LINK_ID and TRIG_LINK: in any case this evaluation causes the PREV_LINK(s) and the TRIG_LINK to be disabled. Several NAND relations may be chained to define more complex enabling conditions for links.

LINK_ID	Identifier of the NAND output link.
PREV_LINK	Identifier of the a NAND input link.
TRIG_LINK	Identifier of a trigger link used to force evaluation of the NAND.

PD_VAR_LINK: This table is used to express variable related link enabling conditions. When the trigger link TRIG_LINK is enabled, if the value of the variable is equal to the VALUE of the PD_VAR_LINK the output link LINK_ID will be enabled. In any case, the TRIG_LINK will then be disabled. Several

Table 11.11. PD_NAND_LINK

Column	Format	Constraint
LINK_ID	Numeric	References PD_LINK
PREV_LINK	Numeric	References PD_LINK
TRIG_LINK	Numeric	References PD_LINK

Table 11.12. PD_VAR_LINK

Column	Format	Constraint
LINK_ID	Numeric	References PD_LINK
VAR_ID	Numeric	References PD_VARIABLE
TRIG_LINK	Numeric	References PD_LINK
VALUE	Alphanumeric	

VAR_LINK and NAND relations may be chained to define more complex enabling condition of a link.

LINK_ID	Identifier of the NAND output link.
VAR_ID	Identifier of the related variable.
TRIG_LINK	Identifier of the trigger link.
VALUE	Value to be checked for equality with the related PD_VARIABLE value.

Table 11.13. PD_PARTICPANT

Column	Format	Constraint
PARTIC_ID	Numeric	Primary key
PROC_ID	Numeric	References PD_PROCEDURE
NAME	Alphanumeric	NOT NULL
GROUP_ID	Numeric	References ADM_GROUP_PROFILE

11.2.9 PD_PARTICIPANT

This table describes the logical participants in a procedure, i.e. roles that may be involved in some of its tasks.

There are formal or logical users and real MMTCA users. Formal users can be defined in the programming phase and be replaced by real users at instantiation or run-time.

PARTIC_ID	Identifier of the participant. The system will automatically assign a unique identifier for every participant.
PROC_ID	Identifier of the procedure.
NAME	Logical name that identifies the participant in the procedure definition.
GROUP_ID	The user group the participant belongs to.

11.2.10 PD_TASK_POT_PARTIC

Table 11.14. PD_TASK_POT_PARTIC

Column	Format	Constraint
TASK_ID	Numeric	References PD_TASK
PARTIC_ID	Numeric	References PD_PARTICIPANT
ROLE	Enumerated	PD_ENUM_ROLE
PRIORITY	Enumerated	PD_ENUM_PRIOR_FL
PRESENCE_REQ	Enumerated	PD_ENUM_PRESENCE

This table describes the potential participants in a task. On run-time, the actual participants will be set from the group of potential participants.

TASK_ID	Identifier of the task.
PARTIC_ID	Identifier of the participant.
ROLE	Role in the task of the -potential- participant (enumerated value supported by the auxiliary table PD_ENUM_ROLE). Possible values for this field are: 'CHAIRMAN': Chairman in the cooperative session. 'NONE': Non-Chairman in the CS or not applicable (asynchronous task).
PRIORITY	Participant priority to be used on the prioritised floor policy (numeric enumerated value supported by the auxiliary table PD_ENUM_PRIOR_FL). Possible values for this field are: 'HIGH': High priority. 'NORMAL': Normal priority. 'LOW': Low priority.
PRESENCE_REQ	Indication of the need of the presence of this participant in the cooperative session (enumerated value supported by the auxiliary table PD_ENUM_PRESENCE). Possible values for this field are: 'ESSENTIAL': The cooperative session can not take place without the presence of this participant. 'OPTIONAL': The presence of this participant is not essential for the cooperative session to start.

11.2.11 PD_PROF_FILES

This table describes all the profile files associated to an application or tool on procedure definition.

Table 11.15. PD_PROF_FILES

Column	Format	Constraint
APPL_ID	Numeric	References PD_APPLICATION
NAME	Alphanumeric	NOT NULL
DESCRIPTION	Alphanumeric	OPTIONAL
PATH	Alphanumeric	NOT NULL
REF_PATH	Alphanumeric	NOT NULL
TYPE	Enumerated	ADM_ENUM_PROF_TYPE

APPL_ID	Identifier of the application to which the profile file is related.
NAME	Name of the profile file.
DESCRIPTION	Description of the purpose and contents of the profile file.
PATH	The path where the profile physical file is located.
REF_PATH	The path to the profile file in the server disks.
TYPE	Indication of the need of the presence of the profile file (enumerated value supported by the auxiliary table ADM_ENUM_PROF_TYPE). Possible values for this field are: 'MANDATORY': The profile file presence is mandatory. 'OPTIONAL': The profile file presence is optional. 'ON_CREATION_ONLY': The profile file presence is needed only on creation.

11.2.12 Procedure Definition (PD) auxiliary tables and sequences

Some auxiliary tables have been defined to support the enumerated types for the enumerated fields, namely: PD_ENUM_PRIOR_LEV, PD_ENUM_TASK_TYPE, PD_ENUM_FLOOR_POL, PD_ENUM_PATH_TYPE, PD_ENUM_FNAME_TYPE, PD_ENUM_ROLE, PD_ENUM_EDIT_ACT, PD_ENUM_MEET_TYPE, PD_ENUM_PRESENCE, PD_ENUM_PRIOR_FL.

A number of ORACLE Sequences have been defined to generate unique keys automatically.

11.3 Metadocument (MD) tables description

11.3.1 MD_METADOCUMENT

This table will contain all the metadocuments (procedure instances) in the MMTCA environment.

METADOC_ID	Identifier of the metadocument. The system will assign a unique identifier for each metadocument created within the MMTCA environment.
PROC_ID	Identifier of the procedure which the metadocument is an instance of.

Table 11.16. MD_METADOCUMENT

Column	Format	Constraint
METADOC_ID	Numeric	Primary Key
PROC_ID	Numeric	References PD_PROCEDURE
METADOC_STAT	Enumerated	MD_ENUM_PROC_STAT
NAME	Alphanumeric	NOT NULL
DESCRIPTION	Alphanumeric	OPTIONAL
TYPE	Enumerated	PD_ENUM_PROC_TYPE
ORGANIZER	Numeric	References ADM_MMTCA_USER
FOLDER_PATH	Alphanumeric	NOT NULL
START_DATE	Alphanumeric	
START_TIME	Alphanumeric	
PRIORITY_LEVEL	Enumerated	PD_ENUM_PRIOR_LEV
DURATION	Numeric	OPTIONAL

METADOC_STAT State of the instance procedure (enumerated value supported by the auxiliary table MD_ENUM_PROC_STAT). There are three states:

- 'SCHEDULED': The instance has been created, but the start time has not yet arrived.
- RUNNING': Some tasks in the procedure are in the active, running, or interrupted state.
- 'TERMINATED': There are no pending tasks in the metadocument task in-tray. All the activated tasks in the metadocument are in the terminated state.

NAME Descriptive name of the instance.

DESCRIPTION Description of the purpose of the instance.

TYPE Type of the metadocument procedure (enumerated value supported by the auxiliary table PD_ENUM_PROC_TYPE). Possible values for this field are:

- 'NORMAL': Standard MMTCA procedure.
- 'CS_PROCEDURE': Ready-to-run Cooperative Session procedure.

ORGANIZER Identifier of the user who is responsible for this instance (i.e. the user that instantiated the procedure).

FOLDER_PATH When specified, is the default directory where the document files are located depending on its PATH_TYPE. The initial value of this field is taken from the DEFAULT_PATH of the PD_PROCEDURE table.

START_DATE	Instance scheduled start date.
START_TIME	Instance scheduled start time.
PRIORITY_LEVEL	Priority level of execution of this instance (numeric enumerated value supported by the auxiliary table PD_ENUM_PRIOR_LEV). Possible values for this field are 0 (Low), 1 (Medium) and 2 (High).
DURATION	Estimated duration of the procedure instance.

11.3.2 MD_INTRAY_TASK

This table describes the set of tasks (task instance) that are activated (scheduled, ready to start, executing or terminated) in the metadocument.

The table Primary key is the triple (METADOC_ID, TASK_ID, SEQ_ACTIVATION).

METADOC_ID	Identifier of the metadocument to which the task instance belongs.
TASK_ID	Identifier of the task definition corresponding to the instance.
SEQ_ACTIVATION	Number of times this task has been activated in the execution of this metadocument.
TASK_STATE	State of the task instance (enumerated value supported by the auxiliary table MD_ENUM_TASK_STAT). The states are:

'SCHEDULED':	The task is waiting for activation (i.e. its start time has no been reached).
'READY':	the task is ready for execution.
'RUNNING':	the task is being executed by the user.
'SUSPENDED':	the task has been interrupted by the user.
'TERMINATED':	the task has finished its execution.

FLOOR_POLICY	Exchange floor policy (enumerated value supported by the auxiliary table PD_ENUM_FLOOR_POL). Possible values

Table 11.17. MD_INTRAY TASK

Column	Format	Constraint
METADOC_ID	Numeric	References MD_METADOCUMENT
TASK_ID	Numeric	References PD_TASK
SEQ_ACTIVATION	Numeric	
TASK_STATE	Enumerated	MD_ENUM_TASK_STAT
FLOOR_POLICY	Enumerated	PD_ENUM_FLOOR_POL
MEETING_TYPE	Enumerated	PD_ENUM_MEET_TYPE
DURATION	Numeric	OPTIONAL

for this field are:

'CHAIRMAN_DRIVEN':	The chairman is responsible of allocating the floor to one of the participants who ask for it.
'FLOOR_DRIVEN':	The floor holder is responsible of allocating the floor to one of the participants who ask for it.
'FCFS':	Floor allocation follows First Come First Served once the floor holder releases it.
'PRIORITIZED':	The floor is allocated to the requester participant with higher priority once the floor holder releases it.
'NONE':	No applicable floor policy (asynchronous task).

MEETING_TYPE — Meeting type in a cooperative session (enumerated value supported by the auxiliary table PD_ENUM_MEET_TYPE). Possible values for this field are:

'OPEN':	Open meeting, where joining an on-going session is allowed.
'CLOSED':	Closed meeting, where joining an on-going session is not allowed.

DURATION — Estimated duration of the task instance.

11.3.3 MD_DOCUMENT

This table describes the set of actual documents used or produced in the procedure instance execution, in front of the logical documents described in the Document Definitions.

The table Primary key is the pair (METADOC_ID, DOC_ID).

Table 11.18. MD_DOCUMENT

Column	Format	Constraint
METADOC_ID	Numeric	References MD_METADOCUMENT
DOC_ID	Numeric	References PD_DOCUMENT
PATH	Alphanumeric	NOT NULL
FILE_NAME	Alphanumeric	NOT NULL
STATUS	Enumerated	MD_ENUM_DOC_STAT
REF_PATH	Alphanumeric	NOT NULL
LOCK_TASK_ID	Numeric	References PD_TASK
LOCK_SEQ_ACT	Numeric	

METADOC_ID	Identifier of the metadocument to which the document instance belongs.
DOC_ID	Identifier of the document definition corresponding to the instance.
PATH	The directory where the document physical file is located.
FILE_NAME	The document's physical file name in the node.
STATUS	State of the document instance (enumerated value supported by the auxiliary table MD_ENUM_DOC_STAT). The states are: 'NOT_CREATED': The document has not been created. 'UP_TO_DATE': The file copy in the server is up-to-date. 'IN_A_NODE': The file has been sent to one node with modification permissions.
REF_PATH	The path to the document file in the server disks.
LOCK_TASK_ID	Identifier of the active task or instance that has locked this document because it is creating or updating it.
LOCK_SEQ_ACT	SEQ_ACTIVATION of the locking task.

Table 11.19. MD_LINK

Column	Format	Constraint
METADOC_ID	Numeric	References MD_METADOCUMENT
LINK_ID	Numeric	References PD_LINK

11.3.4 MD_LINK

This table describes the link instances.

METADOC_ID	Identifier of the metadocument to which the link instance belongs.
LINK_ID	Identifier of the link definition corresponding to the instance.

Table 11.20. MD_VARIABLE

Column	Format	Constraint
METADOC_ID	Numeric	References MD_METADOCUMENT
VAR_ID	Numeric	References PD_VARIABLE
VALUE	Alphanumeric	

11.3.5 MD_VARIABLE

This table describes the container of the run-time values of global variables defined or used during the programming phase, in front of the logical variables described in the Variable Definitions.

The table Primary key is the pair (METADOC_ID, VAR_ID).

METADOC_ID	Identifier of the metadocument to which the link instance belongs.
VAR_ID	Identifier of the variable definition corresponding to the instance.
VALUE	Variable instance value.

Table 11.21. MD_PARTICIPANT

Column	Format	Constraint
METADOC_ID	Numeric	References MD_METADOCUMENT
PARTIC_ID	Numeric	References PD_PARTICIPANT
USER_ID	Numeric	References ADM_MMTCA_USER

11.3.6 MD_PARTICIPANT

This table describes the actual participants in a procedure instance.

The table Primary key is the triple (METADOC_ID, PARTIC_ID, USER_ID).

METADOC_ID	Identifier of the metadocument to which the participant instance belongs.
PARTIC_ID	Identifier of the participant definition corresponding to the instance.
USER_ID	Identifier of the actual user description.

11.3.7 MD_TASK_PARTIC

This table describes the instantiated participants involved in a task.

METADOC_ID	Identifier of the metadocument to which the participant instance belongs.
TASK_ID	Identifier of the task definition corresponding to the instance.
SEQ_ACTIVATION	Number of activation of the related task instance.

Table 11.22. MD_TASK_PARTIC

Column	Format	Constraint
METADOC_ID	Numeric	References MD_METADOCUMENT
TASK_ID	Numeric	References PD_TASK
SEQ_ACTIVATION	Numeric	
PARTIC_ID	Numeric	References PD_PARTICIPANT
USER_ID	Numeric	References ADM_MMTCA_USER
ROLE	Enumerated	PD_ENUM_ROLE
PRIORITY	Enumerated	PD_ENUM_PRIOR_FL
PRESENCE_REQ	Enumerated	PD_ENUM_PRESENCE

PARTIC_ID — Identifier of the participant definition corresponding to the instance.

USER_ID — Identifier of the actual user description.

ROLE — Role in the task of the potential participant (enumerated value supported by the auxiliary table PD_ENUM_ROLE). Possible values for this field are:

- 'CHAIRMAN': Chairman in the cooperative session.
- 'NONE': Non-Chairman in the CS or not applicable (asynchronous task).

PRIORITY — Participant priority to be used on the prioritised floor policy (enumerated value supported by the auxiliary table PD_ENUM_PRIOR_FL). Possible values for this field are:

- 'HIGH': High priority.
- 'NORMAL': Normal priority.
- 'LOW': Low priority.

PRESENCE_REQ — Indication of the need of the presence of this participant in the cooperative session (enumerated value supported by the auxiliary table PD_ENUM_PRESENCE). Possible values for this field are:

- 'ESSENTIAL': The cooperative session can not take place without the presence of this participant.
- 'OPTIONAL': The presence of this participant is not essential for the cooperative session to start.

11.3.8 MD_RUN_TASK_PARTIC

This table describes the real participants executing the task.

Table 11.23. MD_RUN_TASK_PARTIC

Column	Format	Constraint
METADOC_ID	Numeric	References MD_METADOCUMENT
TASK_ID	Numeric	References PD_TASK
SEQ_ACTIVATION	Numeric	
USER_ID	Numeric	References ADM_MMTCA_USER

METADOC_ID Identifier of the metadocument to which the participant instance belongs.

TASK_ID Identifier of the task definition corresponding to the instance.

SEQ_ACTIVATION Number of activation of the related task instance.

USER_ID Identifier of the actual user description.

11.3.9 MD_COOPERATIVE_SESS

This table describes the properties of cooperative sessions (corresponding to synchronous task instances).

Table 11.24. MD_COOPERATIVE_SESS

Column	Format	Constraint
METADOC_ID	Numeric	References MD_METADOCUMENT
TASK_ID	Numeric	References PD_TASK
SEQ_ACTIVATION	Numeric	
CHAIRMAN_ID	Numeric	References ADM_MMTCA_USER
FLOOR_OWNER_ID	Numeric	References ADM_MMTCA_USER
FLOOR_POLICY	Enumerated	PD_ENUM_FLOOR_POL

The table Primary key is the triple (METADOC_ID, TASK_ID, SEQ_ACTIVATION).

METADOC_ID Identifier of the metadocument to which the task instance belongs.

TASK_ID Identifier of the task definition corresponding to the instance.

SEQ_ACTIVATION Number of activation of this task in the metadocument execution.

CHAIRMAN_ID Identifier of the cooperative session chairman.

FLOOR_OWNER_ID Identifier of the current holder of the floor.

FLOOR_POLICY	Exchange floor policy (enumerated value supported by the auxiliary table PD_ENUM_FLOOR_POL). Possible values for this field are:

'CHAIRMAN_DRIVEN':	The chairman is responsible of allocating the floor to one of the participants who ask for it.
'FLOOR_DRIVEN':	The floor holder is responsible of allocating the floor to one of the participants who ask for it.
'FCFS':	Floor allocation follows the First Come First Served once the floor holder releases it.
'PRIORITIZED':	The floor is allocated to the requester participant with higher priority once the floor holder releases it.
'NONE':	No applicable floor policy (asynchronous task).

11.3.10 MD_PROF_FILES

This table describes all the profile files associated to an application or tool at run-time.

Table 11.25. MD_PROF_FILES

Column	Format	Constraint
METADOC_ID	Numeric	References MD_METADOCUMENT
APPL_ID	Numeric	References PD_APPLICATION
NAME	Alphanumeric	NOT NULL
PATH	Alphanumeric	NOT NULL
REF_PATH	Alphanumeric	NOT NULL
TYPE	Enumerated	ADM_ENUM_PROF_TYPE

METADOC_ID	Identifier of the metadocument to which the application instance is attached.
APPL_ID	Identifier of the application to which the profile file is related.
NAME	Name of the profile file.
PATH	The path where the profile physical file is located.
REF_PATH	The path to the profile file in the server disks.

TYPE — Indication of the need of the presence of the profile file (enumerated value supported by the auxiliary table ADM_ENUM_PROF_TYPE). Possible values for this field are:

'MANDATORY':	The profile file presence is mandatory.
'OPTIONAL':	The profile file presence is optional.
'ON_CREATION_ONLY':	The profile file presence is needed only on creation.

11.3.11 Metadocument (MD) auxiliary tables and sequences

Some auxiliary tables have been defined to support the enumerated types for the enumerated fields, namely: MD_ENUM_PROC_STAT, MD_ENUM_TASK_STAT, MD_ENUM_DOC_STATUS.

A number of ORACLE Sequences have been defined to generate unique keys automatically.

11.4 Administration (ADM) tables description

11.4.1 ADM_MMTCA_NODE

This table describes the nodes connected to the MMTCA environment.

Table 11.26. ADM_MMTCA_NODE

Column	Format	Constraint
NODE_ID	Numeric	Primary Key
NAME	Alphanumeric	
ADDRESS	Alphanumeric	
STATUS	Enumerated	ADM_ENUM_NODE_STATUS
LOCATION	Alphanumeric	

NODE_ID	Identifier of the node. The system will assign a unique identifier for each node in the MMTCA environment.
NAME	Unique name that identifies the node.
ADDRESS	Node network address.

STATUS Known status of the node (enumerated value supported by the auxiliary table ADM_ENUM_NODE_STATUS). The values are 'ON_LINE' and 'OFF_LINE'.

Table 11.27. ADM_MMTCA_USER

Column	Format	Constraint
USER_ID	Numeric	Primary Key
NAME	Alphanumeric	UNIQUE
PASSWORD	Alphanumeric	NOT NULL
FULL_NAME	Alphanumeric	
PERMISSION	Enumerated	ADM_ENUM_PERMISS
DEFAULT_NODE	Numeric	References ADM_MMTCA_NODE

11.4.2 ADM_MMTCA_USER

This table describes actual users allowed to login into the MMTCA system.

USER_ID Identifier of the user. The system will assign a unique identifier for each user in the MMTCA environment.

NAME System name of the user (must be unique).

PASSWORD MMTCA access password.

FULL_NAME Administrative name of the user.

PERMISSION User permission level (enumerated value supported by the auxiliary table ADM_ENUM_PERMISS). The values are:

- 'ADMINISTRATOR': This user can perform all the administrative activities including making modifications in the database objects (user, nodes, etc.) at the server site and re-edit already downloaded procedures in the node.
- 'PROGRAMMER': This user can program new procedures in the node and download it to the server.
- 'ORGANIZER': This user can instance and start procedures.
- 'USER': This user can start task in which he is involved.

DEFAULT_NODE Node where the user normally works (for administrator information).

11.4.3 ADM_LOGIN

This table describes the current connections to the MMTCA environment.

Table 11.28. ADM_LOGIN

Column	Format	Constraint
USER_ID	Numeric	References ADM_MMTCA_USER
NODE_ID	Numeric	References ADM_MMTCA_NODE
LOGIN_DATE	Alphanumeric	
LOGIN_TIME	Alphanumeric	

NODE_ID	Identifier of the login node.
USER_ID	Identifier of the user who is logged in.
LOGIN_DATE	Login date.
LOGIN_TIME	Login time.

11.4.4 ADM_LOGIN HISTORY

This table describes the history of connections to the MMTCA environment.

Table 11.29. ADM_LOGIN_HISTORY

Column	Format	Constraint
USER_ID	Numeric	References ADM_MMTCA_USER
NODE_ID	Numeric	References ADM_MMTCA_NODE
LOGIN_DATE	Alphanumeric	
LOGIN_TIME	Alphanumeric	
LOGOUT_DATE	Alphanumeric	
LOGOUT_TIME	Alphanumeric	

NODE_ID	Identifier of the node where the login was made.
USER_ID	Identifier of the user who logged in.
LOGIN_DATE	Login date.
LOGIN_TIME	Login time.
LOGOUT_DATE	Logout date.
LOGOUT_TIME	Logout time.

Table 11.30. ADM_GROUP_PROFILE

Column	Format	Constraint
GROUP_ID	Numeric	Primary key
NAME	Alphanumeric	UNIQUE
DESCRIPTION	Alphanumeric	

11.4.5 ADM_GROUP_PROFILE

This table describes the actual group of users (user profiles) in the organisation.

GROUP_ID — Identifier of the user group. The system will assign a unique identifier for each group in the MMTCA environment.

NAME — Name of the user group (unique).

DESCRIPTION — Description of the user group.

Table 11.31. ADM_USER_GROUP

Column	Format	Constraint
USER_ID	Numeric	References ADM_MMTCA_USER
GROUP_ID	Numeric	References ADM_GROUP_PROFILE

11.4.6 ADM_USER_GROUP

This table-relation describes the relation between the actual users and the group(s) they belong to.

USER_ID — Identifier of the user.

GROUP_ID — Identifier of the group.

11.4.7 ADM_PROF_TEMPLATE

This table describes the profile templates associated to any application executable on MMTCA.

Table 11.32. ADM_PROF_TEMPLATE

Column	Format	Constraint
PROF_ID	Numeric	Primary key
NAME	Alphanumeric	NOT NULL
FULL_NAME	Alphanumeric	NOT NULL

GROUP_ID — Identifier of the tool profile template. The system will assign a unique identifier for each profile template in the MMTCA environment.

NAME — Name of the profile template.

FULL_NAME — The full name (path and name) of the profile template.

11.4.8 ADM_PROF_FILES

This table describes all the profile files associated to an application profile template.

Table 11.33. ADM_PROF_FILES

Column	Format	Constraint
PROF_ID	Numeric	References PD_APPLICATION
NAME	Alphanumeric	NOT NULL
DESCRIPTION	Alphanumeric	
PATH	Alphanumeric	NOT NULL
TYPE	Enumerated	ADM_ENUM_PROF_TYPE

PROF_ID — Identifier of the application profile template to which the profile file is related.

NAME — Name of the profile file.

DESCRIPTION — Description of the purpose and contents of the profile file.

PATH — The path where the profile physical file is located.

TYPE — Indication of the need of the presence of the profile file (enumerated value supported by the auxiliary table ADM_ENUM_PROF_TYPE). Possible values for this field are:

- 'MANDATORY': The profile file presence is mandatory.
- 'OPTIONAL': The profile file presence is optional.
- 'ON_CREATION_ONLY': The profile file presence is needed only on creation.

11.4.9 Administration (ADM) Auxiliary Tables and Sequences

Some auxiliary tables have been defined to support the enumerated types for the enumerated fields, namely: ADM_ENUM_PERMISS, ADM_ENUM_NODE_STAT and ADM_ENUM_PROF_TYPE.

A number of ORACLE sequences have been defined to automatically generate unique keys.

11.5 Concepts of Operation

When the procedure designer uses ViEW to define a procedure, the details are entered in the procedure definition (PD) tables described above. The metadocument (MD) tables are used at run time to control an activation of the procedure. In this section we explain the rationale for the database tables by discussing what happens at run time.

Tasks are ready to run, and will be visible in somebody's Intray, when a record with that TASK_ID and state='READY' is in the MD_INTRAY_TASK table. The first task(s) in a procedure are put there when the procedure in initiated (metadocument is created). Otherwise, MMTCA places tasks in MD_INTRAY_TASK only during the ComputeWorkflow function (this is just a matter of consistency of style: no damage will occur if someone puts an entry there themselves, provided they respect the database structure).

The ComputeWorkflow function will place an entry in MD_INTRAY_TASK if a link to that task is enabled. Links are automatically enabled when preceding tasks terminate. (They can also be enabled manually: a good way of getting a task to run is to use links and place an entry in MD_LINK that will enable the task.)

11.5.1 A Two-task Example

The example procedure shown in Fig. 11.2 is probably the simplest possible. All procedure, task etc identifiers are integers in the database, but letters are used in the following discussion for clarity.

If a user starts up this procedure, this creates a new metadocument (record in the MD_METADOCUMENT table), and activates the first task(s) (an entry for the first task in MD_INTRAY_TASK).

When task T1 eventually completes, the status field in the MD_INTRAY_TASK table will be changed to terminated:

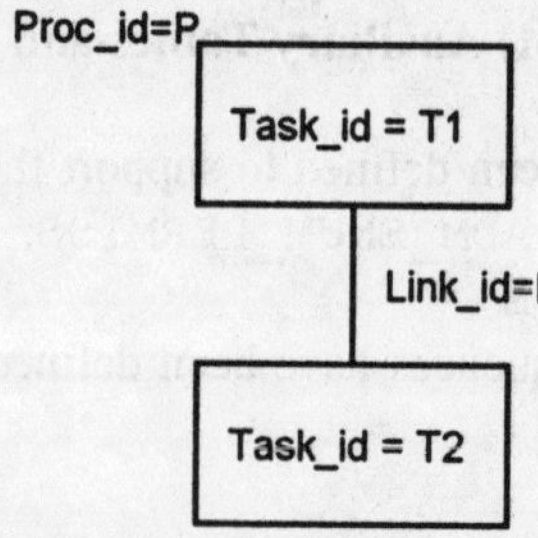

Fig. 11.2. An example procedure

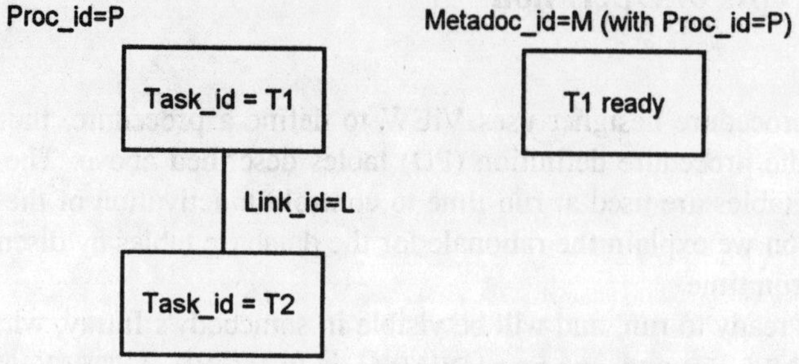

Fig. 11.3. Instantiation of the procedure

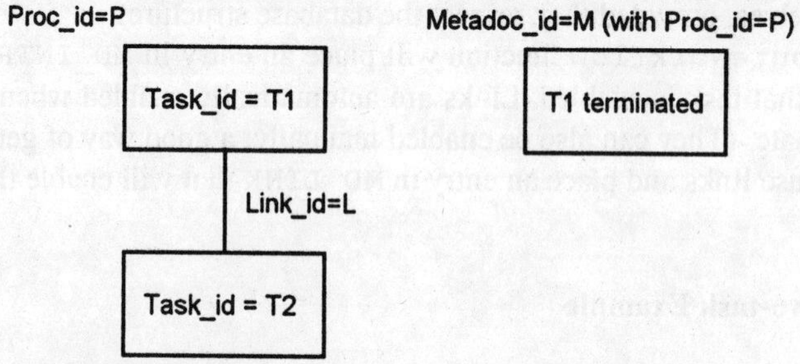

Fig. 11.4. On completion of T1

Now the `ComputeWorkflow` function does its work. It has two phases. In the first phase, the links whose predecessors are terminated tasks are activated (a record is inserted in `MD_LINK`) and these tasks are deleted from `MD_INTRAY_TASK`:

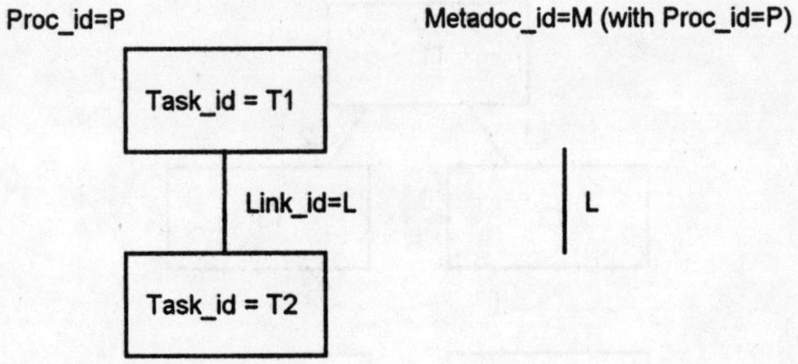

Fig. 11.5. Compute Workfolw, phase 1.

The second phase of `ComputeWorkflow` activates the tasks which are

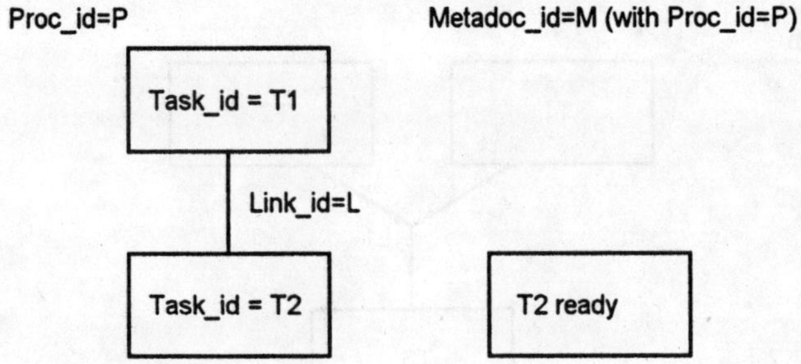

Fig. 11.6. Compute Workflow, phase 2

successors of the active links (by placing a record in `MD_INTRAY_TASK`), and removes the links thus used.

Task T2 now appears in the appropriate Intrays. In this case, when T2 finishes, the ComputeWorkflow function will simply remove the terminated task from `MD_INTRAY_TASK`, since there are no links leaving T2 in the procedure.

11.5.2 Parallelism

A fork operation occurs whenever a task is predecessor to more than one link, as in Fig. 11.7.and a join operation occurs when a task is successor to more than one link, as in Fig. 11.8.

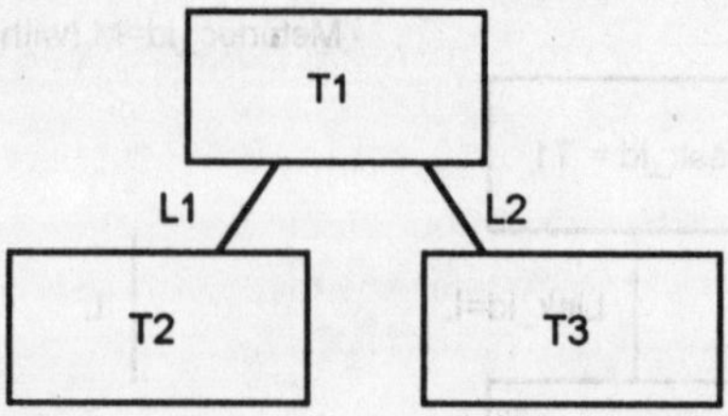

Fig. 11.7. Fork

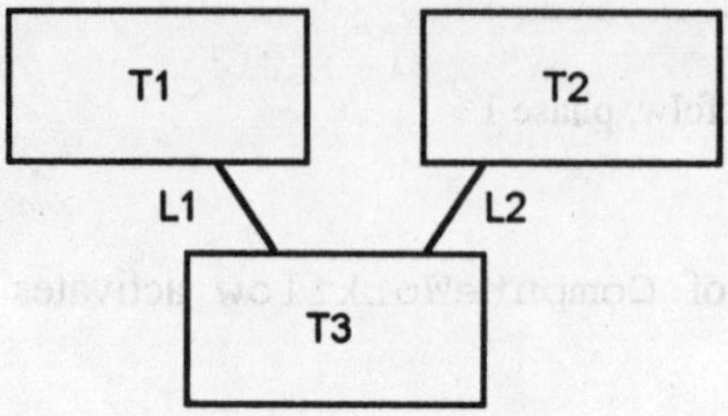

Fig. 11.8. Join

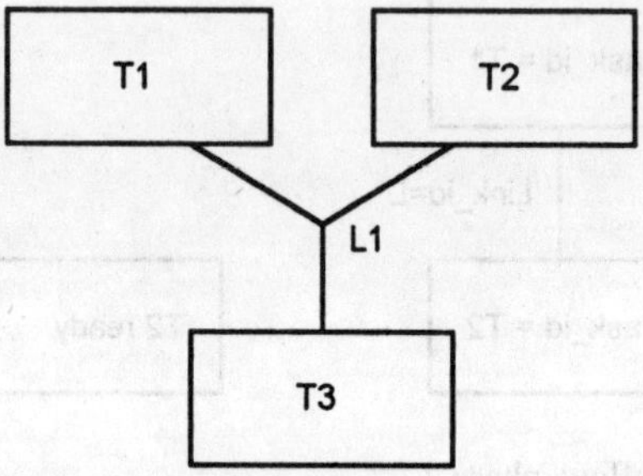

Fig 11.9. T3 should start on completion of T1 or T2.

In this case T3 will not start until both T1 and T2 terminate. It is perhaps worth examining what happens within the `ComputeWorkflow` function here. When this last procedure is started up, both

If it is required that task T3 should start whenever T1 or T2 finishes, the same link should be used. This is not yet supported by ViEW, but can be arranged by altering entries in the database tables (`PD_SUCC_LINK` and `PD_PREV_LINK`).

11.6 Task Script Executor

The role of the task script executor (TSE) in this version of the MMTCA prototype is currently taken by MMBATCH. This is given a task script to run, typically a series of statements which run the actions for that task. MMBATCH calls the command processor functions directly (the command processor is implemented as a DLL).

MMBATCH is a basic Windows application which takes a task script name as a command line parameter, as well as task information (metadoc_id, task_id, seq_activation). It then runs the script, and terminates when the script finishes.

MMBATCH supports a limited number of script commands. The task script syntax is given below, where ┤ denotes end-of-file, and characters in bold face are in the script (case is not significant).

```
Program       = {Statement} ┤.
Statement     = DDEExecute|StrCat|DDETimeout|DDETerminate|
                DDEInitiate| WinWaitClose|Comment .
DDEExecute    = [VarName =]
                DDEExecute(IntegerOrVar,StringOrVar).
StrCat        = VarName = StrCat(StringOrVar{,StringOrVar}).
DDETimeout    = [ VarName =] DDETimeout(IntegerOrVar).
WinWaitClose  = [ VarName =] WinWaitClose(StringOrVar).
DDEInitiate   = VarName =
                DDEInitiate(StringOrVar,StringOrVar).
DDETerminate  = [VarName =] DDETerminate(IntegerOrVar).
IntegerOrVar  = Number | KnownVarName.
StringOrVar   = String | KnownVarName.
```

Number is any sequence of numeric characters.

String starts and ends with the double quote character (") and contains any printing characters with the following restrictions:

- the string cannot contain the newline or carriage return character.
- if a double quote should appear in the string it should be preceded by a double quote character; thus ("") does **not** denote the end of the string.
- maximum string length is 255 characters.

VarName begins with a letter and contains letters, digits, and underscores. A *KnownVarName* is similar but

- the name should match a previously used *VarName*
- that the value of the variable should be of the type expected.

Comment starts with a semi-colon and continues to the end of the line.

With the exception of the functions **StrCat**, **DDEExecute** and **WinWaitClose**, no action is taken on parsing a function.

StrCat catenates the denoted parameters into the receiver variable. A receiver variable must be nominated. The catenated string currently has a maximum length of 1024 characters. Parameters may be either strings or named variables. If the parameter is not delimited by double quotes it must match the name of a previously declared variable. This variable may contain either numeric or string data.

DDEExecute calls the Task Command Processor module (the SA DLL) of the MMTCA node software. The "channel" parameter is ignored, the second parameter defines the action to be performed by the SA module.

WinWaitClose ignores the parameter data, and asks MMTCA to be notified when an action terminates. Since there is only one action being performed at one time, this will be the action which would be performed in the nominated window. Parsing of the input task script file is suspended until notification is received that the action has terminated.

11.6.1 Task Command Processor

The task command processor is a DLL which implements DDE server capabilities for the MMTCA Intray application. Currently it only processes a limited set of DDE commands, and is used to control the execution of actions in the task script. The commands which are implemented are:

- **StartAction** - this command starts an action in the task.
- **ActionComplete** - this command signals the completion of the currently running action.
- **StartNsAction** - this command starts a non-shared action in a CS task.
- **SetConditionLink** - this command allows the user to set the output for a condition box link.
- **EndTask** - this commands signals the end of the currently running task.

The first four commands are also made available as exported DLL functions. The DDE format for the task commands is given below:

[**StartAction(***Type*,*ActionID*,*MetadocID*,*TaskID*,*SeqActivation***)**
]

where *Type* is **SYNC** or **ASYNC**

[**ActionComplete**]

This command takes no parameters.

[**StartNsAction(***Type*,*ActionID*,*MetadocID*,*TaskID*,*SeqAct***)**]

where *Type* is **SYNC** or **ASYNC**

[**SetConditionLink(***ConditionName*,*MetadocId*,*Status*,*AskUser***)**]

where *ConditionName* = name of the condition box
MetadocId=metadocument ID (or **0** for current task metadocument)
Status = **TRUE** or **FALSE** for the output of the condition
AskUser = **TRUE** or **FALSE** (if **TRUE**, *Status* is ignored)

[**EndTask(**{*Status*{, *ResultsOption*>}}**)**]

where *Status* = **COMPLETE** or **INCOMPLETE**.
ResultsOption = **SAVE** or **DISCARD**

The function prototypes for the exported DLL functions are given below:

```
BOOL FAR PASCAL SA_StartAction (LPTASK_ID lpTaskID,
        WORD ActionID, int iType);
```

```
BOOL FAR PASCAL SA_ActionComplete (void);
BOOL FAR PASCAL SA_StartNsAction (LPTASK_ID lpTaskID,
        WORD ActionID, int iType);
```

11.6.2 Additional Task Functions

There are some additional task functions which can be called as exported DLL functions. These allow control of information on variable values from within a task, and setting of workflow condition box output values. The functions provided allow:

- Retrieval of a variable value from the MMTCA database.
- Setting of a variable value in the MMTCA database.
- Enabling of variable links in the MMTCA database.
- Setting of condition box output value for calculating workflow in the MMTCA database.

The first three of the above functions identify their variable by name, and for the instance of the variable in the procedure of the currently running task. The last function allows specification of the procedure instance, but will default to the instance for the currently executing task if zero is supplied. The function prototypes for the additional task functions are given below:

```
BOOL FAR PASCAL MMTCA_GetVariable (LPSTR name, LPSTR buf,
     int len);
BOOL FAR PASCAL MMTCA_SetVariable (LPSTR name, LPSTR buf,
     int len);
BOOL FAR PASCAL MMTCA_EnableVarLinks (LPSTR name);
BOOL FAR PASCAL MMTCA_SetConditionLink (LPSTR lpszLinkName,
     WORD wMetadocID, BOOL bStatus, BOOL bAskUser);
```

11.7 Event management

The Event Manager (EM) module is a collection of three DLLs that provides the functionality for the registration of the applications being executed and the recording and playing back of the events. It consists of three different components:

- The ***Event Manager*** dynamic link library, includes the Event Manager interface and has the control of the hooks' activation,
- The ***EMHooks*** dynamic link library, includes the functions related with the hooks mechanism,

- The *Queue* dynamic link library, encapsulates the queue of incoming events and a second queue to store temporally events between a mouse click down and a mouse click up.

The overall design of the EM along with the relationships with other module's components are shown in fig. 11.10:

The EM module provides the following functionality:

- Event Management.
- Floor mechanism control.

This functionality allows the full control of the CS. The event management is in charge of recording all the events in the floor holder's node and sending them to other participant's nodes, where they are played back. The floor mechanism control is in charge of controlling the floor requesting, passing or grabbing. All possible floor policy schema have been implemented in the MMTCA Toolbox ver. 4.

The EM application is based on the use of hooks, which represent a mechanism to intercept events. This mechanism is needed for the following operations:

- Registration of the applications taking part in an action.
- Detection of the new Cooperative Applications that are started from another running Cooperative Application, i.e., MS-Draw in MS-Word or any Help application. (These applications will appear in the same position with the same size).

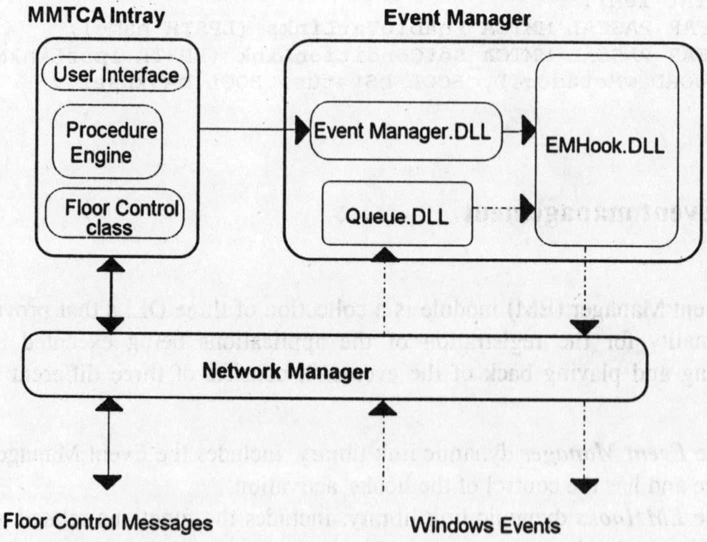

Fig. 11.10. Overall EM Design

- Interception of keyboard and mouse events in the floor-holder node during a CS.
- Transmission only of necessary the events related to the Cooperative Applications.
- Inhibition of any operation on the cooperative window in the non-floor-holder nodes.
- Reproduction of these events in the participating nodes of a CS.
- Detection of the action's finishing.
- Use of an accelerator key (F2) for the floor changing mechanism.
- Disabling minimization for cooperative windows.
- Disabling the use of the Task List and ALT+TAB and ALT+ESC operations for a CS.
- Handling the scroll operations in Cooperative Windows.

11.8 Cooperative Session Control

This section describes the design of the Cooperative Session Manager module of the server-running part of the MMTCA application, from now on called CS Manager.

The CS Manager module is an ANSI C application. It provides some services that are invoked by the Network Manager Message Dispatcher module upon receiving some Floor Control, Event Control and Task Control messages coming from the MMTCA nodes involved in a MMTCA Cooperative Task execution.

The CS Manager services perform some processing with the information received in these messages, and some of them also return some values to be included in the messages that the NM server sends back to other MMTCA nodes involved in the CS.

The overall design of the CS Manager is shown in Fig. 11.11.

Each CS is characterized by a Floor Policy, that specifies the protocol for floor exchange among users. Regardless of the floor policy, all changes in floor ownership are carried out through the server.

Two main floor control policies are specially noticeable: Designation Floor Policy and Queue-Managed Floor Policy.

- ***Designation Floor Policy***: Participants' requests to grab the floor are not attended in a First Come First Served manner. A privileged user is responsible for deciding the next user to hold the floor. The floor token may be granted to a user that has not requested it previously.

  Two modes of Designation floor policy can be identified:

  - `CHAIRMAN_DRIVEN` floor policy, the Chair is the only user that may grant the floor token. So, when the current Floor Holder yields the floor,

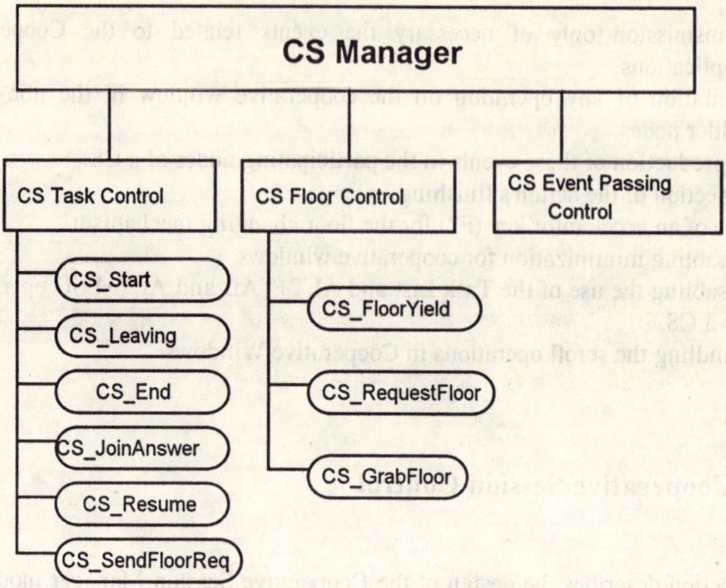

Fig. 11.11. Overall CS Manager Design

it must come back to the chairman who decides who is the new Floor Holder.

- FLOOR_HOLDER_DRIVEN floor policy, the Floor Holder has some privileges to grant the floor to another user. So, s/he can perform either a Pass Floor action indicating the new floor holder or simply a Floor Release action.
  As in the previous case, when the current Floor Holder just yields the floor, without specifying any user, it must come back to the chairman that can decide who is the new Floor Holder.

- ***Queue-Managed Floor Policy***: Participants' requests to grab the floor are attended by the Server. So the server implements a queue-based mechanism to decide at each moment who is the next Floor Holder. When the current Floor Holder yields the floor, it is relayed to another user who has requested it, if there exits, otherwise the chairman must be granted the floor token.
  Two modes of Queue_Managed floor policy can be identified:
  - FIRST_COME_FIRST_SERVED (FCFS) floor policy, the system keeps track of any participants' requests to grab the floor token. When the current floor holder releases the floor, the first participant to ask for the token takes its control. The Floor Token is passed according to a queue

of requests in a First-In-First-Out manner. The advantage of this model is its fairness. Everybody gets an equal chance to hold the floor.

- PRIORITIZED floor policy, users' floor requests include some priority field that is used by the MMTCA server to include them in certain positions at the Request Queue. The Floor Token is passed according to this queue of requests.

Both floor policies with their different modes have been be implemented in this MMTCA Toolbox version.

All the above floor policies show some common points:

- The chairman is the initial Floor Holder and s/he can always grab the floor immediately by removing it from the current floor holder.
- Any participant may request the Floor Token if s/he is not the current owner but it is not possible to have two requests of the same user in the queue.
- Participants' requests to grab the floor are relayed to the rest of cooperative nodes to be displayed at the MMTCA user interface.
- When a user releases the floor and there is no user waiting to hold it, the chairman must take control of it.

12. Application Program Interface

All of the interface functions described in this chapter are defined in dynamic-link libraries (DLLs), and so are available for use by applications while MMTCA is running. They can be used in specially written macros or complete applications that wish to take advantage of MMTCA's workflow and cooperation facilities. The chapter includes worked examples to indicate, for example, how procedure can be instantiated or tasks completed.

Use of these functions avoids the use of the dialogue boxes described in Part 2 of this book, and allows naive end users to be supported in completely tailored ways. There is always a trade-off between making the organisational steps easy for users (procedure designers), and making the cooperative applications easy for their users (end-users): in practice the more complexity is hidden from the end-user, the more work needs to be done by the procedure designer. The extremes are represented by on the one hand using standard Windows applications and no tailoring, where things are as simple as they can be for the procedure designer (e.g. a manager) at the cost of some run-time dialogues; and at the other extreme where specially-written single-user applications (in, say Visual Basic) have been integrated into fully-automated procedures including cooperation.

Using MMTCA technology, true multi-user applications can be easily developed from single-user programs simply by including them in suitable tasks model and making some judicious calls to floor-passing and task control functions.

The functions described here can be declared and used in Visual C++, Visual Basic, Word Basic, Excel, Access Basic and many other end-user oriented macro interfaces, and in this way end users can develop sophisticated applications that automatically take advantage of the facilities offered by MMTCA.

The MMTCA API allows user applications to access and use the functionality of the MMTCA toolbox.

12.1 Server Connection and Login Functions

The connection and login functions allow connection to the MMTCA server, and login and logout from the server.

12.1.1 Login

Defined in SERVICES.DLL.

```
#include login.h
LG_Error FAR PASCAL Login (user, password)
char far * user
char far * password
```

Logs the user into the MMTCA server.

Parameter	Description
user	name of the user.
password	password for the user.

Returns

An LG_Error return code indicating the status of the login.

Comments

This function logs the user into the MMTCA server. Logging in makes the user's presence visible to the server and other users, so they can take part in asynchronous and synchronous tasks. It should be noted that the node needs to have connected to the server with NMConnect before a login can take place.

See Also

NMConnect, NMDisconnect, SLogout

12.1.2 NMConnect

Defined in: WCLIENT.DLL

```
#include wclient.h
BOOL FAR PASCAL NMConnect (hWnd, hostname, server_number)
HANDLE hWnd
char far * hostname
int server_number
```

Connects the node to the MMTCA server.

Parameter	Description
hWnd	the main window handle for the application.
hostname	the name of the host for the MMTCA server.
server_number	the port number on which the MMTCA server is listening for connections.

Returns

TRUE if the connection succeeds, otherwise **FALSE**.

Comments

If another application has already connected the node to the MMTCA server, the function will return **TRUE**, and increment a count of the number of node applications which have requested connection to the server. The count is decremented when NMDisconnect is called - a real disconnect is only done when there are no applications requiring a connection to the server.

See Also

NMDisconnect, Login, SLogout

12.1.3 NMDisconnect

Defined in: WCLIENT.DLL

```
#include wclient.h
BOOL FAR PASCAL NMDisconnect (HANDLE hWnd)
HANDLE hWnd
```

Disconnects the node from MMTCA server.

Parameter	Description
hWnd	the main window handle for the application.

Returns

TRUE if the disconnection succeeds, otherwise **FALSE**.

Comments

A count is kept of the number of applications that have performed an NMConnect. Calling this function decrements the count, and when the count reaches 0, a real disconnection from the MMTCA server is performed.

See Also

NMConnect, Login, SLogout

12.1.4 Logout

Defined in: SERVICES.DLL

```
#include login.h
LG_Error FAR PASCAL Logout (void)
```

Logs the user out from the MMTCA server.

Returns

An LG_Error return code indicating the status of the logout.

Comments

This function logs the user out from the MMTCA server.

See Also

NMConnect, NMDisconnect, Login

12.1.5 LG_Error

```
#include login.h
```

These are the possible login return values.

Value	Meaning
LG_ERROR_ACCESS_NODE_TABLE	Error accessing node in the MMTCA database
LG_ERROR_ACCESS_USER_TABLE	Error accessing user in the MMTCA database
LG_ERROR_INVALID_NODE	Node not in the MMTCA database
LG_ERROR_INVALID_PASSWD	Incorrect user password
LG_ERROR_INVALID_USER	User not in the MMTCA database
LG_ERROR_USER_ALREADY_CONN	User already connected from another node
LG_NO_ERROR	the login was successful

12.2 Workflow Functions

The workflow functions in the MMTCA API allow various aspects of the workflow of a procedure instance to be controlled. This includes the manipulation of variables, the starting and ending of actions for a task, and the setting of task links and condition boxes workflow control structures.

12.2.1 MMTCA_EnableVarLinks

Defined in: SA.DLL

```
#include sa.h
BOOL FAR PASCAL MMTCA_EnableVarLinks (name)
```

```
LPSTR name
```

Enables variable trigger links for the given variable for the currently running procedure instance.

Parameter	Description
name	name of the variable.

Returns

TRUE if the function succeeds, FALSE if it fails.

Comments

This function causes low-level manipulation of the workflow by enabling the trigger links of any variable links for the given variable name in the current procedure instance. If there is no task running, the function will fail. Use of this function is not recommended.

See Also

MMTCA_GetVariable, MMTCA_SetVariable, MMTCA_SetConditionLink

12.2.2 MMTCA_GetMetadocName

Defined in: SA.DLL

```
#include sa.h
BOOL FAR PASCAL MMTCA_GetMetadocName (namebuf,
namebuflen)
LPSTR namebuf
int namebuflen
```

Gets the name of the currently running metadocument.

Parameter	Description
namebuf	buffer to receive the metadocument name.
namebuflen	length of the buffer to receive the metadocument name.

Returns

TRUE if the function succeeds, FALSE if it fails.

Comments

This function retrieves the name of the metadocument for the currently executing task. If there is no task running, then no value will be returned in the *namebuf* buffer.

12.2.3 MMTCA_GetVariable

Defined in: SA.DLL

```
#include sa.h
BOOL FAR PASCAL MMTCA_GetVariable (name, buf, len)
LPSTR name
LPSTR buf
int len
```

Gets the value of the given variable for the currently running procedure instance.

Parameter	Description
name	name of the variable.
buf	buffer to receive the variable value.
len	length of the buffer to receive the variable value.

Returns
TRUE if the function succeeds, FALSE if it fails.

Comments
This function retrieves the value of the named variable for the metadocument of the currently running task. If there is no task running, the function will fail. If the variable is not instantiated for the procedure instance, the function will also fail. The variable name does not have to be unique for all procedures, but it does have to be unque within the procedure instance.

See Also
MMTCA_SetVariable

12.2.4 MMTCA_SetConditionLink

Defined in: SA.DLL

```
#include sa.h
BOOL FAR PASCAL MMTCA_SetConditionLink
      (lpszLinkName, wMetadocID, bStatus, bAskUser)
LPSTR lpszLinkName
WORD wMetadocID
BOOL bStatus
BOOL bAskUser
```

Sets the condition for a given condition box link.

Parameter	Description
lpszLinkName	the name of the condition box link.
wMetadocID	the ID of the metadocument, or 0 for the currently running metadocument.

bStatus	the status value for the condition box output - **TRUE** or **FALSE**.
bAskUser	if **TRUE**, the *bStatus* parameter will be ignored, and the user will be asked to specify the condition value - if **FALSE** the condition box output value will be set to the value given by the *bStatus* parameter.

Returns

TRUE if the function succeeds, FALSE if it fails.

Comments

This is the run-time support for ViEW's decision boxes. It provides support for the high-level workflow decision box construct by allowing the user to set the output value of the condition box to **TRUE** or **FALSE**. This value will enable the relevant output task.

If the *wMetadocID* parameter is 0, then the ID of the metadocument for the currently running task will be used - if no task is running, the function will fail.

If the *bAskUser* parameter is TRUE, then a message box will be used to ask the user to set the condition box output value. The condition specified in the workflow will be given in the text of the message.

See Also

MMTCA_GetVariable, MMTCA_SetVariable, MMTCA_EnableVarLinks, SetConditionLink

12.2.5 MMTCA_SetVariable

Defined in: SA.DLL

```
#include sa.h
BOOL FAR PASCAL MMTCA_SetVariable (name, buf, len)
LPSTR name
LPSTR buf
int len
```

Sets the value of the given variable for the currently running procedure instance.

Parameter	Description
name	name of the variable.
buf	buffer containing the new variable value.
len	length of the buffer containing the new variable value.

Returns

TRUE if the function succeeds, FALSE if it fails.

Comments

This function sets the value of a variable for the metadocument of the currently running task. If there is no task running, the function will fail. If the variable is not instantiated for the procedure instance, the function will also fail. The variable name does not have to be unique for all procedures, but it does have to be unque within the procedure instance.

See Also

MMTCA_GetVariable

12.2.6 SA_ActionComplete

Defined in: SA.DLL

```
#include sa.h
BOOL FAR PASCAL SA_ActionComplete(void)
```

Completes the currently running action.

Returns

TRUE if the function succeeds, FALSE if it fails.

Comments

This function signals that the currently running action has been completed. When an action is run from the task script, the task script executor (TSE) application waits for the action to complete before moving on to the next command in the task script. Calling this function signals the TSE that the action has completed and it can progress to the next command in the script.

See Also

SA_StartAction, SA_StartNsAction, ActionComplete

12.2.7 SA_StartAction

Defined in: SA.DLL

```
#include sa.h
BOOL FAR PASCAL SA_StartAction(lpTaskID, ActionID,
                               iType)
LPTASK_ID lpTaskID
WORD ActionID
int iType
```

Starts the given action for a task.

Parameter	Description
lpTaskID	far pointer to a TASK_ID structure for the current task.
ActionID	ID of the action to be started.
iType	type of the task - **ASYNC** or **SYNC**.

Returns

TRUE if the function succeeds, FALSE if it fails.

Comments

This function starts an action for a task. The *iType* parameter indicates whether the action is for an asynchronous or a synchronous task - if it is for the latter, then the user calling is the task chairman, as only the chairman runs the task script (and this function should be called from within a task script). When this function is called, the metadocument ID for the specified task will be saved as being the current metadocument, the execution of the task script will be suspended until the action has been completed, and the action will be started.

See Also

SA_ActionComplete, SA_StartNsAction, StartAction

12.2.8 SA_StartNsAction

Defined in: SA.DLL

```
#include sa.h
BOOL FAR PASCAL SA_StartNsAction
                    (lpTaskID, ActionID, iType)
LPTASK_ID lpTaskID
WORD ActionID
int iType
```

Starts the given action for a task, but does not register the applications as being shared.

Parameter	Description
lpTaskID	far pointer to a TASK_ID structure for the current task.
ActionID	ID of the action to be started.
iType	type of the task - **ASYNC** or **SYNC**.

Returns

TRUE if the function succeeds, FALSE if it fails.

Comments

This function starts an action for a task. The *iType* parameter indicates whether the action is for an asynchronous or a synchronous task - if it is for the latter, then the user calling is the task chairman, as only the chairman runs the task script (and this function should be called from within a task script). When this function is called, the metadocument ID for the specified task will be saved as being the current metadocument, and the action will be started. Unlike SA_StartAction, the execution of the task script will **not** be suspended until the action has been completed - the script execution will continue normally. The applications which are started for the action will not be logged as shared applications in the MMTCA application table by the **Event Manager** (EM), so they will not be available as shared applications in a Cooperative Session. This allows applications such as a videoconference application to be started on all nodes in a Cooperative Session by the workflow specification, but does not include them as shared applications in the Cooperative Session itself.

See Also

SA_ActionComplete, SA_StartAction, StartNsAction

12.3 Cooperative Session Functions

The Cooperative Session functions in the MMTCA API control the various aspects of a CS, including the floor control mechanisms, and the installation of shared applications.

12.3.1 EM_AppClosed

Defined in: EM.DLL

```
#include em.h
BOOL FAR PASCAL EM_AppClosed (void)
```

Checks if all cooperative applications have been closed.

Returns

TRUE if there are no applications logged in the MMTCA application table, otherwise **FALSE**.

Comments

Applications are logged in the MMTCA application table by the Event Manager (EM) for both asynchronous and synchronous actions. When a call is made to EM_InstallApp, the EM starts logging applications which start up in the application table. When EM_FinishInstall is called, it stops logging applications and starts waiting for events from the floorholder node.

See Also
EM_InstallApp, EM_FinishInstall

12.3.2 EM_ChairmanLeaving

Defined in: EM.DLL

```
#include em.h
BOOL FAR PASCAL EM_ChairmanLeaving (void)
```

Stops a Cooperative Session by removing the chairman.

Returns
TRUE if it succeeds, **FALSE** if there is an error. The user must be the chairman of the Cooperative Session, and must currently have the floor, otherwise they will not be able to leave.

Comments
Calling this function effectively stops the Cooperative Session, as the chairman (who must be the current floorholder for the function to succeed) stops sending events, and the Task Engine is notified that the current action has been completed.

See Also
EM_UserLeaving, EM_Quit

12.3.3 EM_CSFreezeOFF

Defined in: EM.DLL

```
#include em.h
BOOL FAR PASCAL EM_CSFreezeOFF (void)
```

Re-enables the sending of events in a Cooperative Session, and re-enables the use of shared applications.

Returns
TRUE if it succeeds, **FALSE** if there is an error.

See Also
EM_CSFreezeON

12.3.4 EM_CSFreezeON

Defined in: EM.DLL

```
#include em.h
BOOL FAR PASCAL EM_CSFreezeON (void)
```

Disables the sending of events in a Cooperative Session, and disables the use of shared applications.

Returns
TRUE if it succeeds, **FALSE** if there is an error.

See Also
EM_CSFreezeOFF

12.3.5 EM_EnableSending

Defined in: EM.DLL

```
#include em.h
BOOL FAR PASCAL EM_EnableSending (void)
```

Sets the user as floorholder of a Cooperative Session, and enables sending of events to other nodes.

Returns
TRUE if it succeeds, **FALSE** if there is an error.

Comments
After this function is called, all events from applications which are logged in the MMTCA application table will be sent to the MMTCA server.

12.3.6 EM_FinishInstall

Defined in: EM.DLL

```
#include em.h
BOOL FAR PASCAL EM_FinishInstall (lpNetMessage)
lpNETMESSAGE lpNetMessage
```

Tells the MMTCA Event Manager (EM) that the applications for the task have all been installed.

Parameter	Description
lpNetMessage	far pointer to a NETMESSAGE structure, containing information on the current task.

Returns

TRUE if it succeeds, **FALSE** if there is an error.

Comments

If the user is a participant in a Cooperative Session, the automatically starts to wait for events from the floorholder node. The *lpNetMessage* parameter should already contain a pointer to a NETMESSAGE structure - this only requires the TASK_ID information to be completed.

See Also

EM_InstallApp

12.3.7 EM_GrabFloor

Defined in: EM.DLL

```
#include em.h
BOOL FAR PASCAL EM_GrabFloor (lpNetMessage)
lpNETMESSAGE lpNetMessage
```

Grabs the floor in a Cooperative Session for the chairman of the CS.

Parameter	Description
lpNetMessage	far pointer to a NETMESSAGE structure, containing information on the current task and message/command.

Returns

TRUE if it succeeds, **FALSE** if there is an error.

Comments

The function sends a message to the MMTCA server to grab the floor for the chairman. The *lpNetMessage* parameter should already contain a pointer to a completed NETMESSAGE structure, containing the **NM_FloorControl** message type, and the **CSGrabFloor** command, as well as the TASK_ID information.

See Also

EM_RequestFloor, EM_TakeFloor, EM_YieldFloor, NETMESSAGE

12.3.8 EM_InstallApp

Defined in: EM.DLL

```
#include em.h
BOOL FAR PASCAL EM_InstallApp (wNodeType)
WORD wNodeType
```

This function initialises the logging of applications for a task in the MMTCA application table.

Parameter	Description
wNodeType	the type of node that is participating in the task

Value	Meaning
`ASYNC`	the node is performing an asynchronous task.
`CHAIRMAN`	the node is the chairman of a Cooperative Session
`PARTICIPANT`	the node is a participant in a Cooperative Session

Returns

TRUE if it succeeds, **FALSE** if there is an error.

Comments

The MMTCA Event Manager (EM) logs all applications used in an action of a task, whether it is an asynchronous or a synchronous task. Calling this functions initialises the EM to look for new applications being started - it will log these in the MMTCA application table until the EM_FinishInstall function is called.

See Also

EM_FinishInstall

12.3.9 EM_Quit

Defined in: EM.DLL

```
#include em.h
BOOL FAR PASCAL EM_Quit (void)
```

Removes a node from a Cooperative Session.

Returns

TRUE if it succeeds, **FALSE** if there is an error.

Comments

The function disables the sending and receiving of events in a Cooperative Session, and removes the event filters.

See Also

EM_ChairmanLeaving, EM_UserLeaving

12.3.10 EM_RequestFloor

Defined in: EM.DLL

```
#include em.h
BOOL FAR PASCAL EM_RequestFloor (lpNetMessage)
```

```
lpNETMESSAGE lpNetMessage
```

Sends a message to the MMTCA server to signal that the user wishes to take the floor.

Parameter	Description
lpNetMessage	far pointer to a NETMESSAGE structure, containing information on the current task and message/command.

Returns

TRUE if it succeeds, **FALSE** if there is an error.

Comments

The function sends a message to the MMTCA server. The *lpNetMessage* parameter should already contain a pointer to a completed NETMESSAGE structure, containing the **NM_FloorControl** message type, and the **CSRequestFloor** command, as well as the TASK_ID information.

See Also

EM_GrabFloor, EM_TakeFloor, EM_YieldFloor

12.3.11 EM_TakeFloor

Defined in: EM.DLL

```
#include em.h
BOOL FAR PASCAL EM_TakeFloor (void)
```

Takes the floor in a Cooperative Session.

Returns

TRUE if it succeeds, **FALSE** if there is an error.

Comments

The function disables the reception of events from other nodes, and enables the sending of events to other nodes.

See Also

EM_GrabFloor, EM_RequestFloor, EM_YieldFloor

12.3.12 EM_UserLeaving

Defined in: EM.DLL

```
#include em.h
BOOL FAR PASCAL EM_UserLeaving (void)
```

Stops the user from taking part in a Cooperative Session.

Returns

TRUE if it succeeds, **FALSE** if there is an error. The user must be a participant of the Cooperative Session (i.e. not the Chairman), and must not be the current floorholder, otherwise they will not be able to leave.

Comments

The function disables the reception of events from the floorholder node in a Cooperative Session.

See Also

EM_ChairmanLeaving, EM_Quit

12.3.13 EM_YieldFloor

Defined in: EM.DLL

```
#include em.h
BOOL FAR PASCAL EM_YieldFloor (lpNetMessage)
lpNETMESSAGE lpNetMessage
```

Releases the floor in a Cooperative Session.

Parameter	Description
lpNetMessage	far pointer to a NETMESSAGE structure, containing information on the current task and message/command.

Returns

TRUE if it succeeds, **FALSE** if there is an error.

Comments

The function disables sending of events to other nodes, enables reception of events, and sends a message to the MMTCA server informing it that the user has yielded the floor. The *lpNetMessage* parameter should already contain a pointer to a completed NETMESSAGE structure, containing the **NM_FloorControl** message type, and the **CSFloorYield** command, as well as the TASK_ID information.

See Also

EM_GrabFloor, EM_RequestFloor, EM_TakeFloor, NETMESSAGE

12.4 Database Access Functions

The SQL functions in the MMTCA API give access to the tables in the MMTCA database, and allow inspection and manipulation of the database contents.

12.4.1 Commit

Defined in: SERVICES.DLL

```
#include dbclient.h
void FAR PASCAL Commit (void)
```

Performs an SQL **COMMIT** on the MMTCA database.

Returns
No return value.

See Also
RollBack

12.4.2 ErrInfo

Defined in: SERVICES.DLL

```
#include dbclient.h
char FAR * FAR PASCAL ErrInfo (void)
```

Returns an error string for the last SQL command carried out on the MMTCA database.

Returns
A far pointer to the error string buffer – if there was no error, the buffer will be empty.

12.4.3 FreeTable

Defined in: SERVICES.DLL

```
#include dbclient.h
void FAR PASCAL FreeTable (pt)
Table far * pt
```

Frees the memory for the given Table.

Parameter	Description
pt	far pointer to a Table structure which was previously allocated using the Select function.

Returns
No return value.

Comments
When a successful Select call is made, memory is allocated for the Table returned. This function needs to be called to free that memory when the table is no longer needed.

See Also
Select, Table

12.4.4 nSql

Defined in: SERVICES.DLL

```
#include dbclient.h
int FAR PASCAL nSql (sql_sentence)
char FAR * sql_sentence
```

Executes multiple SQL statements in the MMTCA database.

Parameter	Description
sql_sentence	far pointer to a buffer containing multiple SQL statements, separated by semi-colons (';').

Returns
The numbers of rows changed, or 0 if nothing has been altered.

Comments
This function allows multiple SQL statements to be sent to the MMTCA server in a batch, to change the contents of the MMTCA database, namely **INSERT**, **UPDATE**, and **DELETE** statements. These operations need to be followed by a call to Commit to permanently write the changes to the database.

See Also
Commit, Sql

12.4.5 RollBack

Defined in: SERVICES.DLL

```
#include dbclient.h
int FAR PASCAL RollBack (void)
```

Performs an SQL **ROLLBACK** statement on the MMTCA database.

Returns

The numbers of rows changed, or 0 if nothing has been altered.

Comments

Some of the databases supported by MMTCA might not have rollback capability.

See Also

Commit

12.4.6 Select

Defined in: SERVICES.DLL

```
#include dbclient.h
Table FAR PASCAL Select (select_sentence)
char FAR * select_sentence
```

Performs an SQL **SELECT** on the MMTCA database, and returns the resulting table.

Parameter	Description
select_sentence	far pointer to a buffer containing an SQL **SELECT** statement.

Returns

A Table structure containing the result of the SQL SELECT, or NULL if there was an error.

Comments

This is the function used to retrieve data from the MMTCA database. The table returned will contain the results of the SQL query, even if this is an empty table. After the table has been used, the memory allocated for it should be freed using the FreeTable function.

See Also

FreeTable, Table

12.4.7 Sql

Defined in: SERVICES.DLL

```
#include dbclient.h
int FAR PASCAL Sql (sql_sentence)
char FAR * sql_sentence
```

Executes an SQL statement in the MMTCA database.

Parameter	Description
sql_sentence	far pointer to a buffer containing an SQL statement.

Returns

The numbers of rows changed, or 0 if nothing has been altered.

Comments

This function is used for sending SQL statements to change the contents of the MMTCA database, namely **INSERT**, **UPDATE**, and **DELETE** statements. These operations need to be followed by a call to Commit to permanently write the changes to the database.

See Also

Commit, nSql

12.5 File Transfer Functions

The file transfer functions allows transfer of files to and from the MMTCA server, for use in procedure definitions and running instances of procedures.

12.5.1 FT_CopyFile

Defined in: SERVICES.DLL

```
#include file_tra.h
FT_Error FAR PASCAL FT_CopyFile(node_whole_path,
                                server_whole_path)
char far * node_whole_path
char far * server_whole_path
```

Copies the given file to the MMTCA server.

Parameter	Description
node_whole_path	path and name of the file on the node.
server_whole_path	path and name of the file on the server.

Returns

An FT_Error return code indicating the status of the file transfer operation.

See Also

FT_RetrieveFile

12.5.2 FT_CreateMetadocDirs

Defined in: SERVICES.DLL

```
#include file_tra.h
FT_Error FAR PASCAL FT_CreateMetadocDirs (proc_id,
                        metadoc_id, metadoc_dir_wpath)
int proc_id
int metadoc_id
char far * metadoc_dir_wpath
```

Creates the directory for a metadocument on the MMTCA server, and copies any existing procedure definition document files into it.

Parameter	Description
proc_id	ID of the procedure.
metadoc_id	ID of the metadocument.
metadoc_dir_wpath	buffer to receive the path of the metadocument directory on the MMTCA server.

Returns

An FT_Error return code indicating the status of the file transfer operation.

See Also

FT_DeleteMetadocDirs

12.5.3 FT_CreateProcDirs

Defined in: SERVICES.DLL

```
#include file_tra.h
FT_Error FAR PASCAL FT_CreateProcDirs
                          (proc_id, proc_dir_wpath)
int proc_id
char far * proc_dir_wpath
```

Creates the directories for a procedure on the MMTCA server.

Parameter	Description
proc_id	ID of the procedure.
proc_dir_wpath	buffer to receive the path of the procedure directory on the MMTCA server.

Returns

An FT_Error return code indicating the status of the file transfer operation.

See Also

FT_DeleteProcDirs

12.5.4 FT_CreateTPTDirs

Defined in: SERVICES.DLL

```
#include file_tra.h
FT_Error FAR PASCAL FT_CreateTPTDirs
                         (tpt_id, tpt_dir_wpath)
int tpt_id
char far * tpt_dir_wpath
```

Creates the directories for a tool profile template on the MMTCA server.

Parameter	Description
tpt_id	ID of the tool profile template.
tpt_dir_wpath	buffer to receive the path of the tool profile template directory on the MMTCA server.

Returns

An FT_Error return code indicating the status of the file transfer operation.

See Also

FT_DeleteTPTDirs

12.5.5 FT_DeleteDocFile

Defined in: SERVICES.DLL

```
#include file_tra.h
FT_Error FAR PASCAL FT_DeleteDocFile (metadoc_id, doc_id,
                     task_id, edit_action, force_deletion)
int metadoc_id
int doc_id
int task_id
int seq_act
char far * edit_action
int force_deletion
```

Deletes a document for a running procedure instance.

Parameter	Description
metadoc_id	ID of the metadocument.
doc_id	ID of the document.
task_id	ID of the task.
seq_act	sequence activation of the task.
edit_action	edit action for the document.
force_deletion	flag to indicate whether or not deletion of the document should be forced.

Returns

An FT_Error return code indicating the status of the file transfer operation.

See Also

FT_RetrieveDocFile, FT_SaveDocFile

12.5.6 FT_DeleteMetadocDirs

Defined in: SERVICES.DLL

```
#include file_tra.h
FT_Error FAR PASCAL FT_DeleteMetadocDirs (proc_id,
                        metadoc_id, metadoc_dir_wpath)
int proc_id
int metadoc_id
char far * metadoc_dir_wpath
```

Deletes the directory for a metadocument on the MMTCA server.

Parameter	Description
proc_id	ID of the procedure.
metadoc_id	ID of the metadocument.
metadoc_dir_wpath	not used.

Returns

An FT_Error return code indicating the status of the file transfer operation.

See Also

FT_CreateMetadocDirs

12.5.7 FT_DeleteProcDirs

Defined in: SERVICES.DLL

```
#include file_tra.h
FT_Error FAR PASCAL FT_DeleteProcDirs (proc_id,
      metadoc_dir_wpath)
int proc_id
char far * proc_dir_wpath
```

Deletes the directories for a procedure on the MMTCA server.

Parameter	Description
proc_id	ID of the procedure.
proc_dir_wpath	not used.

Returns

An FT_Error return code indicating the status of the file transfer operation.

See Also

FT_CreateProcDirs

12.5.8 FT_DeleteTPTDirs

Defined in: SERVICES.DLL

```
#include file_tra.h
FT_Error FAR PASCAL FT_DeleteTPTDirs (tpt_id,
           tpt_dir_wpath)
int tpt_id
char far * tpt_dir_wpath
```

Deletes the directories for a tool profile template on the MMTCA server.

Parameter	Description
tpt_id	ID of the tool profile template.
tpt_dir_wpath	not used.

Returns

An FT_Error return code indicating the status of the file transfer operation.

See Also

FT_CreateTPTDirs

12.5 9 FT_RetrieveDocFile

Defined in: SERVICES.DLL

```
#include file_tra.h
FT_Error FAR PASCAL FT_RetrieveDocFile (metadoc_id,
   doc_id, task_id, edit_action, force_retrieval)
int metadoc_id
int doc_id
int task_id
int seq_act
char far * edit_action
int force_retrieval
```

Retrieves a document for a running procedure instance from the MMTCA server.

Parameter	Description
metadoc_id	ID of the metadocument.
doc_id	ID of the document.
task_id	ID of the task.
seq_act	sequence activation of the task.
edit_action	edit action for the document.

force_retrieval	flag to indicate whether or not retrieval of the document should be forced.

Returns

An FT_Error return code indicating the status of the file transfer operation.

See Also

FT_SaveDocFile, FT_DeleteDocFile

12.5.10 FT_RetrieveFile

Defined in: SERVICES.DLL

```
#include file_tra.h
FT_Error FAR PASCAL FT_RetrieveFile(node_whole_path,
                    server_whole_path)
char far * node_whole_path
char far * server_whole_path
```

Retrieves the given file from the MMTCA server.

Parameter	Description
node_whole_path	path and name of the file on the node.
server_whole_path	path and name of the file on the server.

Returns

An FT_Error return code indicating the status of the file transfer operation.

See Also

FT_CopyFile

12.5.11 FT_RetrieveProfFile

Defined in: SERVICES.DLL

```
#include file_tra.h
FT_Error FAR PASCAL FT_RetrieveProfFile (metadoc_id,
      appl_id, force_retrieval)
int metadoc_id
int appl_id
int force_retrieval
```

Retrieves a tool profile file from the MMTCA server.

Parameter	Description
metadoc_id	ID of the metadocument.
appl_id	ID of the application for the tool profile file.
force_retrieval	flag to indicate whether or not retrieval of the document should be forced.

Returns

An FT_Error return code indicating the status of the file transfer operation.

See Also

FT_SaveProfFile

12.5.12 FT_SaveDocFile

Defined in: SERVICES.DLL

```
#include file_tra.h
FT_Error FAR PASCAL FT_SaveDocFile (metadoc_id, doc_id,
                    task_id, force_saving)
int metadoc_id
int doc_id
int task_id
int seq_act
int force_saving
```

Saves a document for a running procedure instance to the MMTCA server.

Parameter	Description
metadoc_id	ID of the metadocument.
doc_id	ID of the document.
task_id	ID of the task.
seq_act	sequence activation of the task.
force_saving	flag to indicate whether or not saving of the document should be forced.

Returns

An FT_Error return code indicating the status of the file transfer operation.

See Also

FT_RetrieveDocFile, FT_DeleteDocFile

12.5.13 FT_SaveProfFile

Defined in: SERVICES.DLL

```
#include file_tra.h
FT_Error FAR PASCAL FT_SaveProfFile (metadoc_id,
           appl_id)
int metadoc_id
int appl_id
```

Saves a tool profile file to the MMTCA server.

Parameter	Description
metadoc_id	ID of the metadocument.
appl_id	ID of the application for the tool profile file.

Returns

An FT_Error return code indicating the status of the file transfer operation.

See Also

FT_RetrieveProfFile

12.5.14 FT_Error

Defined in: SERVICES.DLL

```
#include file_tra.h
```

These are the return codes used by the file transfer functions.

Value	Meaning
`FT_ERROR_BAD_ACTION`	edit action argument is bad.
`FT_ERROR_BAD_MD_APPL_ID`	application ID argument is bad.
`FT_ERROR_BAD_MD_DOC_ID`	document ID argument is bad.
`FT_ERROR_BAD_STATUS`	status argument is bad.
`FT_ERROR_DB_ACCESS`	error in database access.
`FT_ERROR_DIR_CREAT`	error in creating directory.
`FT_ERROR_DIR_REMOVE`	error in removing directory.
`FT_ERROR_FILE_CREAT`	error in creating file.
`FT_ERROR_FILE_DELETE`	error in deleting file.
`FT_ERROR_FILE_OPEN`	error in opening file.
`FT_ERROR_FILE_READ`	error in reading file.
`FT_ERROR_FILE_STAT`	error in file status.
`FT_ERROR_FILE_UTIME`	error in file timestamp.
`FT_ERROR_FILE_WRITE`	error in writing to file.
`FT_ERROR_FILES_COPY`	error in copying files.
`FT_ERROR_FILES_UNLINK`	error in unlinking files.
`FT_ERROR_LOCKED_DOC`	document is already locked.
`FT_ERROR_METADOCS_EXIST`	tried to delete procedure with metadocuments.
`FT_NO_ERROR`	no error in file transfer operation.

12.6 Server Messaging Functions

The server messaging functions allows the distribution of network messages to other nodes through the MMTCA server, and the reception of messages from other nodes.

12.6.1 FreeNetMessage

Defined in: SERVICES.DLL

```
#include net_msg.h
void FAR PASCAL FreeNetMessage (msg)
NetMessage far * msg
```

Frees a network message structure that has been allocated when a message is received from the MMTCA server.

Parameter	Description
msg	far pointer to a NETMESSAGE structure.

Comments

When a message is received from the MMTCA server, memory is allocated for the message, and the application registered to receive such a message is passed a pointer to it. Once the application has finished processing the message, it should call this function to free the memory.

See Also

InitSendMessages, RegisterModuleHandle

12.6.2 InitSendMessages

Defined in: SERVICES.DLL

```
#include net_msg.h
void FAR PASCAL InitSendMessages (void)
```

Initialises the node to receive network messages from the MMTCA server.

Comments

This function needs to be called by at one node application to initialise the node services for receiving messages from the MMTCA server.

See Also

FreeNetMessage, RegisterModuleHandle

12.6.3 RegisterModuleHandle

Defined in: HANDLES.DLL

```
#include handles.h
void FAR PASCAL RegisterModuleHandle (app, hWnd)
int app
HWND hWnd
```

Registers a window handle with the MMTCA services.

Parameter	Description
app	indicates the application role to be taken - **IN_TRAY** for receiving control messages, **EVENT_MANAGER** for processing CS events.
hWnd	window handle of the window to receive the notification messages.

Comments

This function is most useful from an API point of view if an application wishes to process the NETMESSAGE messages normally sent to the MMTCA Intray. These are the **NM_TaskControl**, **NM_ActionControl**, and **NM_FloorControl** messages. Note that the first two types of messages are used in the setup of Cooperative Sessions, and these will not work properly if the messages are not being processed.

After a module has called this function to register itself to receive the network messages, any subsequent messages will be notified to the window handle given by the sending of the user-defined Windows message **MMTCA_NET_MESSAGE** (defined in **MMTCAMSG.H**). The LPARAM of the message will be a far pointer to a NETMESSAGE structure – after the message has been processed, the structure should be freed using FreeNetMessage.

See Also

InitSendMessages, FreeNetMessage

12.6.4 RetrieveModuleHandle

Defined in: HANDLES.DLL

```
#include handles.h
HWND FAR PASCAL RetrieveModuleHandle (app)
int app
```

Retrieves the window handle currently registered for the MMTCA service.

Parameter	Description
app	indicates the application role to be taken - **IN_TRAY** for receiving control messages, **EVENT_MANAGER** for processing CS events.

Returns

The window handle of the application registered for the MMTCA service, or NULL if no application has registered.

See Also

RegisterModuleHandle

12.6.5 SendNetworkMessagetoServer

Defined in: SERVICES.DLL

```
#include net_msg.h
void FAR PASCAL SendNetworkMessagetoServer (msg)
NetMessage far * msg
```

Sends a network message to the MMTCA server.

Parameter	Description
msg	far pointer to a NETMESSAGE structure.

Comments

The function sends the given NETMESSAGE structure to the MMTCA server – the server will distribute it to the appropriate group of nodes depeneding on the message and command types.

12.7 DDE Commands

The DDE commands in the MMTCA API give access to some of the workflow control functionality from within a running task, using the standard DDE interface for executing commands. Before using the DDE commands, a DDE client must connect to the MMTCA DDE server.

12.7.1 ActionComplete (DDE Command)

ActionComplete ()

DDE command that completes the currently running action.

Comments

This command signals that the currently running action has been completed. When an action is run from the task script, the task script executor (TSE) application waits for the action to complete before moving on to the next command in the task script. Using this command signals the TSE that the action has completed and it can progress to the next command in the script.

See Also

StartAction, StartNsAction, SA_ActionComplete

12.7.2 EndTask (DDE Command)

EndTask (***status, results_options***)

Ends the currently running task.

Parameter	Description
status	the new status for the task - either `COMPLETE` or `INCOMPLETE`.
results_options	the option which should be used for the task results (i.e. documents) - either `SAVE` or `DISCARD`.

Comments

The command is used to allow automatic ending of a task. Normally when a task (either asynchronous or synchronous on the chairman node) ends, the End Task dialog is displayed, allowing the user to specify the new *status* of the task, and whether the *results_options* should be for saving or discarding document changes for the task. However, this DDE command can be used in a task script (or from a DDE client application running in a task) to automatically end the task with the specified parameters. If either of the parameters is not valid, the End Task dialog will be invoked to get a valid response from the user.

12.7.3 SetConditionLink (DDE Command)

SetConditionLink (*link_name, metadocl_id, status, ask_user*)

Sets the condition value for a workflow TRUE/FALSE condition box.

Parameter	Description
link_name	the name of the condition box link.
metadocl_id	the ID of the metadocument, or 0 for the currently running metadocument.
status	the status of the condition box output - TRUE or FALSE.

ask_user	if TRUE the *status* parameter will be ignored, and the user will be asked to specify the condition value.

Comments

This is the DDE run-time support for ViEW's decision boxes. It provides support for the high-level workflow decision box construct by allowing the user to set the output value of the condition box to `TRUE` or `FALSE`. This value will enable the relevant output task.

If the *metadocI_id* parameter is 0, then the ID of the metadocument for the currently running task will be used - if no task is running, the command will fail.

If the *ask_user* parameter is TRUE, then a message box will be used to ask the user to set the condition box output value. The condition specified in the workflow will be given in the text of the message.

See Also

MMTCA_SetConditionLink

12.7.4 StartAction (DDE Command)

StartAction (*type, actionID, metadocID, taskID, seq_activation*)

Starts the given action for a task.

Parameter	Description
type	type of action - `ASYNC` or `SYNC`.
actionID	the ID of the action to be started.
metadocID	the ID of the procedure instance for the action.
taskID	the ID of the task for the action.
seq_activation	the sequence activation of the task for the action.

Comments

This command starts an action for a task. The *type* parameter indicates whether the action is for an asynchronous or a synchronous task - if it is for the latter, then the user calling is the task chairman, as only the chairman runs the task script (and this command should be called from within a task script). When this command is used, the metadocument ID for the specified task will be saved as being the current metadocument, the execution of the task script will be suspended until the action has been completed, and the action will be started.

See Also

ActionComplete, StartNsAction, SA_StartAction

12.7.5 StartNsAction (DDE Command)

StartNsAction (*type, actionID, metadocID, taskID, seq_activation*)

Starts the given action for a task, but does not register the applications as being shared.

Parameter	Description
type	type of action - ASYNC or SYNC.
actionID	the ID of the action to be started.
metadocID	the ID of the procedure instance for the action.
taskID	the ID of the task for the action.
seq_activation	the sequence activation of the task for the action.

Comments

This command starts an action for a task. The *type* parameter indicates whether the action is for an asynchronous or a synchronous task - if it is for the latter, then the user calling is the task chairman, as only the chairman runs the task script (and this command should be called from within a task script). When this command is used, the metadocument ID for the specified task will be saved as being the current metadocument, and the action will be started. Unlike StartAction, the execution of the task script will **not** be suspended until the action has been completed - the script execution will continue normally. The applications which are started for the action will not be logged as shared applications in the MMTCA application table by the **Event Manager** (EM), so they will not be available as shared applications in a Cooperative Session. This allows applications such as a videoconference application to be started on all nodes in a Cooperative Session by the workflow specification, but does not include them as shared applications in the Cooperative Session itself.

See Also

ActionComplete, StartAction, SA_StartNsAction

12.8 MMTCA API Examples

In this section some examples are given for using the MMTCA API functions from C and from macro languages such as Word Basic.

12.8.1 Example of Using Simple SQL

This is an example of using the MMTCA API to do some simple SQL to update the MMTCA database. It removes all the live links for a metadocument "Example Metadoc", which is an instance of procedure "Example Procedure".

The example is first given in 'C':

```
char szDelete [] = "DELETE FROM MD_LINKS A WHERE \
 A.METADOC_ID IN (SELECT B.METADOC_ID FROM \
 MD_METADOCUMENT B, PD_PROCEDURE C \
 WHERE B.NAME='Example Metadoc' \
 AND C.NAME='Example Procedure' \
 AND C.PROC_ID=B.PROC_ID)";
if (Sql (szDelete))
   CommitCommit ();
```

This example could also be done from a macro language such as Microsoft Word Basic:

```
Declare Function Sql Lib "SERVICES.DLL" (sql_statement$
As String) As Integer
Declare Function Commit Lib "SERVICES.DLL" As Integer
Sub MAIN
sql_delete$ = "DELETE FROM MD_LINKS A WHERE A.METADOC_ID
IN ( \
  SELECT B.METADOC_ID \
  FROM MD_METADOCUMENT B, PD_PROCEDURE C \
  WHERE B.NAME='Example Metadoc' \
  AND C.NAME='Example Procedure' \
  AND C.PROC_ID=B.PROC_ID)"
res = Sql (sql_delete$)
If res Then
res = Commit
End If
End Sub
```

12.8.2 Example of Automatic Procedure Instantiation

This is an example of using the MMTCA API to automatically instantiate a procedure definition from the MMTCA database.

Before instantiating a procedure, the steps that are involved in this should be understood. These are:

- Create the metadocument
- Create the metadocument directory on the MMTCA server
- Instantiate the documents
- Instantiate the variables
- Instantiate the tool profiles
- Instantiate the starting intray tasks
- Commit the database changes

The step which has been missed out from the above process is that of instantiating the participants. If this is done at procedure instantiatioin time, each participant defined for the procedure needs to be bound to an actual user for the duration of the metadocument. Since there can be an arbitrary number of participants for any given procedure, there is no generic way of instantiating them. This could be done for specific cases where the procedure participants are known, or they could be left unbound (as in this example) and instantiated on a per-task basis at a later time.

For each of the database update steps involved in the instantiation of a procedure, the information which needs to be provided is the name of the procedure, and the name of the new metadocument. Additionally, the creation of the metadocument must specify a user who will be the organiser for the metadocument, and might also specify the node folder path for the new metadocument, rather than using the default path for the procedure, and starting date and time.

The example is also slightly database specific in the creation of the metadocument, due to the different ways in which Oracle, Informix, and Ingres implement the unique ID values for the metadocument table. Examples are given for all three databases.

- SQL to Create the metadocument
- SQL to Instantiate the documents
- SQL to Instantiate the variables
- SQL to Instantiate the tool profiles
- SQL to Instantiate the starting intray tasks

These SQL statements can be executed using the Sql function, as shown in the Simple SQL example.

Example 'C' Code: To perform all of the stages in a 'C' program, it is assumed that the above SQL statements have been constructed and stored in character arrays, and we have pointers to these arrays:

```
void InstantiateProcedure (
 LPSTR lpszProcName,
 LPSTR lpszMetadocName,
 LPSTR lpszOrganiserName)
 {
 char szSelect [300];

 wsprintf (szSelect, lpszCreateMetadoc,
  lpszMetadocName,
  lpszProcName,
  lpszOrganiserName);

 if (Sql (szSelect)) // nSql for Ingres, 2 statements
  {
  WORD wProcID;
  WORD wMetadocID;
  char szMetadocPath [100];
```

```
wProcID = GetProcedureID (lpszProcName);
wMetadocID = GetNewMetadocID (lpszProcName,
  lpszMetadocName);
FT_CreateMetadocDirs (wProcID, wMetadocID,
  szMetadocPath);

wsprintf (szSelect, lpszInstDocuments, szMetadocPath,
  wMetadocID);
Sql (szSelect);
wsprintf (szSelect, lpszInstVariables, wMetadocID);
Sql (szSelect);
wsprintf (szSelect, lpszInstToolProfiles,
  wMetadocID);
Sql (szSelect);
wsprintf (szSelect, lpszInstIntrayTasks, wMetadocID);
Sql (szSelect);
Commit ();
}
}

WORD GetProcedureID (LPSTR lpszProcName)
{
Table t;
WORD wProcID;
char szSelect [100];

wsprintf (szSelect,
 "SELECT PROC_ID FROM PD_PROCEDURE WHERE NAME='%s'",
 lpszProcName);

if ((t = Select (szSelect)) == NULL ||
 t->nrows < 1)
 return 0;

wProcID = atoi (t->rows [0][0]);
return wProcID;
}

WORD GetNewMetadocID (LPSTR lpszProcName,
     LPSTR lpszMetadocName)
{
Table t;
WORD wMetadocID;
char szSelect [100];

wsprintf (szSelect,
 "SELECT METADOC_ID \
 FROM MD_METADOCUMENT A, PD_PROCEDURE B \
 WHERE A.NAME='%s' AND A.PROC_ID=B.PROC_ID \
 AND B.NAME='%s'",
 lpszMetadocName,
 lpszProcName);

if ((t = Select (szSelect)) == NULL ||
```

```
    t->nrows < 1)
    return 0;

  wMetadocID = atoi (t->rows [0][0]);
  return wMetadocID;
  }
```

SQL Example to Create the Metadocument: The SQL statements for creating a new metadocument are given below, for each of the three databases. The three %s arguments should be replaced by the name of the new metadocument, the name of the procedure it is based on, and the name of the organiser for the new metadocument respectively.

Oracle

```
INSERT INTO MD_METADOCUMENT (METADOC_ID, PROC_ID,
   METADOC_STAT, NAME, DESCRIPTION, ORGANIZER, FOLDER_PATH)
  SELECT MD_SEQ_METADOC_ID.NEXTVAL, A.PROC_ID, 'SCHEDULED',
   '%s', A.DESCRIPTION, B.USER_ID, A.DEFAULT_PATH
  FROM PD_PROCEDURE A, ADM_MMTCA_USER B
  WHERE A.NAME='%s' AND B.NAME='%s';
```

Informix

```
INSERT INTO MD_METADOCUMENT (METADOC_ID, PROC_ID,
   METADOC_STAT, NAME, DESCRIPTION, ORGANIZER, FOLDER_PATH)
  SELECT 0, A.PROC_ID, 'SCHEDULED', '%s', A.DESCRIPTION,
   B.USER_ID, A.DEFAULT_PATH
  FROM PD_PROCEDURE A, ADM_MMTCA_USER B
  WHERE A.NAME='%s' AND B.NAME='%s';
```

Ingres

```
UPDATE MD_SEQ_METADOC_ID SET ID=ID+1;
INSERT INTO MD_METADOCUMENT (METADOC_ID, PROC_ID,
   METADOC_STAT, NAME, DESCRIPTION, ORGANIZER, FOLDER_PATH)
  SELECT DISTINCT MD_SEQ_METADOC_ID.ID, A.PROC_ID,
   'SCHEDULED',
   '%s', A.DESCRIPTION, B.USER_ID, A.DEFAULT_PATH
  FROM PD_PROCEDURE A, ADM_MMTCA_USER B
  WHERE A.NAME='%s' AND B.NAME='%s';
```

SQL Example to Instantiate the Documents: The SQL statement for instantiating the documents for a new metadocument is given below. The %s argument should be replaced by the path for the new metadocument on the server (obtained when the server directories are created using FT_CreateMetadocDirs) - this is concatenated with the filename of the document to create the reference path for the document on the MMTCA server. The %d argument is the ID of the new metadocument.

```
  INSERT INTO MD_DOCUMENT (METADOC_ID, DOC_ID,
    PATH, FILE_NAME, STATUS, REF_PATH)
```

```
SELECT A.METADOC_ID, B.DOC_ID, A.FOLDER_PATH,
 B.FILE_NAME, 'UP_TO_DATE', '%s/'||B.FILE_NAME
FROM MD_METADOCUMENT A, PD_DOCUMENT B
WHERE A.PROC_ID=B.PROC_ID
 AND A.METADOC_ID=%d
```

SQL Example to Instantiate the Variables: The SQL statement for instantiating the variables for a new metadocument is given below. The %d argument is the ID of the new metadocument.

```
INSERT INTO MD_VARIABLE (METADOC_ID, VAR_ID, VALUE)
  SELECT A.METADOC_ID, B.VAR_ID, B.DEF_VALUE
  FROM MD_METADOCUMENT A, PD_VARIABLE B
  WHERE A.PROC_ID=B.PROC_ID
    AND A.METADOC_ID=%d
```

SQL Example to Instantiate the Tool Profiles: The SQL statement for instantiating the tool profiles for a new metadocument is given below. The %d argument is the ID of the new metadocument

```
INSERT INTO MD_PROF_FILES (METADOC_ID, APPL_ID, NAME, PATH,
    REF_PATH, TYPE)
  SELECT A.METADOC_ID, B.APPL_ID, B.NAME, B.PATH,
    B.REF_PATH, B.TYPE
  FROM MD_METADOCUMENT A, PD_PROF_FILES B,
    PD_APPLICATION C, PD_ACTION D, PD_TASK E
  WHERE B.APPL_ID=C.APPL_ID
    AND C.ACTION_ID=D.ACTION_ID
    AND D.TASK_ID=E.TASK_ID
    AND E.PROC_ID=A.PROC_ID
    AND A.METADOC_ID=%d
```

SQL Example to Instantiate the Starting Intray Tasks: The SQL statement for instantiating the starting intray tasks for a new metadocument is given below. The %d argument is the ID of the new metadocument.

```
INSERT INTO MD_INTRAY_TASK (METADOC_ID, TASK_ID,
    SEQ_ACTIVATION, TASK_STATE, MEETING_TYPE, FLOOR_POLICY)
  SELECT A.METADOC_ID, B.TASK_ID, 1,
    'READY', B.MEETING_TYPE, B.FLOOR_POLICY
  FROM MD_METADOCUMENT A, PD_TASK B, PD_SUCC_LINK C
  WHERE A.METADOC_ID=%d
    AND B.PROC_ID=A.PROC_ID
    AND B.TASK_ID=C.TASK_SUCC
    AND NOT EXISTS
      (SELECT D.LINK_ID FROM PD_PRED_LINK D WHERE
         D.LINK_ID=C.LINK_ID)
    AND NOT EXISTS
      (SELECT E.LINK_ID FROM PD_VAR_LINK E WHERE
         E.LINK_ID=C.LINK_ID)
    AND NOT EXISTS
      (SELECT F.LINK_ID FROM PD_NAND_LINK F WHERE
         F.LINK_ID=C.LINK_ID);
```

12.8.3 Example of Setting a Conditional Link Output

This is an example of using the MMTCA API to set the output value of a conditional link in the workflow of a procedure instance.

To set the output of a conditional link from within a running task, all that is required is the link name, and the status which the link output is to be set to (TRUE or FALSE).

The function to use is:

MMTCA_SetConditionLink (*LinkName, MetadocID, Status, AskUser*)

If we wished to set the output of the conditional link "Example Condition" to TRUE, then in 'C' the function would be called as:

```
MMTCA_SetConditionLink ("Example Condition", 0,
    TRUE, FALSE);
```

To accomplish the same call in a Microsoft Word macro, the macro would be:

```
Declare Function MMTCA_SetConditionLink Lib "SA.DLL"
  (linkname$ As String, metadoc_id As Integer, status As
   Integer, ask_user As Integer) As Integer
Sub MAIN
res = MMTCA_SetConditionLink("Example Condition",0,1,0)
End Sub
```

Note that for this macro to work properly it has to be run when the current directory for Word is the MMTCA\RUN directory, or the directory is in the search path.

12.9 Structures

12.9.1 Table

```
#include dbclient.h
typedef struct table {
  int ncols, nrows;
  char FAR * FAR *cols;
  char FAR * FAR *rows[1];     /* ncols wide */
} FAR * Table;
```

The Table structure contains information returned from an SQL **SELECT** statement.

Member	Description
ncols	the number of columns in the table.
nrows	the number of rows in the table.
cols	far pointer to the array of column names.
rows	far pointer to the array of rows of the table.

See Also

Select

12.9.2 NETMESSAGE

```
#include mmtca.h
typedef struct {
  int iMessageType;
  int iCommand;
  TASK_ID TaskId;
  union {
    EVENTMSG _ev;
    WORD _dt[MAX_LENGTH];
  }U;
} NETMESSAGE;
```

The structure used for carrying MMTCA messages between the MMTCA server and client nodes.

Member	Description
iMessageType	the type of control message that is being sent. This can be one of: **NM_FloorControl** – a message used for floor control in a Cooperative Session **NM_TaskControl** – a message used for control of the setting up and execution of an asynchronous or synchronous task. **NM_ActionControl** – a message used for the execution of an action in a task. **NM_EventFromFloor** – a message used for passing events during a Cooperative Session.
iCommand	the command that is being sent in the control message. This can be one of: **ATaskStart** – an NM_TaskControl command type indicating that a user has started an asychronous task. **ATaskAbort** – an NM_TaskControl command type indicating that a user has aborted an asychronous task. **UpdateIntray** – an NM_TaskControl command type indicating that an event has occurred which means that the user's intray of tasks may need to be updated. **RemoteActionStarted** – an NM_TaskControl command type indicating to the chairman that a participant in a Cooperative Session has started an action in the CS.

LoggedInUser – an NM_TaskControl command type indicating that a user has logged in to the MMTCA server.

LoggedOutUser – an NM_TaskControl command type indicating that a user has logged out from the MMTCA server

CSInvite – an NM_TaskControl command type indicating that the chairman of a Cooperative Session has invited users to register for the CS.

CSRegister – an NM_TaskControl command type indicating that a user has registered for a Cooperative Session.

CSAbort – an NM_TaskControl command type indicating that a Cooperative Session has been aborted.

CSStart – an NM_TaskControl command type indicating that a Cooperative Session has been started.

CSExpired – an NM_TaskControl command type indicating that the registration deadline for a Cooperative Session has expired.

CSReady – an NM_TaskControl command type indicating that a user is ready to start a Cooperative Session.

CSLeaving – an NM_TaskControl command type indicating that a user is leaving a Cooperative Session.

CSEnd – an NM_TaskControl command type indicating that a Cooperative Session has ended.

CSJoin – an NM_TaskControl command type indicating that a user has requested to join a Cooperative Session which is already in progress.

CSJoinAnswer – an NM_TaskControl command type indicating the chairman of a Cooperative Session's response to a user's request to join the CS.

CSResume – an NM_TaskControl command type indicating that a Cooperative Session is resuming after a user has joined.

CSFreezeON - an NM_TaskControl command type indicating that event sending in a Cooperative Session is to be suspended.

CSFreezeOFF - an NM_TaskControl command type indicating that event sending in a Cooperative Session is to be restarted.

CSFloorGranted - an NM_FloorControl command type indicating that the floor in a Cooperative Session has been granted to a user.

CSRequestedFloor - an NM_FloorControl command type indicating that the floor in a Cooperative Session has been requested by a user.

CSLostFloor - an NM_FloorControl command type indicating that the floor in a Cooperative Session has been lost by a user.

CSFloorYield - an NM_FloorControl command type indicating that the floor in a Cooperative Session has been released by a user.

CSRequestFloor - an NM_FloorControl command type indicating that a user in a Cooperative Session is requesting the floor.

CSGrabFloor - an NM_FloorControl command type indicating that the chairman of a Cooperative Session is grabbing the floor.

CSFloorInform - an NM_FloorControl command type indicating that a user in a Cooperative Session has grabbed or passed the floor.

TaskId a TASK_ID structure containing information on the task to which the control message refers.

_ev the Windows **EVENTMSG** structure that contains a hardware event being sent during a Cooperative Session in an **EventFromFloor** type message.

_dt an array containing additional data for control messages - the data is dependent on the message and command type. **MAX_LENGTH** is currently defined as 5.

See Also

TASK_ID

12.9.3 TASK_ID

```
#include mmtca.h

typedef struct {
  WORD wMetadocId;
  WORD wTaskId;
  WORD wSeq_activation;
} TASK_ID;
```

This structure holds information about a task in an instance of procedure.

Member	Description
wMetadocId	the **metadocument** of which the task is a member.
wTaskId	the **task**.
wSeq_activation	the sequence activation of the task in the current metadocument.

Glossary

Action: An action corresponds to the activation of one, or more, applications. Each application is associated with one, or more, documents.

ADM: The administration tool in MMTCA which supports the adding to the database of nodes, users, user groups and their authorisation to use the system.

API (Application Program Interface): Any collection of functions that can be called from applications. Lists of such functions are important when writing applications or macros.

Application: Any computer program that can be started up by a user on their workstation. In MMTCA all applications are assumed to be Windows-compatible.

Asynchronous Task: A task that a user carries out independently from other users.

CCT (Cooperative Control Toolbox): A small window indicating floor holder status and allowing users to request or grant the floor, depending on the floor policy in use.

CS see Cooperative Session.

CSRR (Cooperative Session Registration Request): A pop-up dialogue that appears on the screen of all potential participants when a cooperative session is started up.

Combo Box: A standard control in Windows which consists of an editable value field and a pull-down list to display a set of suitable values: selecting one of this values places it in the editable field.

Cooperative Session: The actual execution of a synchronous task.

CS (Cooperative Session): q.v.

DDE (Dynamic Data Exchange): One of the mechanisms provided by Windows for communication between applications.

Dialogue: A Windows primitive, used to request from the user information about a task s/he is performing. There are various types of dialogues in MMTCA, such as information dialogues, confirmation dialogues and error message dialogues.

DLL (Dynamic Link Library): A file with suffix .DLL in a standard location which is automatically loaded by Windows when one of its functions is referenced by an application. DLLs can be shared by several applications, and so can be configured to allow communication between applications.

Document: A (possibly multimedia) object in the computer store whose information content can be examined or modified using an application.

Event Manager (EM): A part of the MMTCA environment that coordinates workstations in cooperative sessions.

Floor: In a meeting or cooperative session, the speaker is said to "have the floor", so the floorholder is simply the person speaking at the moment. All other participants in the meeting can watch and listen; they may also request the floor.

Floor Policy: Any mechanism for deciding who the next floorholder should be.

Instantiation: A procedure or business process can be executed many times, for example, a number of employees may apply for holidays using a routine procedure. Each time any procedure is invoked or instantiated, there are potentially documents created to record its progress, for example a form requesting particular holidays, or a memo agreeing to them. The metadocument comprises all such documents. In MMTCA metadocuments are in one-to-one correspondence with procedure instantiations, and the two concepts are identified.

Intray: The user interface to MMTCA which by default shows the tasks that user should consider starting up. It is like an office in-tray containing folders of documents for the user's attention.

Links: In MMTCA links indicate the dependencies between tasks.

List Box: A List Box displays a list of choices. If there are more choices that can fit in the box, scroll bars are provided.

Login: The process of identifying a user to MMTCA, by means of a user name and a password.

Logout: The process of breaking the connection with MMTCA.

Metadocument: An instance of a procedure. A metadocument can be thought of as a notional collection of documents generated by or used in that instance or occurrence of the procedure.

Metadocument Browser: A tool which allows users to examine the database records of completed and currently-active metadocuments, their tasks and associated participants and documents.

MMTCA (Multimedia Toolbox for Cooperative Applications): The acronym for the Esprit project whose results are described in this book.

Network Manager: A part of the MMTCA environment which manages communication between nodes and the server (including the database).

Node: A workstation on a network.

Participant: A user filling (or bound to) a role in a procedure instance, i.e. working on the associated metadocument.

Procedure: A procedure describes how a group of people may carry out some activity. Each time the procedure is instantiated, a new metadocument is created.

Procedure Designer: Someone who organises work to be done, by specifying a procedure (using ViEW) or setting up a Ready-to-Run Cooperative Session

PTA (Procedure Task Action model): A method for describing workflow in MMTCA.

Ready-to-Run Cooperative Session: An ad hoc cooperative session that is started up as soon as it is defined.

Role: A place for a user in a procedure.

Stand-alone Cooperative Session: same as Ready-to-Run Cooperative Session, so called because it is not part of a larger procedure.

Synchronous Task: A single-action task carried out concurrently by more than one user, where the users are working jointly on the same document.

Task: A task represents the work that a user, or a number of users, may perform.

Tool Profile Editor: A tool in the MMTCA environment that supports the integration of single-user applications so that they can be used in a WYSIWIS mode, and the tailoring of their initialisation state.

TPE see Tool Profile Editor.

TPT (Tool Profile Template): see Tool Profile Editor.

User: A person using a workstation.

Variables: in MMTCA these are places to store values specific to a metadocument. A set of variables is defined for the procedure; each metadocument has potentially a set of cooresponding values.

ViEW (Visual Editor for Workflow): The procedure design tool in the MMTCA environment.

WYSIWIS (What You See Is What I See): A style of cooperative working in which the computer hardware and software ensures that a given collection of windows is displayed identically on a collection of desktop workstations, so that mouse movements, keystrokes etc controlling the applications on one machine (the floor holder for the time being) have effect on all participants displays.

Workflow: Any mechanism for arranging the orderly execution of tasks by a group of people collaborating on a project, including distribution or forwarding of relevant documentation.

TPC (Tool Profile Compiler): see Tool Profile Editor.

References

Ahuja, S.R., et al. (1990): A comparison of application sharing mechanisms in real-time desktop conferencing systems, *Conference on office information systems*, 238-248.

Bannon, L., and Schmidt, K. (1991): CSCW: Four characters in search of a context, *Studies in computer-supported cooperative work: theory, practice and design*. J. Bowers and S. Benford (Eds.), Elsevier, Netherlands, 3-16

Benford, S. (1989) Requirements of activity management, in J.M. Bowers and S.D. Benford (Eds), *Proceedings of the first European conference on computer supported cooperative work*, Dec. 89, North Holland Elsevier Science, Amsterdam.

Berman, T. and Thorensen, K. (1988): Can networks make an organisation?, in *Proceedings of CSCW'88*, Association of Computing Machinery Baltimore, MD.

Bodker, S. and Gronbek, K. (1989): Cooperative prototyping experiments, in J.M. Bowers and S.D. Benford (Eds), *Proceedings of the first European conference on computer supported cooperative work*, Dec. 89, North Holland Elsevier Science, Amsterdam.

Bowers, J., Churcher, J. and Roberts, T. (1988): Structuring computer mediated communication in COSMOS, in R. Speth (ed) *EUTECO'88: Research into networks and distributed applications*, Vienna, Austria.

Bowers, J. and Churcher, J. (1988): Local and global structuring of computer mediated communication: developing linguistic perspectives on CSCW in Cosmos, in *Proceedings of CSCW'88*, Association of Computing Machinery, Baltimore, MD.

Bowers, J. (1990): Preliminary procedure for group work design in central government departments, Version 1.0, Advanced Concepts Branch, CCTA, London.

Bullen, C.V., Bennett, J.L. (1990): Learning from user experience with groupware, *ACM conference on computer-supported cooperative work*, p. 291-302; reprinted in *Groupware: software for computer-supported cooperative work*, ed. Marca, D., Bock, G. (1992), Los Alamitos, CA: IEEE Computer Society Press, p. 11-22.

Christie, A.M. (1993): A graphical process definition language, *Information and Software Technology*, 35.

de Cindio, F., de Michelis, G, et al. (1986): CHAOS as a coordinating technology, *Proc. CSCW '86*, Austin Tx.

Crowe, M.K. and Tian, S. (1994): Introduction to multimedia toolbox for cooperative applications (MMTCA), *Proceedings of Broadband Islands '94*, Hamburg, Germany, to appear.

Crowley, T., Milazzo, P., Baker, E., Forsdick, H. and Tomlinson, R. (1990): MMConf: an infrastructure for building shared multimedia applications, *CSCW 90 Proceedings*, p.329-342.

Danielson, T., Panoke-Babtz, U. et al (1986): The AMIGO project: advanced group communication model for computer-based communication environment, *Proc. CSCW '86*, Austin Tx.

Delisle, N.M. and Schwartz, M.D. (1986): Neptune: A hypertext system for CAD applications, *Proc. 1986 ACM-SIGMOD Int. Conf. Management of Data* (Washington, DC, USA) ACM, 132-143.

Dwight, B.D. (1991): Software that makes your work flow, *Datamation*, April 1991, 75-78.

Ellis, C.A. and Bernal, M. (1982): Officetalk-D: An experimental office information system, *Proceedings ACM-SIGOA conference on office information systems*, 131-140.

Ellis, C.A., Gibbs, S.J., Rein G.L. (1991): Groupware: some issues and experiences, *Communications of the ACM*, **34**, p.38-58; reprinted in *Groupware: software for computer-supported cooperative work*, ed. Marca, D., Bock, G. (1992), Los Alamitos, CA: IEEE Computer Society Press, p.23-43.

Fafchamps, D., Reynolds, D. and Kuchinsky, A. (1989): The dynamics of small group decision making over the e-mail channel, in J.M. Bowers and S.D. Benford (Eds), *Proceedings of the first European conference on computer supported cooperative work*, Dec. 89, North Holland Elsevier Science, Amsterdam.

Fischer, G., and Stevens, C. (1991): Information access in complex, poorly structured information spaces. In *Proceedings of the CHI '91 Conference on Human Factors in Computing Systems.* ACM, New York, 63-70

Gale, S. (1992): Desktop video conferencing: technical advances and evaluation issues, *Computer Communications*, **15** pp 517-526.

Garret, L.N., Smith, K. and Meyrowitz (1986): Intermedia: issues strategies and tactics in the design of hypermedia document system, *Proceedings of CSCW'86* (Austin, TX, USA).

Greenberg, S. (1990): Sharing views and interactions with single-user applications, *Proceedings of the Conference on Office Information Systems '90.* ACM, New York, 227-237

Greif, I. (1988): *Computer-supported cooperative work: a book of readings*, Morgan Danfmann Publishers, Inc. ISBN 0-934613-57-5.

Gronbaek, K., Kyng, M. and Mogensen, P. (1993): CSCW challenges: cooperative design in engineering projects, *Communications of the ACM*, **36**, 67-77.

Grudin, J. (1991): CSCW - introduction, *Communications of the ACM*, 34, p. 31-34.

Harper, R.A. (1989): Working in harmony: an examination of computer technology in air traffic control, in J.M. Bowers and S.D. Benford (Eds), *Proceedings of the First European Conference on Computer Supported Cooperative Work*, Dec. 89, North Holland Elsevier Science, Amsterdam.

Henderson, A., et alia (1986): Rooms: the use of multiple virtual workspaces to reduce space contention in a window-based graphical user interface, *ACM Transactions on Graphics*, **5**, pp 211-243.

Hiltz, S.R., Turoff, M. (1978): The network nation: human communication via computer, Addison Wesley, Boston, M.A..

Ishii, H., Miyaki, N. (1991): Towards an open shared workspace: Computer and video fusion approach of Teamworkstation, *Communications of the ACM*, **34** (12).

Jackson, M C (1992): *Systems methodology for the management sciences*, Plenum Press, New York.

Jeffay, K., Lin, J.K., Menges, J.B., Smith, F.D. (1992): *Architecture of the artifact-based collaboration system matrix*, Dept of Computer Science, University of North Carolina at Chapel Hill, TR92-012.

Johansen, R. (1988) *Groupware: computer support for business teams*, The Free Press, 866 Third Avenue, New York, N.Y. 10022; ISBN 0-02-916491-5.

Kaashoek, M.F., et al. (1989): An efficient reliable broadcast protocol, *ACM operating system review*, **23**, pp 5-19.

Kraemer, K.L. and Kling, J.L. (1988): Computer based systems for cooperative work and group decision making, *ACM Computing Surveys,* **20**, 2.

Kreifelts, T., and Woetzel (1986): Distribution and error handling in an office procedure system, *Proc. IFIP WG 8.4 Working conference on office systems methods and tools*, Pisa, p.197-208.

Lantz, K.A. (1986): An experiment in integrated multimedia conferencing, *Proc. CSCW*, pp 533-552.

Lauwers, J.C., Joseph, T.A., Lantz, K.A., and Romanow, A.L. (1990): *Replicated architectures for shared window systems: a critique*, ACM 089791-358-2/90/0004/0249, 249-260.

Lyytinen, K (1987): A taxonomic perspective of information systems development: theoretical constructs and recommendations, *Critical Issues in Information Systems Research*, ed. Boland, R.J., Hirschheim R.A. (Wiley) p.3-41

Malone, T.W., Crowston, K. (1990): What is coordination theory and how can it help design cooperative work systems?, Proc. CSCW '90, ACM, Los Angeles, p. 357-370.

Malone, T.W., Grant, K.R., Turbak, F.A., Brobst, S.A., and Cohen, M.D. (1987) Intelligent information-sharing systems. *Communications of the ACM,* **30**, 390-402

Malone, T.W. and Lai, K. (1988): Object Lens: a spreadsheet for cooperative work, *Proc. CSCW'88*, Portland, OR, USA.

Marca, D. and Bock, G. (1992): *Groupware: software for computer-supported cooperative work*, IEEE Computer Society Press.

Marchionini, G. and Schneiderman, B. (1988): Finding facts vs browsing knowledge in hypertext systems, *IEEE Computer*, 70-79.

Mayer, E. (1992) Concurrent multicast checkpointing, *Upper layer protocols, architectures and applications*, Elsevier Science Publishers B.V. (North-Holland), 1992 IFIP, pp. 321-335.

Nelson, T.H. (1980): Replacing the printed word: a complete literary system, *IFIP Proc.*, 1013-1023.

Olphert, C.W. and Powrie, S.E. (1990): ORDIT: a cooperative methodology for the definition of organisational requirements, in *IFIT 8.4 Conference on multi-user interfaces and applications*, Heraklion, Crete.

Ould, M. A. (1992): Process Modelling with RADs, *IOPENER*, **1**.

Ovum Ltd (1993): *Groupware: market strategies*, London.

PC Plus (1993): Nov. 1993, Workgroup computing, 29-30.

Perin, C. (1991): Electronic Social Fields in Bureaucracies, *Communications of the ACM*, **34**, 75-82.

Pinella, P. (1990) Organisational computing arrives, *Datamation*, **15**, pp 42-48.

Rash, W. (1994): Virtual meetings at the desktop, *Windows Sources*, Jan 1994, p. 235-264.

Rodden, T. (1991): A survey of CSCW systems, *Interacting with Computers*, **3**, 319-353.

Sarin, S.K., Abbott, K.R. and McCarthy, D.R. (1991): A process model and system for supporting collaborative work, ACM 0-89791-456-2/91/0010/0213, 1991, 213-224.

Schrage, M (1990): *Shared minds: the new technologies of collaboration*, Random House.

Shepherd, A., Mayer, N., Kuchinsky, A. (1990): Strudel – an extensible electronic converstaion toolkit, *Proc. CSCW '90*, Los Angeles, CA.

Stefik, M., Foster, G., Bobrow, D.G., Kahn, K., Lanning, S., and Suchman, L. (1987): Beyond the chalkboard: computer support for collaboration and problem solving in meetings, *Communications of the ACM*, **30** pp 32-47; reprinted in *Groupware: software for computer-supported cooperative work*, ed. Marca, D., Bock, G. (1992), Los Alamitos, CA: IEEE Computer Society Press.p.334-349

Stefik, M., Bobrow, D.G. et al. (1987): WYSIWIS revised: early experiences with multiuser interfaces, *ACM Trans. Office Information Systems*, **5**, 147-168.

Trigg, R., Suchman, L. and Halasz, F. (1986): Supporting collaboration in NOTECARDS, in *CSCW'86 - Proceedings of the conference on computer-supported cooperative work*, MCC Software Technology Program, Austin, TX, 1986.

Unicom (1993): *Collaborative work: the desktop multimedia network paradigm for group working*, Unicom Seminars Ltd, Uxbridge

Wilson, P. (1990): Computer supported cooperative work: an overview, *Intelligent Tutoring Media*, 1, pp. 103-116.

Wilson, P. (1991): *Computer supported cooperative work*: An Introduction, Oxford, Intellect.

Winograd, T. and Flores, F. (1986): Understanding computers and cognition, Ablex, Norwood, NJ.

Winograd, T. (1987): A language/action perspective on the design of cooperative work, *Stanford University Department of Computer Science Technical Report, STAN-CS-87-1158.*

Zisman, M.D (1977). *Representation, specification, and automation of office procedures*, PhD dissertation, Wharton School, Univ. Pennsylvania.

Subject Index

Printing: Weihert-Druck GmbH, Darmstadt
Binding: Theo Gansert Buchbinderei GmbH, Weinheim